Managing
Quality

Mihaela Kelemen

1:00 LMX 220

McD 120

Managing Quality

Managerial and Critical Perspectives

Mihaela Kelemen

SAGE Publications
London • Thousand Oaks • New Delhi

© Mihaela Kelemen 2003

First published 2003

SAGE Publications Ltd
6 Bonhill Street
London EC2A 4PU

SAGE Publications Inc
2455 Teller Road
Thousand Oaks, California 91320

SAGE Publications India Pvt Ltd
B-42, Panchsheel Enclave
Post Box 4109
New Delhi - 100 017

British Library Cataloguing in Publication Data

A catalogue record for this book is available from the British
Library

ISBN 0 7619 6903 9
ISBN 0 7619 6904 7 (pbk)

Library of Congress Control Number available

Typeset by Photoprint, Torquay, Devon
Printed and bound in Great Britain by the Athenaeum Press, Gateshead

Contents

Figures and table

Acknowledgements

The idea of writing this book came as I was teaching a group of MBA students three years ago: they asked me to recommend a book on quality management that is both prescriptive and critical of such prescriptions. As such a book did not exist, the students asked me to write it. So here I am, three years later completing this ambitious task: whether my students will find this book meets their expectations remains to be seen. This is what quality is about: it lies in the eyes of the beholder.

I have been fascinated by the topic of quality since my undergraduate years. In my last year I wrote an undergraduate dissertation on product reliability, as part of the requirements for a BA in applied economics. Since then, my focus has shifted away from the technical and statistical aspects of quality to its softer and more controversial aspects. It was Keith Grint, at Oxford University, who initially introduced me to sociological debates within management. It is thanks to his erudite supervision and wealth of knowledge which he generously shared, that my horizons expanded away from a positivist framework to a more interpretative way of understanding organizations. If it were not for Keith, I would have probably not left my economics paradigm to venture into the dangerous waters of social constructivism.

Having moved to Keele University in 1996, my understanding of organizational issues widened further to include among others, postmodernist and poststructuralist approaches, discourse analysis, feminism and actor-network-theory. I would like to thank my colleagues for providing such an inspiring and intellectually challenging work environment. In particular, I would like to thank Valerie Fournier for her friendship, moral support and stimulating ideas on theory, research and life in general. It has been immensely rewarding to be her friend and colleague over the past six years. Also, I would like to thank Martin Parker for reading virtually every single piece of work that I have written in the last five years. His careful and critical commentary and genuine belief in my abilities have meant a lot to me. Gordon Pearson deserves special thanks for the countless insightful discussions on organizations, ethics and life. His sense of humour and endless kindness have, on many occasions, brightened up my life. Thanks are also due to Rolland Munro who not only helped me to think through my positioning *vis-à-vis* poststructuralism with encouragement along the way, but also, as Head of Department, facilitated the timing of my sabbatical leave in such a way that I could match it with a visiting position at the Pennsylvania State University. Many other colleagues in the department deserve special thanks for giving me inspiration to entertain new ideas and explore new areas which proved essential to the completion of the book: Dirk Bunzel, Simon Lilley, Geoff Lightfoot, Peter Armstrong, Gavin Jack and Matthias Klaes must be thanked for such inspiration. Particular thanks are also due to John Hassard (now at UMIST) and Paul Forrester (now at Birmingham University) for their team spirit and encouragement to stay with the discipline of operations and quality management, in my early years at Keele.

My PhD students, some of whom have already graduated, deserve special acknowledgement for challenging me intellectually and keeping me always alert to what is happening in other fields of research, in particular, Dr Rosmimah Mohd-Roslin, Dr Ioanna Papasolomou-Doukakis, Colin Rigby and Andrew Christmas. Andrew Christmas was very kind to also help me with graphical support. My undergraduate and MBA students, too many to be acknowledged by name, have also played an important role as sounding boards for some of my most controversial ideas. Their feedback and suggestions have always been given most careful consideration and have helped me discern what is useful and important to them.

The empirical research that underpins some of the chapters would not have been possible without the generous financial support from the Horia Georgescu Foundation and Citibank. Patricia Georgescu deserves special thanks for being such a wonderful individual who has done so much for the Romanian cause, in the memory of her husband, Horia, a Romanian diplomat and journalist. Ian Cormack and Malcolm Parker (ex-Citibankers) need special mention for taking an interest in my ideas and academic career. Most of this book was written during my sabbatical at the Pennsylvania State University. I have been fortunate to have had a most wonderful host there: Professor Martin Kilduff who not only orchestrated the mechanics of my sabbatical and ensured that my time at 'Penn State' was productive and intellectually stimulating but he and his wife, Conni Johnson, generously welcomed me in their home on so many occasions. To Martin, I owe my reconfigured understanding of postmodernism and deconstruction as well as my renewed interest in philosophy.

I have asked three collaborators to write their own case studies on quality management for this book and would like to take this opportunity to thank them: Dr Ioanna Papasolomou-Doukakis whose area of expertise is service marketing, Duthika Perera whose MBA research focused on empowerment and customer satisfaction in the public sector and Joan Durose, an NHS expert and management consultant whose depth and breadth of knowledge on the management of change are hard to match. Joan is also a close friend who has been extremely supportive during past year, particularly as I was going through difficult times caused by illness and death in the family: her positive attitude towards life and generosity as a friend will not be forgotten.

My closest friends, some of whom have opted for an academic career, while others have chosen the practical world of management, have also contributed immensely to this project. Dr Tima Bansal, from Ivey Business School in Canada has been a constant source of inspiration and moral support, since the time we were completing our doctoral dissertations at Oxford. She took the time to read this book and made insightful comments which sharpened my arguments and improved the logical flow of my thoughts. Marcus Scott deserves special thanks for keeping me in good spirits by constantly challenging some of my taken-for-granted beliefs and e-mailing useful materials for my lectures on feminism. I thank him for finding space in his very busy investment banking schedule to read and make comments on the book. Last, but not least, Dr Gregg Robins, a specialist in banking and Eastern European studies, has been of great help in sharpening my ideas about capitalist ideology, market economies and consumerism. For this and his friendship, I thank him.

The most important people in making this project come alive are the ex-Sage editor, Rosemary Nixon who has been extremely interested in this book and was instrumental in helping me sign the contract; and Kiren Shoman, the current Sage editor, whom I thank for her enthusiasm, kindness, patience and practical help on getting the book through the publishing hurdles.

My family: parents, brother, sister-in-law, mother-in-law and brother-in-law must also be thanked for their unconditional and everlasting love and moral support. Without them, I would not be who I am today: special thanks to my parents who have always believed in me and encouraged me to assert my independence of thought from a very early stage.

This book is dedicated to my husband, Csaba Sinka, for being here, always and forever.

Introduction

This book is about the meanings, implementation and consequences of quality. The concept of quality has been contemplated through history and continues to be of much interest today. On a superficial level, quality means making useful things or behaving in a way that contributes to achieving a desirable set of relationships between individuals. On a more philosophical level, quality is intrinsic to the very notion of human existence. There is, however, no universally agreed definition of quality: different definitions highlight different aspects of quality. Quality has been defined as, among others, value for money, fitness for use, consistency, excellence and product integrity. To gain a sound understanding of the meanings of quality, we have to familiarize ourselves with the theoretical perspectives from which quality has been defined in the literature.

Most of these perspectives (the product-based approach, the manufacturing-based approach, the value-based approach and the user-based approach) view quality as a technical, operational achievement: we call these perspectives, managerial perspectives. In contrast, other perspectives (the transcendental approach, the social constructivist approach, the discursive approach and the slogan approach) regard quality as a complex and contested social and political phenomenon, which acquires its meanings via processes of intersubjective communication in which organizational and societal power configurations play a substantial role: we call these critical perspectives. The book draws on both managerial and critical perspectives in an attempt to provide a more comprehensive and culturally sensitive analysis of quality.

More specifically, the book aims to:

1 Introduce readers to key concepts and issues in quality management.
2 Provide an overview of both managerial and critical perspectives on quality management.
3 Present the 'wisdom' of quality management gurus.
4 Document the way quality is pursued in manufacturing, service and public sector organizations.

5 Compare and contrast existing 'hard and soft' technologies of quality management.
6 Critically review the rhetoric and practice of total quality management (TQM) and business process re-engineering (BPR).
7 Examine the consequences of quality on a wide number of stakeholders in order to assess whether quality is an ethical project.
8 Subject the language of quality management to scrutiny.
9 Document the mundane nature of quality management practices that take place in organizations via the presentation of real-life case studies.

The book is aimed at undergraduate and postgraduate students studying quality and operations management. It may also appeal to quality management practitioners and consultants interested in challenging the managerial perspective that dominates much of the rhetoric and current practice of quality management.

The book has four parts: Part 1, Theoretical Perspectives on Quality, introduces the reader to a number of theoretical debates and controversies in the field of quality. Four managerial perspectives and four critical perspectives on quality are introduced in Chapter 1. An assessment is also provided of the consequences of these quality perspectives on the experiences of various organizational stakeholders, in particular, managers, employees, customers and shareholders. Chapter 2 provides a short history of the principles underlying the concept of quality (i.e., measurement, standardization, inspection, interchangeable parts, precision and feedback) and examines the contribution of a number of American and Japanese quality management gurus (e.g., Deming, Juran, Ishikawa, Taguchi and so on) to the development of quality management as a scientific discipline. These gurus tend to view quality from a managerial perspective, as a process or outcome that can be planned, managed and controlled with the help of technical and/or managerial knowledge. Throughout the book such managerial perspectives are subjected to criticism for failing to grasp the elusive, complex and political nature of quality. While traditionally quality has belonged to the field of operations management, more recently it started to be recognized as important for the efficient functioning of other organizational functions such as strategy, marketing, human resource management (HRM), design and accounting (a position which will be explored in more detail in Chapter 3).

In Part 2, Practical Approaches to Quality, the book moves on to discuss ways in which quality is implemented and managed in manufacturing, service and public sector organizations via a number of 'hard and soft technologies' of quality management (Chapter 4). Hard technologies (e.g., quality standards, quality costs and quality assurance), discussed in Chapters 5, 6 and 7, are typically associated with direct and technical control. Direct control refers to coercive mechanisms by which individuals are made to do things they would not do otherwise. Technical control is a form of indirect control which relies on the use of technology to get people to conform. Soft technologies (e.g., employee involvement, teamwork, leadership and culture) tend to be aligned with notions of bureaucratic and disciplinary control. Bureaucratic control refers to the internalization of rational rules and routines by organizational selves. Disciplinary control is a form of post-bureaucratic control which appears not to control but to offer a high degree of individual autonomy at work; it works through the internalization of a complex set of norms and standard practices which provide common sense and self-evident experience to individuals (Chapters 8, 9 and 10).

Part 3, Consequences of Quality, ponders the consequences and morality of quality. Proponents of soft technologies to managing quality suggest that none of the hard technologies work unless individuals are persuaded by the relevance and legitimacy of quality. Persuasion is however a social and political process in which some interests are elevated and others are pushed down. If we view quality as constituted at the intersection of opposing interests and agendas, it is important that such interests are reconciled prior to any actual engagement in quality programmes. Chapter 11 asks whether it is indeed possible to pursue quality in an ethical manner, that is, in a way that accounts for the interests of all organizational stakeholders, not only for the interests of the customer. Chapter 12 subjects the language of quality management to close scrutiny in an attempt to shed light on the consequences of the language in use on the experiences and identities of both managers and employees. These two chapters draw on critical perspectives to quality.

The book ends with Part 4: Case Studies on Quality Management. Here the author of the book and her collaborators present real-life examples which attempt to weave in some of the conceptual matters presented in the book. For example, Joan Durose's sensitive analysis of the NHS asks whether the political focus in the NHS changes the relationship between the user, the health professional and the manager. Duthika Perera's case study continues this strand of inquiry by posing the question of the extent to which the standardization of health care provision and empowerment programmes can go hand in hand in the NHS. Mihaela Kelemen's case shifts away from issues in the public sector to concerns faced by the private sector, discussing the role of teamleaders in managing quality in a logistics organization. Duthika Perera's analysis of the relationship between new technology and customer satisfaction is critical of the uses to which new technology is put: to discriminate between various types of customers and treat consumers as commodities. Ioanna Papasolomou-Doukakis's case of the UK retail banking sector throws light on the rhetoric of internal marketing and the extent to which it helps to improve quality. Finally, I look at the ways in which quality standards have been implemented in a UK insurance company and the responses this process has triggered from the various organizational stakeholders. These cases document the complex and multi-faceted nature of quality and the consequences it has upon a number of organizational stakeholders.

PART ONE

Theoretical perspectives on quality

Re-defining quality 1

This chapter introduces the readers to various theoretical controversies in the quality management literature. It starts by suggesting that there are four managerial perspectives on quality (the product-based approach, the manufacturing-based approach, the value-based approach and the user-based approach) and four critical ones (the transcendental approach, the social constructivist approach, the discursive approach and the slogan approach). Managerial perspectives view quality as a self-contained entity or process that can be planned, managed, controlled with the help of technical and managerial knowledge. Critical perspectives assert that quality is a complex and multifaceted concept which escapes a definitive definition. Quality has multiple, contradictory meanings which arise from processes of intersubjective communication. Hence, quality is a political, cultural and social process rather than a technical, operational issue.

The chapter charts the strengths and weaknesses of each of the above approaches to quality, by placing them in their broader social and cultural context (Reeves and Bednar, 1994). In reviewing such strengths and weaknesses, the chapter asks two questions:

1 For which organizational stakeholders (i.e., manager, employee, shareholder, customer) do they constitute strengths and/or weaknesses?
2 To what extent does each approach to quality account for the interests of all organizational stakeholders?

The concept of quality has been contemplated throughout history and continues to be a subject of great interest today. Remember the story of the *Titanic*, the unsinkable ship that sank in 1912 as a result of colliding with an iceberg? *Titanic* was built to be the most technologically advanced, the fastest and most luxurious ship on the highly competitive North Atlantic mail and passenger route. The ship was made out of the finest steel and had a double-hulled bottom and automatic watertight doors that could be closed from the bridge. This, coupled with its elegant features such as deep plush carpeting, a gymnasium, an automatic dishwasher, a squash court and a swimming pool made the *Titanic* a symbol of excellence. Yet, what was supposed to provide a pleasurable experience ended up in tragedy for so many of the crew and passengers. The reasons may have little to do with the quality of design and manufacturing and more with the quality of the decisions taken by the people in command. Indeed, too much confidence in the *Titanic*'s technological superiority led the people in command to take the ship through an ice field at top speed instead of slowing down, as was the common practice. The result was disastrous. Therefore, it was not the quality of the technology that failed the *Titanic*: the quality of decision-making failed her (Bond, 2001).

Remember also the *Challenger*'s accident? On 28 January 1986 the space shuttle *Challenger* burst into flames 73 seconds after being launched into space. The loss of the space shuttle was caused by the failure of the joint between the two lower segments of the right solid motor. Subsequent investigation showed that the failure of the pressure seal called the O-ring was due to a faulty design relating to a number of physical and technical factors. Moreover, the people who made the decision to launch *Challenger* were not aware of the problems concerning the O-rings or of the advice given by the contractor against launching the shuttle at temperatures below 53 degrees Fahrenheit. They also did not take into consideration concerns expressed that it was not safe to launch because of ice on pads. What was supposed to be a marvellous technological achievement ended up destroying not only people's lives but also NASA's reputation as a quality-driven business (Bank, 1992).

Quality is by no means a modern invention: quality has always been important to human survival and progress. The quality of the crops, the quality of houses and roads, of medical care were as important to our ancestors as they are to us. What is different, however, is the fact that in the last century or so, quality has become a scientific discipline of its own, safeguarded by a professional elite of managers, designers, engineers and marketers. And as a scientific discipline, it has its own vocabulary, techniques and rules that must be endorsed by those interested in pursuing its cause. Moreover, quality has become an institutional norm central to the effective functioning of the market: a norm that organizations (be they private, public or voluntary) are expected to endorse if they are to gain legitimacy in the eyes of society.

In recent decades, organizations have eagerly embraced the cause of quality in the belief that quality can offer new opportunities for competitive advantage. Critics, however, are quick to point out that organizations' over-concern with quality usually translates into the bureaucratic implementation of standards, leading to the commodification of organizational relations (i.e., a situation where organizational members and relationships between them are treated as commodities to be sold and bought on the internal market). In contemporary Britain, quality appears to hold a central place in political, economic and social debates: politicians, policy-makers, consumers, managers, trade unions, and eco-activists call upon the imagery of quality in an attempt to give weight to their cause. Such parties allege that they pursue quality for and in the name of the consumer. The consumer has become a Godlike icon before whom markets and politicians alike bow (Gabriel and Lang, 1995). But sometimes this notion of consumer is too abstract and has little to do with the real needs and concerns of the actual consumer.

In western societies, but increasingly so in other societies, individuals are socialized into thinking of themselves and each other as consumers rather than producers. The market is both the common glue that keeps individuals together, for in order to exist they must engage in exchanges; and the differentiator between individuals as they can choose certain exchanges and not others, and thus, assemble a unique bricolage of products and services that may set them apart from the others by conferring them a unique identity.

The literature on quality is full of controversial perspectives and lacks clear conceptualizations. The purpose of this chapter is not merely to support some perspectives, or to criticize others from a particular vantage point but to suggest that different definitions may be appropriate under different circumstances. Furthermore, the chapter urges the reader to abandon the search for a universal definition of quality and accept that quality is an elusive, multifaceted and socially contingent concept.

To guide the reader in a more effective manner, the chapter builds upon and expands Garvin's (1984) framework concerning approaches to quality. The boundaries between these approaches are rather artificial and various writers may in fact belong to more than one approach. The first four approaches – namely, the product-based approach, the manufacturing-based approach, the value-based approach and the user-based approach – seem to be very popular with organizations and quality management gurus alike. We term them managerial for they view quality as a technical, operational and manageable matter. The latter four approaches – namely, the transcendental approach, the social constructivist approach, the discursive approach and the slogan approach – broaden the analysis of quality: here, quality is seen as a social, cultural and political process which has multiple meanings.

MANAGERIAL PERSPECTIVES ON QUALITY

The product-based approach

This managerial approach views quality as a precise and measurable variable. According to Abbott, 'differences in quality amount to differences in the quantity of some desired ingredient or attribute' (1955: 126–7). Thus, the better the quality of cocoa in a chocolate cake, the higher the quality of the cake, providing that the attribute in question is considered desirable by all buyers. Product-based definitions first appeared in the economic literature, supplementing the theory of competitive markets. While the theory of competitive markets viewed the principle of price competition as the driving force in an exchange, quality competition drew attention to the fact that buyers and sellers did not engage in exchanges of homogeneous or standardized goods. Therefore, buyers are not only interested in agreeing the right price but are adamant that the good in question provides them with the expected experience (Knight, 1921). If products and services were homogeneous, they would all provide the same experience. It is the difference in quality that makes products and services capable of providing different experiences and in so doing, of meeting the diverse needs of the buyers. With a few exceptions, most economic theories on quality focused exclusively on durability (Levhari and Srinivasan, 1969; Swan, 1970), for increased durability ensured more of the same for longer and this was seen to contribute directly to improved quality.

Strengths and weaknesses of the product-based approach   The product-based approach was the first approach to acknowledge the possibility of measuring and controlling the quality of a product by measuring and controlling the quantities of a desired ingredient. Although focused on the ingredients and capabilities of the product, this approach hinted at the role played by the customers and their needs in defining quality. This approach has been relatively popular during the craft manufacturing period but has lost its significance during the mass production era and thereafter. Hence, it is of little relevance to contemporary organizations and remains confined to the drawers of management history.

The manufacturing-based approach

This managerial approach defines quality as the degree to which a specific product conforms to a design or specification (Gilmore, 1974). Crosby (1979), for example, defines quality as conformance to requirements. Process and design variation are seen to be a constant thread to achieving conformance to requirements. While according to some commentators, variation can be totally eliminated (see, for example, Crosby's 'zero defects' philosophy), for others (Deming and Juran), only a certain type of variation is controllable, others are not. Both camps agree, however, that if the design and the production process are stable and reliable, quality is inherent. To achieve consistency in design, companies can employ Taguchi methods of design engineering that assume that any deviation from the centre, no matter how small, increases a product's ultimate cost, including warranty, liability, lost customer goodwill (for a more detailed discussion of the Taguchi method see Chapters 3 and 4). In the production stage, statistical process control (SPC) enables workers to tell the difference between avoidable errors (due to special causes) and unavoidable ones (due to random causes) and track down the causes of controllable problems (see Chapter 7). Source inspection (or *poka-yoke*) is another technique that ensures that errors are caught at the outset before they materialize into defects (see Chapter 3). This approach to quality is engineering driven and relies on the application of statistical methods to controlling variation in design, processes and final products. The idea of controlling variation statistically sprang from agricultural research carried out by statistician R.A. Fisher at the beginning of the twentieth century. To speed up the development of crop-growing methods, Fisher perfected scientific short cuts for sifting through mountains of data to spot key cause–effect relationships. Fisher's work inspired W.A. Shewhart, a physicist at AT&T Bell Laboratories who transformed Fisher methods into a quality control discipline for factories. Such methods of quality control were first implemented on a large scale in Japanese factories after the Second World War and then spread to the rest of the world.

Strengths and weaknesses of the manufacturing-based approach

Quality as 'conformance to specifications' has numerous advantages for managers and consumers but less so perhaps for employees. Most technical advances in quality are due to standardization and mass production. The very first technical advances in quality were achieved in the US armament industry. The crafts approach that had been dominant in Europe in the nineteenth century did not allow for quantity production, leading major American firms to adopt a version of mass production where the key to quality was conformance to specifications: if parts did not conform to specifications then the whole production system would fail. Given that inspection was too expensive, there was a need to make the processes more predictable and error freer: quality control techniques were thus introduced. While standardization benefited the managers, the shareholders and to a large extent the consumers (through more affordable prices and less defect prone products), workers were reduced to mere extensions of the machinery. The mass production regime led eventually to the deskilling of work and a decreasing role for workers and trade unions in organizing the production process. Moreover, taking all necessary steps to ensure a product conforms to internal specifications does not necessarily lead to customer satisfaction. For the customer, the quality of a product/service is a subjective perception and 'conforming to specifications' sometimes plays only a minor role in affecting such perceptions.

The value-based approach

This managerial perspective considers quality as being the degree of excellence at an acceptable price or the control of variability at an acceptable cost. Numerous writers subscribe to this perspective, among them Feigenbaum (1951) and Abbott (1955). According to Abbott (1955), quality and price are inextricably bound together in economic choice. The relationship between quality and cost is, however, complex: there is little agreement in the literature as to whether the relationship is direct or inverse. Such a state of affairs is typically attributed to definitional problems and the inconsistency of cost collection procedures. Japanese manufacturers take the view that quality and cost are inversely related because resources put into improving quality are more than matched by the savings made with respect to rework, scrap and customer complaints. In the western manufacturing paradigm, however, the relation between costs and quality is held to be a direct one, that is, better quality presupposes higher costs. The relationship between quality and price is similarly fraught with difficulties. It is widely accepted that price affects people's perceptions of quality but there are no models to account for the complexity built into this relationship: for some consumers, for example, smaller prices couched under the veneer of 'value for money' signal reasonable quality at competitive prices. On the other hand, at the upper end of the market, high prices signal uniqueness and exquisite quality reserved only for the few who can afford it. In such a market, the higher the price, the higher the desirability of the good/service.

Strengths and weakness of the value-based approach   The value-based approach attempts to relate two distinct concepts: quality and price, resulting in the hybrid concept of 'affordable excellence'. This notion lacks, however, well defined boundaries and is often highly subjective (Garvin, 1988: 46). In the marketplace, consumption decisions are based on both price and quality. The value-based approach attempts to capture the intricate relation between these two aspects. Defining quality as value allows one to compare widely disparate goods and experiences, for example, staying a night at the Plaza Hotel in New York or spending it at the YMCA. This definition also facilitates cross-company and cross-industry analyzes as well as better knowledge of how purchase decisions are made by the customers. From a company's point of view, the value-based definition requires high levels of efficiency that usually translate into cost reduction programmes and increased levels of productivity. This could put a strain on both managers and employees. The consumer, however, is the one most certainly benefiting from having access to products and services that are better value for money. Companies tend to advertise their products as offering both value and quality.

The user-based approach

This last managerial perspective on quality focuses on the capacity of a good/service to satisfy or exceed the wants of a specific customer. Quality is typically defined as meeting and exceeding customer expectations (Gronroos, 1983; Parasuraman et al., 1985). Although the impetus for such conceptualizations of quality comes from the service marketing literature, some quality thinkers have also pointed to the importance of the end-user as early as 1960, defining quality as 'the degree to which the product in use will meet the expectations of the customer' (Feigenbaum, 1961: 13) and 'the extent to which a product successfully serves the purposes of the user' (Juran et al., 1974: 22). While some of the quality gurus (Shewhart, Juran and Feigenbaum) have highlighted the importance of customer needs, they have provided little advice as to how customer wants are to be translated into appropriate product and services specifications. The difficulty of such processes of translation is magnified if we consider that what counts as satisfaction is a subjective matter and varies according to one's tastes, standards, beliefs and objectives; these themselves vary greatly with the individual personality and the cultural environment (Abbott, 1955). Marketers have done a great deal to identify the needs of the customers through 'preference testing' in order to sensitize the manufacturers to what is significant for consumers (Bayton, 1958; Bucklin, 1963). More recently, service marketers have developed quality tools and techniques that had as the primary ingredient an understanding of customer's expectations and needs (e.g., SERVQUAL: for a more detailed discussion see Chapter 4).

Strengths and weakness of the user-based approach   The user-based definition signals the role of the consumer as the ultimate judge of quality. Customers can articulate how satisfied or dissatisfied they are with a product/service, though pinning down the rationale behind such a judgement is usually very difficult. Nevertheless, there are numerous marketing instruments that allow managers and researchers to include subjective factors (i.e., courtesy, helpfulness, confidence, appearance) into the definition of quality. The SERVQUAL instrument developed by Parasuraman et al. (1985) is a generic tool designed to measure the gap between customers' perceptions and expectations. Although heavily criticized, SERVQUAL is a useful exercise in drawing managers' and employees' attention to the dynamics of the market. Meeting and exceeding customers' expectations is the most challenging definition of quality for a company: on the one hand, the company has to be externally oriented, on the other hand, it must translate customers' demands into internal operational demands. Furthermore, there is no guarantee that the trade-off between an external and internal focus will in fact lead to customer satisfaction. Oliver (1981) argues that pre-purchase attitudes play a major role in the subsequent evaluation of quality by the customer; thus, customers will evaluate the quality of a product or service more favourably if their initial expectations are high. Most research findings regarding the concepts of customer satisfaction and service quality are, however, contradictory. In some studies, service quality is an outcome of customer satisfaction, in others the opposite is held to be the case. Although these concepts have been often treated as separate constructs in the literature, their typical operationalization makes it difficult to distinguish between them. The user-based definition favours the consumer but poses important challenges for the managers who must be in a position to measure customers' subjective perceptions and then translate them into operational efficiency.

CRITICAL PERSPECTIVES ON QUALITY

The transcendental approach

This perspective considers quality as synonymous with 'innate excellence'. On the one hand, quality is universally and absolutely recognizable, on the other hand, it escapes precise definitions and measurements. Pirsig's (1974: 185, 213) definition of quality is a powerful illustration of this approach: 'quality is neither mind, nor matter, but a third entity independent of the two . . . even though Quality cannot be defined'. Garvin (1984) contends that this understanding of quality borrows heavily from Greek philosophy. Quality is regarded as something beyond definition, a direct experience that can be understood only after one has been exposed to a set of objects that display its characteristics. Thus quality is an embodied phenomenon and therefore cannot be approached merely through cognition. Indeed, quality triggers in individuals not only a rational response but also emotions and feelings such as pleasure, pain, hate, and happiness.

Strengths and weakness of the transcendental approach   Quality as excellence is one of the oldest approaches to quality: it was a source of inspiration for the Greek philosophers such as Socrates, Plato and Aristotle and it still acts as one in contemporary society. Peters and Waterman's book *In Search of Excellence* (1982) proved to be such a bestseller mainly because of our fascination with the idea of achieving excellence in private and organizational lives. An organizational vision articulated around the imagery of excellence has a deeper impact upon the employees than one based on conformance to requirements, for example. The former is loosely defined and provides scope for individual interpretation and creativity (thus securing commitment), while the latter is constraining and tends to be perceived as lacking inspiration. Customers also take pride in owning excellent products or enjoying excellent services: numerous advertising campaigns stress that their products excel (see, for example, Singaporean Airlines, British Airways, Mercedes, BMW, Chiva Regal). While quality as excellence is an orienting meaning device, pointing to a desired state, the transcendental approach to quality fails to provide the blueprint as to how to control and measure quality. Excellence is difficult to pin down, measure and render controllable. Indeed, how could one assess whether and to what extent excellence has been achieved? Who determines what is excellent and what is not? If one has to rely on the expertise of the manager or the worker, who is to say that the same result will be obtained if the customer was asked? While the elusiveness and seduction of excellence may favour the customer, it certainly does not favour the manager who may need more specific procedures and techniques to be in a position to control quality. Ultimately, in some cases, the imagery of excellence (when not based on meeting safety and technical standards) may also fail the consumer: the example of Concorde discussed by Muschamp (2000) is an illustrative one.

For more than three decades Concorde was considered to be an aesthetic masterpiece. Indeed, the contrast between its elongated fuselage and wide swept-back wings, the proportions of the windows to the fuselage and the triangular configuration formed by its needlepoint nose and the wing tips made the Concorde the most elegant and sumptuous aircraft for passengers (Muschamp, 2000). This coupled with its supersonic speed and the amounts of champagne and caviar served on board may explain its image of excellence and exquisiteness (it may also explain the typically £7,000 charged for a return trip between London and New York). This image of excellence arose partly from the craft's technical abilities (speed, elegance of design) and partly from the service provided on board. But because there had been no competition in the supersonic transport of the civilians, there was little incentive to technically upgrade the aircraft. Thus, Concorde pilots had to use manual controls to a larger extent than necessary. On 25 July 2000, an Air France Concorde carrying German tourists to New York crashed into a hotel outside Paris, killing 113 people. An engine burst into flames when the plane was trying to take off: a piece of fuselage dropped by another aeroplane which had already taken off was sucked in by the Concorde engine. As the engine was close to the fuel tank, it erupted in flames: the technical obsolescence of the aircraft made it impossible for the pilots to detect the fire in time and stop the take off. Thus, what was thought for years to be an icon of excellence proved in fact to be a fallible product (Muschamp, 2000).

The concerns regarding the uncontrollability of 'excellence' did not constitute a problem during the time of craftsmanship when each product was made individually, but with the advent of mass manufacturing and the factory system, the prevailing view of quality as a measure of excellence was too vague for practical purposes. Quality had to be quantifiable if manufacturers were going to be able to measure and control it. Thus, the definition of quality turned away from excellence to 'conformance to requirements' and later on to 'value for money' and 'customer satisfaction'.

The social constructivist approach

This critical perspective considers quality not as lying in the product or service but as being constructed through the accounts provided by various powerful agents: a product is held to be a quality product not because it is inherently good, but because it has been adjudged good by those in a position to bestow or recognize quality in the product: the customers, top management, a standard certification body and so on. Thus, quality cannot be studied in a neutral, value-free way through an objective lens of research. Rather, it must be viewed as a collective and, therefore, political process which unfolds sinuously both within and outside the organization. The causes and outcomes of this process are difficult to predict or indeed control at a distance. For example, advertising and public relations (PR) campaigns try to enhance the image of goods/services in the marketplace; yet there are no conclusive measurements to confirm that perceived quality and advertising are directly related. Similarly, the relationship between inspirational, quality-driven organizational cultures and customers' perceptions of products or services is equally spurious. In some cases, the reverse may be true: highly bureaucratic, mechanistic organizations such as McDonalds and Disney do in fact provide consistent goods and services which are perceived within a particular market as high quality (here, consistency and value for money are the most important ingredients of quality). The social constructivist approach suggests that the meanings of quality are constructed, negotiated and enacted within a particular context and depend on existing power relations. Thus, there can be no ultimate, universal and objective meaning of quality. Quality acquires diverse and occasionally contentious meanings in the process by which employees, managers, customers, citizens attempt to make sense of what is going on around them.

Strengths and weakness of the social constructivist approach
The social constructivist approach to quality stresses the processual and social nature of quality. Here quality is something in the making, a process to which a number of parties contribute but whose effects are difficult to predict or control at a distance. Although this definition may have little practical relevance from the point of view of improving organizational performance, it draws attention to the most powerful voices within and outside the organization. Such voices usually win out at the expense of the rest and are taken to be the 'the reality of quality'. Although within the organization managerial perspectives are usually the most powerful ones, in the marketplace it is usually the voice of the consumer or of the quality certification body. Rather than searching for a definitive definition of quality, organizations must attempt to democratize their quality-related practices to the extent that marginal voices (e.g. employees) become heard. In turn, researchers are urged to move beyond the benign vision of managerial perspectives on quality and question the ways quality is identified and pursued in organizations and uncover some of the unchallenged assumptions and implicit power relations hidden within this allegedly neutral concept.

The discursive approach

This approach makes language central to the social construction of quality. It is through and with language that people in organizations make meaning, construct, negotiate and enact certain realities. Language is a socially conditioned process which determines (rather than reflects) reality, being itself determined by the existing social conventions and power relations. The discursive approach to quality emphasizes this interdependence between language, power and reality. This literature views quality as one of the many discourses present in organizations. While for some researchers, quality is a language game (de Cock, 1998) or a sign (Xu, 1999) beyond which there is no material reality, for others (Kelemen, 2000, 2001) quality is a discursive resource whose effects upon individual and collective identities are both material and linguistic, both durable and transient at the same time. Many discursive conceptualizations of quality find resonance with Michel Foucault's writings on power, knowledge and the self (Foucault, 1977, 1980) and have been mirrored in recent literature on total quality management and business process re-engineering (Knights and McCabe, 1998a, 1998b; Kelemen, 2001).

Strengths and weaknesses of the discursive approach This approach could again be discredited for its lack of practical usefulness for, indeed, who could measure discourse? If quality resides only in language as some researchers suggest, we could change it by altering the way we speak about it. This in itself could be productive: it has been documented that language is essentially social and dependent on the material practices of a particular society. In turn, by altering the language of quality, one could, in theory change the way people think about it and interact with each other. Such processes of change could be experienced as positive and fulfilling but also as limiting and oppressive. It is hard to imagine that managers, employees, shareholders and consumers will ever refer to quality as discourse: yet, this approach to quality could stimulate researchers to construct more imaginative accounts about the meanings and consequences of quality in organizations.

The slogan approach

Organizations' obsession with quality and the consequent abuse of the term has lead to a situation where quality has become a mere slogan. A slogan is a meaningless platitude with which nobody disagrees; as who could be against quality? As a slogan, quality gives the illusion of a unitary meaning that is endorsed by everyone in the organization; in so doing, it aims to construct a sense of normality and taken-for-granted commonsense among employees. Given its commonsensical message, it becomes harder and harder to ask questions such as: Why is quality a good thing? For whom is quality good? How is quality pursued by organizations? What are its consequences on organizational stakeholders? There is little doubt, for example, that McDonalds burgers are quality ones (providing one likes value-for-money, standardized burgers) but that is not to say that working as a sales assistant at McDonalds is a quality experience (Pearson and Parker, 2001). Furthermore, some companies that are seen to provide quality products and services may do so at the expense of harming the environment. The controversial *Brent Spar* oil platform which was disposed by Shell in 1991 in the North Sea raised awareness of how some corporate practices relating to the environment may go unnoticed. Although Shell disposed of its oilrig in the most ecologically friendly way, the case was picked up by Greenpeace and described as a 'quick and dirty' deepwater disposal, thus stirring public emotion and anger and raising concern over how companies deal with the environment. More and more companies are exporting their manufacturing divisions to Asian and Eastern European countries due to cheap labour and advantageous taxation, destroying western communities and ways of life. Even companies which have built a reputation around the imagery of excellence do sometimes step away from this ideal when they deal with employees' disputes. The British Airways cabin crew strike from July 1997 is such an example: the three day strike organized by the cabin crew because they disliked the way the airline had imposed new working practices without their prior agreement was poorly handled by the leadership of the company who threatened the strikers with legal action (cf. *The Economist*, 7 December 1997).

Therefore, we should remain wary of slogans that urge us to view quality as an inherently morally good project, existing in some void, outside cultural and historical parameters. For the slogan of quality hides the contentious, political nature of the production and consumption practices in which quality is necessarily embedded. It is these practices that we need to understand and challenge in order to arrive at a notion of quality that is more democratic and meaningful.

Strengths and weaknesses of the slogan approach   As a slogan, quality could be mobilized by numerous parties: managers, for example, can use the message of quality to inspire the employees, instil pride in the work they do and provide meaning for otherwise meaningless tasks. Although this could easily be a managerial ploy, it may work, particularly when employees perceive that it is beneficial to their career to be involved in quality programmes. Employees, on the other hand, could have their voice heard more often and more loudly because they now speak in the name of quality rather than in their own name. Given that quality is a company and society-wide concern, their suggestions for improving quality have a better chance of being heard and not pushed under the carpet. Therefore, various parties could pursue various ends, all in the name of quality. This scenario could in fact be a productive one, providing that all interested parties achieve their goals and at the same time the market endorses their efforts as quality. More talk about quality is not bad in itself but it could have disastrous effects when people do not do what they say they do. For example, when companies pledge quality in their advertising campaigns but do not deliver it, the slogan of quality could have negative effects upon organizational image and profits.

SUMMARY

This chapter has reviewed eight definitions of quality: managerial definitions regard quality as a technical issue which can be managed and controlled with the help of statistical and managerial knowledge. Critical approaches shed light on the multifaceted, contentious and political nature of quality. The chapter maps out the strengths and weakness of these eight approaches from the point of view of various stakeholders: that is, managers, employees, customers, shareholders, and so on. The boundaries between these approaches are by no means definitive or clear cut: they reflect the point of view of the author of the book. Chapter 2 provides a short historical overview of the principles that underpin the quality thinking, going back to antiquity, and reviews the wisdom of modern quality gurus.

KEY CONCEPTS

Here are the key concepts covered by this chapter: definitions of quality, managerial perspectives, critical perspectives, social constructivism, discourse, slogan.

QUESTIONS

At the end of this chapter you should be able to answer the following questions:

- What are the most important managerial/critical approaches to quality? Provide a short summary of each approach.
- What are the strengths and weaknesses of each individual approach?
- What is the difference between managerial and critical approaches to quality?
- To what extent can managerial and critical approaches be reconciled?
- What is your own definition of quality? What theoretical perspectives (managerial and/or critical) does it draw upon?

2 The origin and evolution of quality management

Chapter 2 takes a cursory look at the principles underlying the discipline of quality management. Although it is only relatively recent that the concern for quality has been translated into a scientific discipline safeguarded by professional and academic bodies, practical preoccupations with quality run deep in the history of humankind. This chapter outlines the main principles that foreground the management of quality, as we know it today, providing evidence that attests to the ancient roots of quality. The contemporary quality movement and the lessons espoused by modern quality gurus have not emerged out of a void but are the logical continuation of a number of developments in science, technology and management that have started many centuries ago.

PRINCIPLES OF QUALITY MANAGEMENT

In this section we review the principles considered to lie at the basis of quality management, namely: measurement, standardization, inspection, interchangeable parts, precision and feedback (Morrison, 1994).

Measurement   The ability to measure can be traced back to the primitive people. The primitive people used some sort of mental measurement to assess how far a prey was, or how heavy a stone. In fact, the process of comparing an unknown against a standard unit with a divided scale was already in use among late Stone Age people. Quantitative knowledge of a particular object helped decide whether the object was useful for a particular task or not. If a stone was too heavy or too large for a particular house, it had to be adjusted in order to fit the building requirements. Thus, measurement plays an important role in assessing the usefulness (i.e., quality) of a particular object.

Standardization   The uniformity of units of weight and measures has been recorded as early as the Babylonian civilization (*c.* 1800BC). Standards played a significant role in expanding and managing the Roman Empire. Although most of these standards differed to some extent from the type of standards that later emerged in the industrial process, those used in territorial planning and construction came very close to matching the modern ones. The Romans achieved standardization in many fields. The unit of measurement was unified and adopted throughout the empire. This achievement led to measurement becoming a specific component of the production process, particularly in construction works and stone quarrying. In England, there are records to suggest that standards of weight were introduced in Saxon times and defence standards were put in place by Charles I in 1631.

Inspection   Standardization was initially enforced via inspection and can be traced back to the Roman Empire. Historic documents attest that in the eleventh-century England The Guild Act empowered the wardens of the crafts to inspect the work and ensure that it is 'good and right'. In France, a 1689 decree by Louis XIV regarding the navy and the naval arsenal stipulated the duties and obligations of the general commissioner for naval artillery. Here, quality inspection of the manufacturing process was the most important attribution aiming to ensure that the product corresponded to what had been ordered.

Interchangeable parts   The invention of printing from movable type is one of the earliest recorded examples of this principle and the Guttenberg Bible printed in 1454 was the first book to be so produced. One of the most celebrated sixteenth-century factories, the Arsenal of Venice was described by George (1972) as the quintessential example of quality control. The factory, which is thought to have employed around two thousand people, was manufacturing the war fleet for the Venetian state. The philosophy guiding the manufacturing process stressed the importance of standardization and interchangeable parts: all bows were to be made so that arrows would fit any of them and the stern posts were to be built in such a way that each ruder would fit them. In Britain, the standardization of component parts and the development of interchangeable mechanisms were developed to a high degree of perfection in the manufacturing of steam engines at the Soho Engineering Foundry of Boulton and Watt in Birmingham. In fact, the very first standardizing authority in the world was established in Britain in 1901.

Precision   The control of quality necessitates high-precision equipment which can detect any small deviation from the standard. The science of metrology which witnessed rapid progress in the seventeenth and eighteenth centuries and inventions such as the Vernier scale and the screw micrometer have contributed substantially to the development of quality control.

Feedback   This is another principle that lies at the core of quality control: once deviations are detected, they must be fed back and resolved before they became defects. The principle of feed-back was first applied in Britain in 1787 to regulate the speed of windmills via a fly-ball governor. From 1788, the same principle was developed extensively by James Watt with respect to steam engines.

In conclusion, the basic principles of modern quality control – that is, measurement, standardization, interchangeability, precision, inspection and feedback – have a long history. It is perhaps insightful to return to the example of ancient Rome and take a cursory look at its achievements in the field of quality. The Roman building yard represented the place where all Roman achievements regarding design, materials, process and standardization came together (Bigliazzi, 1995). One of the most important elements of quality management on the building site was the co-ordination of the functions performed by various categories of craftsmen such as: stone cutters, sculptors, plasterers, wall builders, roofers, marble decorators, mechanics, surveyors, engineers and architects. Measuring instruments were constantly used on the site and there were housing standards that regulated the builders' business from the time of the Emperor Augustus. The quality of bricks reached such high levels that it was considered more reliable than stone, while at the same time being the cheapest material of construction.

THE EVOLUTION OF QUALITY

Preoccupations for quality are a common thread of both ancient and modern societies; approaches associated with the control and management of quality have evolved constantly as a result of changing economic, social and political conditions and have been heavily influenced by cultural and historical factors. The First and Second World Wars have, for example, given an impetus to quality control due to the strategic importance and the rapid growth of the defence industry.

The First World War stimulated the development of mass production. Inspection, standardization and interchangeable parts became widespread in America. The evolution of automatic dialling forced telephone manufacturing companies to implement quality control in a serious manner. Shewhart's invention of the control chart in 1924 and Dodge's acceptance sampling plans (see Chapter 7) started to be recognized as crucial to quality control, in a move away from inspection to detection of errors prior to becoming product defects. The Second World War provided another impetus to the development of quality control with a clear emphasis on preventive activities rather than the detection of poor quality.

While the American imprint on quality was very obvious throughout and between the two wars, Japan was a relatively obscure player at the time (although it did excel at making beautiful swords and building exquisite battleships). After the Second World War, Japan transformed itself from a country that manufactured mainly shoddy goods into a quality leader in most fields, ranging from car manufacturing to electronics and home appliances. Due partly to an extraordinary ability to quickly and efficiently import and adopt foreign knowledge and know-how, Japan was the first nation to recognize and capitalize on the importance of quality and its strategic role in the global market. Morishima (1982) analysed the historical context of the so-called Japanese miracle, suggesting there may be significant links between a national ideology, very much rooted in Confucianism, and the chosen path of economic development via quality and technological innovation.

Across centuries, China and the West have represented major sources for the import of cultural and technological know-how, for the Japanese. This is not to say that Japanese organizations are mere imitators, copiers of foreign techniques and philosophies. Dahlgaard (1999) argues that there are three stages in the evolution of the Japanese quality movement. During, the first two decades after the war, Japan merely imported ideas on quality from America and spread their adoption throughout companies. The 1960s witnessed a change in this approach towards retaining only what really worked in the Japanese context, adapting Western approaches to suit such context or developing new techniques. In the early 1960s, the ambitious aim of Matsushita Electric was to eliminate all defects, a strategy called 'zero defects'. In 1960 Shingo developed a system called Single (-digit) Minute Exchange of Dies (SMED) that reduced a particular set-up time from four hours to three minutes. He was also the promoter of *poka-yoke* (defect free production). From the 1970s onwards, Japan concentrated on further developing original techniques of quality and exporting them to the rest of the world. By the late 1970s, the Japanese experience of 'zero quality control' (ZQC) demonstrated to the rest of the world that quality control by prevention was more cost-effective and more desirable than quality control by detection (Xu, 1999).

In contrast to Japan and America, the British approach to quality in the twentieth century seemed to be highly fragmented and sporadic. The overall approach was to pay lip service to quality and favour fire-fighting techniques rather than pursue long-term commitments to quality. This is ironic, for a number of reasons: first, Great Britain has been a world leader in technology and manufacturing in the eighteenth and nineteenth centuries. Second, one of the most important contributions to statistical methods for quality was made by Tippett, a British statistician in 1931, the same year that Shewhart had published his book on statistical process control. While Shewhart's work was taken seriously by American corporations, Tippett's work passed almost unobserved by the British industry.

There may be, however, deeper reasons for the loss of industrial leadership suffered by the UK. Morrison (1994) talks about a nationalistic attitude, rooted in the belief that 'British is best', which prevented companies from seeing the dangers posed by foreign competition. As long as Britain kept its captive markets, its colonies, there was nothing to fear. The collapse of the empire, however, had serious consequences on British organizations, forcing them to compete on European, Asian and American markets against competitors which were more aggressive and more tuned to quality.

There may, however, be other reasons: the short-termist approach and a lack of appropriate quality training among senior managers may also explain why British manufacturing had such a hard time surviving in a competitive market. Although things are starting to change with Britain being one of the largest providers of postgraduate MBAs (Master of Business Administration) in the world, the country is seen by some to be still struggling to rejuvenate its private business and the public sector (Caulkin, 2002). According to Caulkin (2002) world-class British managers are rare and so is world-class management research in Britain. Perhaps such analyses are too gloomy and do not capture some of the most current trends. British management has become more proactive and indeed more preoccupied with quality matters in the past few years. Such changes are most obvious in the British service sector (banking, insurance, tourism, retailing) and the Internet infrastructure industries. Meanwhile, Japan and the US appear to have lost some of their initial spark and bases for competitive advantage. New players such as the Asian tigers are attempting to make a name for themselves in the global marketplace by pursuing quality in a most serious manner.

The development of quality as a scientific discipline and practice of management has been multifaceted. The discipline of quality has become more and more complex and its effects more and more significant. If quality used to mean mere conformance to standards, or fitness for use, it now accounts for the expectations and perceptions of the end-user (the customer, the citizen or the society at large). Quality must be approached not only as a technical, rational phenomenon but also as a cultural and political process with significant consequences upon day-to-day activities.

As a practice of management, quality has spread from the fields of manufacturing and engineering to incorporate the entire production chain, from design to marketing to after-sale services. If initially quality was only the concern of a few specialized professionals from the quality assurance department, it has now become everybody's responsibility in the organization, from the front line people to the highest echelon of management. Quality management has also spread to the service, public and voluntary sectors and its focus has shifted away from inspection and detection to prevention, maintenance and improvement.

The widespread concern with quality as a scientific discipline and as a practice of management was given impetus by a number of 'quality gurus' whose models and theories are presented below. The tensions between these models are also highlighted and an explanation is offered as to why different gurus suggest different paths for quality.

Quality gurus could be grouped in three camps based on some notion of chronology (Bendell, 1991):

1   The early American writers subscribe mainly to a managerial approach to quality: W. Edwards Deming and Joseph M. Juran are typically

associated with the manufacturing-based view on quality while Armand V. Feigenbaum is the proponent of the value-based approach to quality. To some extent, however, Juran and Feigenbaum also embrace a user-based view on quality. These early gurus took the message of quality to Japan in the 1950s.

2   The Japanese writers developed new quality concepts in response to the American messages from the late 1950s onwards: K. Ishikawa could be said to have embraced a social constructivist approach to quality while G. Taguchi and S. Shingo subscribed to manufacturing-based models of quality

3   The new Western wave writers, following the Japanese industrial success, have given rise to increased awareness of quality in the West: Phil Crosby embraces a slogan approach to quality while Tom Peters's approach is more in line with transcendental and discursive approaches. Nevertheless, both gurus argue that quality is a manageable and controllable phenomenon: in this sense, they could also be classified as managerialist.

THE EARLY AMERICAN WRITERS

The early American gurus, i.e., W. Edwards Deming and Joseph J. Juran, have had the largest impact on our current understanding of quality management and the ways in which quality is understood and managed in contemporary organizations. Implicit in their work is the view that quality is key to economic survival, social fulfilment and environmental protection.

W.E. Deming

W.E. Deming was born in 1900 and was awarded a doctorate in mathematical physics in 1928 by Yale University. His approach to quality draws heavily on Shewhart's concept of statistical process control. Deming's work had initially no impact in America primarily because in the postwar booming market, everything built was sold. After the war, he went to Japan as an Adviser to the Japanese Census. The Union of Japanese Scientists and Engineers (JUSE) invited him to lecture on quality control techniques to engineers and senior managers. His contribution to rebuilding the Japanese economy was recognized by the Emperor who awarded him the Second Order of the Sacred Treasure (Bendell, 1991).

His main message to the Japanese was that variability is inherent in any process and is due to two types of causes, namely, special causes which are easily assignable, identifiable and solvable by operators themselves, and common causes which are due to design and operation and only management can eliminate. Deming argues that 94 per cent of the quality problems are the

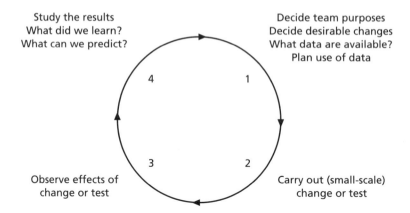

FIGURE 2.1
The PDCA cycle
(adapted from
Bendell, 1991)

responsibility of management. He believes in a quantitative and systematic approach to identifying and solving problems, the so-called plan, do, check, action (PDCA) cycle (see Figure 2.1).

Deming started to be known in the West in the early 1980s when NBC television broadcast a documentary entitled 'If Japan Can Why Can't We?'. Deming's work in the West is best known in respect to the 'Seven Deadly Sins' of Western managers and the 'Fourteen Principles for Transformation' aimed at supporting the implementation of a successful quality initiative. His late work tends to be rather prescriptive offering broad guidelines rather than concrete ideas as to how to improve quality.

Let us first look at the so-called 'deadly sins' which refer to management practices which hinder the achievement of quality. In Deming's view, the seven deadly sins to be avoided at all costs are:

1 Lack of consistency (the organization is managed on a flavour-of-the-month basis, thus lacking a long-term strategy).
2 Short-term profit focus.
3 Too much emphasis on performance appraisals.
4 Regular movement of managers between jobs either within or between organizations, i.e., job-hopping.
5 Over-reliance on visible figures and a neglect of other less tangible aspects of the organization.
6 Excessive medical costs supported by the company.
7 Excessive costs of liability.

While some of these guidelines are self-evident, others are more contentious. It is not clear for, example, what are the defining criteria for 'too much', 'over-reliance' and 'excessive'. Moreover, one has no control over how many employees may fall ill: picking up medical bills, rather than being a deadly sin, could in fact lead to higher morale among the workforce and more loyalty towards the company. Deming presents no clear evidence as to how these deadly sins undermine the quality process in a company. Instead, he proposes 14 principles of transformation to cure the 'deadly sins' and pave the way for the successful implementation of quality programmes, namely:

1 create constancy of purpose to improve product and service;
2 adopt new learning philosophy;
3 cease dependence on inspection;
4 end awarding business on price;
5 improve constantly and for ever the system of production and service;
6 institute training on the job;
7 institute leadership;
8 drive out fear;
9 break down barriers between departments;
10 eliminate slogans, exhortations and numerical targets for the workforce;
11 eliminate quotas or work standards, and management by objectives or numerical goals;
12 remove barriers that rob people of their right to pride of workmanship;
13 institute a vigorous education and self-improvement programme;
14 put everyone in the company to work to accomplish this transformation.

Some of these principles make good business sense but are by no means novel. For example, communication, leadership and company-wide training are regarded by many academics and practitioners as the cornerstone of effective management. The 14 principles of transformation subscribe to the view that management is omniscient and has the ability to predict and control what goes on in the organization.

Deming's approach to quality has been praised, among others, for its systemic logic, sound statistical approaches, its emphasis on leadership and an awareness of the different sociocultural contexts (Flood, 1993; Beckford, 1998). However, Deming adopts a unitary perspective on organizations, saying relatively little about managerial interventions in political and coercive situations and showing a limited understanding of human motivation. Deming's work lacks a well-defined methodology as he merely indicates what to do but not how to do it. Like most managerial approaches to quality, Deming's models are based on a universal notion of quality which is discussed mainly in relation to the product/service. Quality of social relations is considered irrelevant unless it can be shown to contribute to increased bottom line profit.

Joseph M. Juran

Joseph M. Juran was born in 1904 in Transylvania and became a naturalized American soon after. He trained as an engineer and like Deming, he was invited to Japan in the 1950s to conduct seminars for top and middle executives. He was also awarded the Second Order of the Sacred Treasure by the Emperor of Japan. His most important books are *Quality Control Handbook* (Juran et al., 1974) and *Juran On Planning For Quality (Quality Planning, Quality Control, Quality Improvement)* (1988). Juran defines quality as 'fitness for use or purpose' and argues that quality control should be conducted as an integral part of management control. Moreover, quality does not happen by accident but has to be planned. Juran proposes a quality-planning map consisting of the following steps:

1 identify who the customers are;
2 determine the needs of those customers;
3 translate those needs into company language;
4 develop a product that can respond to customer needs;
5 optimize the product features so as to meet company needs as well as customer needs;
6 develop a process which is able to produce the product;
7 prove that the process can produce the product under operating conditions;
8 transfer the process to operations.

Juran is the first quality writer who introduced the internal customer concept, a concept that was consequently singled out by the service marketing and total quality management literature as the backbone of effective organizational relationships. For Juran, the majority of quality problems (around 80 per cent) are the fault of poor management, rather than poor workmanship and the recipe for action should be 90 per cent substance and 10 per cent exhortation, not the reverse. His methodology is typically praised for its focus on continuous improvement as well as for emphasizing the centrality of planning in managing quality and acknowledging the importance of both external and internal customers in the process of managing quality (Flood, 1993). The limitations of his manufacturing-based approach to quality are to a certain extent similar to those of Deming's method. He underrates workers' contribution, views organizations as sites of consensus and common interests, and provides little discussion of motivational, leadership and other social issues. Despite such limitations, Juran has contributed a great deal to raising awareness among Western and Japanese managers of the importance of quality in competing successfully in the global market.

Armand V. Feigenbaum

Armand V. Feigenbaum is perhaps less known than the previous two gurus, yet his contribution to the quality management movement is the most tangible one. His work was discovered by the Japanese in the 1950s at about the same time Juran and Deming were visiting Japan. In his most important book, *Quality Control: Principles, Practice and Administration* (1951) he defines quality from a value-based approach as 'best for the customer use at the right selling price' and views quality control not only as a technical issue but more important as a business method.

Quality control is a management tool with four steps:

1 setting quality standards;
2 appraising conformance to these standards;
3 acting when standards are unmet or exceeded;
4 planning for improvements in the standards.

According to Feigenbaum, there are four types of control:

1 New design control refers to those mechanisms put in place to ensure that the design of a new product or process meets certain standards, as decided by the technical experts and managers.
2 Incoming materials control refers to those procedures by which materials from suppliers are checked against existing standards.
3 Product control is performed usually via acceptance sampling procedures (see Chapter 7 for a more detailed discussion of this procedure).
4 Special process studies are those controls which ensure that the process of production is on target. Statistical process control (see Chapter 7 for a more detailed discussion) is the most widely used technique for controlling and adjusting process variation.

Feigenbaum is also well known for attempting to quantify the cost of quality. He divides costs of quality into:

• prevention costs – costs that relate to those activities aimed to build quality within the system in order to prevent defects and faulty products and services;
• appraisal costs – costs relating to the inspection and control of quality.
• internal failure costs (i.e., scrap, rework).
• external failure costs (i.e., warranty costs, complaints).

Feigenbaum takes a systemic view on organizations, highlighting the importance of the relations between internal organizational subsystems and between these and the environment. The concept of total quality management is typically traced back to his work. Referring to quality control, Feigenbaum, suggested that this must be total and systematic, requiring the involvement of all functions, not just manufacturing. He defined total quality control (TQC) as an agreed company-wide operating work structure, documented in effective, integrated technical and managerial procedures for guiding the co-ordinated actions of the people, the machines and the information within the company in the best and most practical ways to assure customer quality satisfaction and economical cost of quality (Feigenbaum, 1983).

Feigenbaum's approach to quality emphasizes human relations and employee participation to a larger extent than other early American gurus.

For him, quality control is not only a technical tool but also, more importantly, a business method and an organizational practice. His main weakness remains the fact that his method is rather prescriptive and fails to address in detail the implementation and management of quality in organizations. He, like Deming and Juran, views organizations as cohesive entities untouched by conflict and opposing interests.

In his recent work Feigenbaum adopts a rather descriptive tone telling us what quality is. His 'ten crucial benchmarks for total quality success' are enumerated below

1   quality is a company-wide process;
2   quality is what the customer says it is;
3   quality and cost are a sum, not a difference;
4   quality requires both individual and team zealotry;
5   quality is a way of managing;
6   quality and innovation are mutually dependent;
7   quality is an ethic;
8   quality requires continuous improvement;
9   quality is the most cost effective, least capital-intensive route to productivity;
10 quality is implemented with a total system connected with customers and suppliers.

These assume quality to be an iconic, universal value, one that needs to be internalised throughout the organization. Some of these ideas are rooted in the slogan approach to quality for they simply state the obvious in a plain, easy to understand manner, and others find resonances with the user-based approach to quality in their emphasis of the role of the consumer in defining quality.

THE JAPANESE WRITERS

Kaoru Ishikawa

Kaoru Ishikawawas born in 1915 and was awarded a doctorate in engineering. For Ishikawa quality is not only an attribute of the product but also an attribute of after-sale services, of the management, the company itself and its employees. He is an advocater of company-wide quality and a pioneer of the quality circle movement. He says:

> I first considered how best to get grassroots workers to understand and practice quality control. The idea was to educate all people working at factories throughout the country but this was asking too much. Therefore, I thought of educating factory foremen or on the spot leaders in the first place. (quoted by Bendell, 1991: 17)

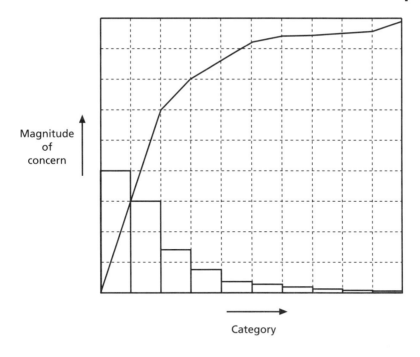

FIGURE 2.2
Pareto chart
(adapted from
Kanji and Asher,
1996)

Magnitude
of
concern

Category

The first quality circle was registered in 1962 at The Nippon Telegraph and Telephone Public. According to Ishikawa, a quality circle is a voluntary group of some five to ten workers from the same workshop who meet regularly and are led by a foreman, assistant foreman, work leader or one of the workers. The original aims of the quality circles were to contribute to the improvement and development of the enterprise; to respect human relations and build a happy working environment offering job satisfaction; and to deploy human capabilities more fully. Where possible quality circles implement solutions themselves or put strong pressures on management to introduce them (Ishikawa, 1985).

Quality circles members are trained to use a number of tools and techniques such as (for these and other tools seen Kanji and Asher, 1996):

• Pareto charts, which take their name from Vilfredo Pareto (1848–1922) whose research was primarily concerned with the distribution of wealth. He found by analysing the distribution of total income among the population of a country that a small proportion of the population (20 per cent) received a large part of the income (80 per cent). In the context of quality control, the Pareto analysis will indicate which areas, if improved, will give the greatest benefit for the least effort (see Figure 2.2). Interestingly, Pareto was rather a conservative, someone who strongly believed that an elite of about 20 per cent of the population should run the other 80 per cent.

FIGURE 2.3
Cause–effect
diagram
(adapted from
Kanji and Asher,
1996)

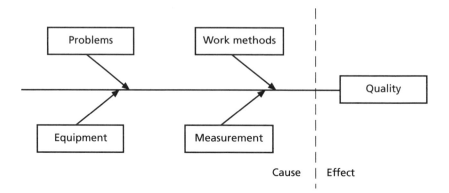

FIGURE 2.4
Process flow
chart (adapted
from Kanji and
Asher, 1996)

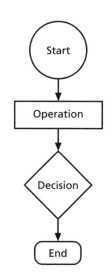

- The cause and effect diagram, also called the Ishikawa diagram is used to reveal the factors/causes which contribute to the achievement of a particular goal or objective. Such causes have been classified by Ishikawa to include methods, equipment, materials, and people issues. There are three steps to this method: first members brainstorm all possible causes of the problem/effect under analysis. Secondly, they classify the causes under the four headings mentioned above and thirdly, they draw the diagram (see Figure 2.3).
- Process flow charting is a technique used to record a series of events and activities, stages and decisions in a form that can be easily understood and communicated to all. It is very helpful in visualizing processes and highlighting where improvements are needed. It allows processes to be challenged and gaps, duplications, and dead ends identified thus leading to process simplification (see Figure 2.4).

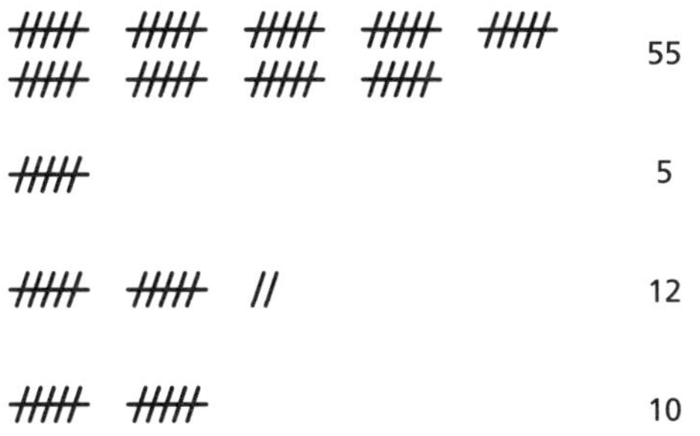

‖‖‖ ‖‖‖ ‖‖‖ ‖‖‖ ‖‖‖
‖‖‖ ‖‖‖ ‖‖‖ ‖‖‖   55

‖‖‖   5

‖‖‖ ‖‖‖ //   12

‖‖‖ ‖‖‖   10

FIGURE 2.5
Check sheet
(adapted from
Kanji and Asher,
1996)

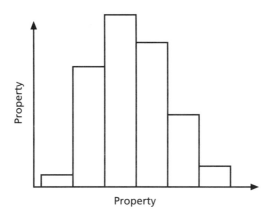

FIGURE 2.6
Histogram
(adapted from
Kanji and Asher,
1996)

- Check sheets are used to record customer requirements and priorities, focusing attention on those elements which are most sought after or appreciated by the customer: they could also be used to visualize defective parts (see Figure 2.5).
- Histograms are ways of visually displaying sets of data and enabling comparisons between two or more characteristics. They are most often used to display frequency distributions and are helpful in summarizing the data, and appreciating measures of central tendency and dispersion (see Figure 2.6).
- Scatter diagrams are used to determine if there is a relationship between two variables: one dependent and one independent. The scattergraph gives a general view on relationships; it does not provide formal measurements of these relationships, nor does it shed light on what causes these relationships (see Figure 2.7).
- Control charts are drawn in order to record the occurrence of a particular event. They consist of upper and lower control and warning limits: when the measurements go above or below these limits, it is said that the process is out of control and one must intervene in order to bring it

FIGURE 2.7
Scatter diagram
(adopted from
Kanji and Asher,
1996)

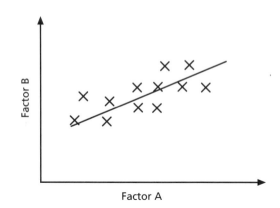

Factor B

Factor A

FIGURE 2.8
Control chart
(adapted from
Kanji and Asher,
1996)

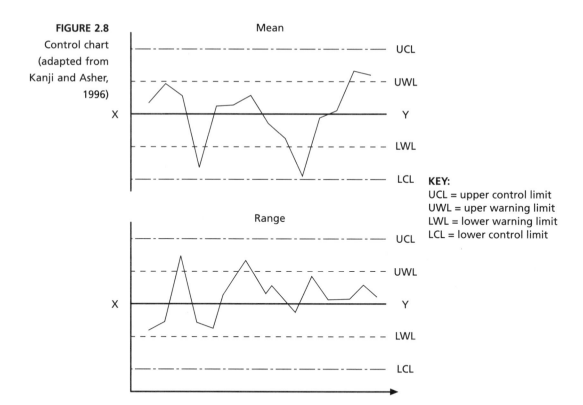

KEY:
UCL = upper control limit
UWL = uper warning limit
LWL = lower warning limit
LCL = lower control limit

back to a normal state (see Chapter 7 for a more detailed analysis) (see Figure 2.8).

The strengths of Ishikawa's approach to quality lie in its emphasis on company-wide participation, and in using a combination of qualitative and quantitative methods to improve quality and in promoting the use of quality circles. Thus, it could be considered a social constructivist approach to quality, one that recognizes the importance of a multitude of voices in defining quality.

Various commentators (including Deming and Juran) have questioned whether quality circles can be transferred successfully to the West. Quality circles have been criticized for failing to break down organizational boundaries as they tend to focus on a single area. It has also been argued that the Ishikawa diagram is too linear and does not account for the interrelationships between causes and/or effects; for example there may be relationships between materials, equipment, people and methods that are not captured by the technique. Furthermore, while some of these tools and techniques may work well in isolation, it is not clear how they interrelate and how they could pull together in the implementation of an Ishikawa quality programme (Beckford, 1998).

Genichi Taguchi

Genichi Taguchi was born in 1924 and worked in a number of prestigious public organizations including The Ministry of Public Health and Welfare and The Institute of Statistical Mathematics before joining the Electrical Communication Laboratory of the Nippon Telephone and Telegraph Company in 1950. It was here that he began to develop his techniques of experimental design. Taguchi was concerned primarily with the optimization of the product and/or process prior to manufacturing. The concepts of quality and reliability were thus pushed back to the design stage where they really belonged. In contrast to existing definitions of quality, Taguchi views quality in terms of quality loss defined as the loss imparted to society from the time the product is shipped. Such loss refers not only to the loss to the company through the cost of reworking and scrapping, maintenance costs, downtime due to equipment failure and warranty claims, but also costs to the customer through poor product performance and reliability. The quality loss is operationalized through the quality loss function, a quadratic function which shows that a reduction in variability around the target leads to a decrease in loss and a subsequent increase in quality. According to this function, loss is minimum when the product is on target (see Chapter 3). The quality loss function can be used to evaluate design decisions on a financial basis in order to decide whether additional costs in production will actually prove to be worthwhile in the marketplace (Taguchi, 1986). Taguchi's approach is manufacturing-based due to the fact that it attempts to secure conformance to technical requirements in the design and production stage.

Taguchi's methodology can be applied online in production and offline in design. The offline quality control, for example, comprises three stages (Bendell, 1991):

1   system design: the creation of the design concept;

2 parameter design: in this phase the nominal design features are tested and those least sensitive to changes in environmental conditions are determined;
3 tolerance design: employed to reduce variation further if required, by tightening the tolerance of those factors shown to have a large impact on variation.

Accordingly, optimizing a product corresponds not only to getting its quality characteristics on target but also minimizing variability away from the target on a piece-to-piece or time-to-time basis.

Taguchi is also famous for codifying the so-called orthogonal arrays, that is, designs for experiments, in such a way that an engineer automatically has a route to a minimum number of prototypes necessary for experimentation. Taguchi's aim was to create a product so 'robust' that it could withstand random fluctuations during manufacturing that would otherwise lead to defects. He identified the controllable and uncontrollable variables most likely to affect quality. He then looked for the most resilient combination of these variables which would ensure the performance of the product irrespective of what else would go wrong in production.

The most important advantage of the method is that it allows for on-line, real-time control. The method has been praised for its practicality: as it was developed and used mainly by engineers rather than statisticians, the method did not have the communication problems associated with many statistical methodologies. Furthermore, the approach recognizes the systemic impact of quality and guides the process of quality control effectively. Among its weaknesses, one could mention the bias towards manufacturing, and in particular, automated processes, and the general lack of guidance on management and organizational issues. In fact, quality is placed in the hands of technical experts (engineers) while workers are not considered a significant factor in the production of quality goods (Beckford, 1998).

Shigeo Shingo

Shigeo Shingo is the least known Japanese quality writer in the West. His approach emphasizes production rather than organizational issues, and it is thus manufacturing-based. He believed that statistical methods detect errors too late in the manufacturing process. Shingo's method emphasises 'zero defects' through good engineering and process investigation and rectification (Shingo, 1986).

His method, *poka-yoke* or zero defects, stops the process whenever a defect occurs, defines the cause and prevents the recurring source of the defect. The method relies on a process of continuously monitoring potential sources of error. The machines used in this process are equipped with feedback instrumentation. If source inspection is employed as an active part of production in order to identify errors before they become defects, statistical sampling is no longer necessary and workers are free to concentrate on more valuable activities. Unlike statistical control systems, in which a fairly long time elapses between the 'check' stage and the execution of feedback and action, *poka-yoke* minimizes defects by carrying out feedback and action immediately at a low cost. It can be used at the source of raw materials and components, at the start of the production process and at production points where errors might occur (for more details, read Kanji and Asher, 1996).

THE NEW WESTERN WAVE OF QUALITY GURUS

Phil Crosby

Phil Crosby is an American consultant whose name is primarily associated with 'do it right first time' and 'zero defects'. Unlike Shingo, Crosby's 'zero defects' emphasises worker's responsibility, exhortations and slogans (Crosby, 1979), and not the technical aspects of the process. In this sense, one can argue that it is a slogan approach: such slogans are seen to help individuals internalize the importance of quality and perform their duties to the customer in a more effective manner.

Crosby defines quality as conformance to requirements which the company itself has established for its products based directly on its customers' needs. Quality is an inherent characteristic of the product, not an added element. Like some of his predecessors, Crosby argues that management is to blame for the vast majority of the quality problems within an organization. Moreover, the most important performance measurement within an organization is the cost of quality and it is cheaper to get things right first time.

He proposes (14) steps to quality improvement, namely:

1   make it clear that management is committed to quality;
2   form quality improvement teams;
3   measure processes;
4   evaluate cost of quality;
5   raise the quality awareness;
6   take actions to correct problems;
7   establish process monitoring;
8   train supervisors;
9   hold a zero defect day;
10 encourage individuals to establish improvement goals for themselves and their groups;
11 encourage communication;
12 recognise and appreciate those who participate;
13 establish quality councils;
14 do it all over again.

Among the strengths of Crosby's approach are his motivational style, the clarity of his approach and the importance placed on workers' involvement and responsibility. His major weaknesses concern the potential for zero defects to be interpreted as zero risks and the ineffectiveness of his model in highly coercive environments. Some commentators also criticize Crosby for the PR style in which companies are supposed to go about quality, by using slogans and exhortations (Flood, 1993).

Tom Peters

Tom Peters is another American consultant who has researched into the secrets of most successful American companies. In his most popular book, *In Search of Excellence* (with Waterman, 1982) he analysed the critical success factors in 43 large American corporations. Excellence is presented as a universal icon that can guide businesses and sift through winners and losers. In this book, Peters and Waterman subscribe to a transcendental approach to quality: excellence is synonymous with quality yet it is indefinable through objective and rational methods of research. In a second book, *A Passion for Excellence* (1985), Peters and Austin identify leadership as central to the quality improvement process. They see management by walk about (MBWA) as the basis of leadership for it enables the leader to keep in touch with the workers, customers and suppliers. The words uttered by leaders are argued to have a large impact on the organizations studied in the book: it is that language and the deeds of the leaders that define other people's sense of reality. In this sense, Peters subscribe to a discursive approach to quality. In his third book, *Thriving on Chaos* (1987) he prescribes ways of bringing about a management revolution in the West. Such ways tend to focus on the end-user as the most important factor in judging quality efforts. Tom Peters has been mainly criticized for his sales-driven approach to quality and for setting and embracing new fashions rather than sticking to his initial models: indeed, from a transcendental approach, he moved on to a discursive one and then to a user-based one. Supporters, on the other hand, defend him by claiming that since the world is changing rapidly, views and models of management must change too: his books and videos still have a wide appeal among managerial audiences.

SUMMARY

The principles reviewed at the beginning of the chapter signal that quality had existed for many thousands of years. Many of the models proposed by the quality gurus subscribe to the view that quality is a universal value, something that can be measured, controlled, planned and mustered via various technical or managerial methods and techniques. It is important to note the contradictions between the various methods and models advocated by the quality gurus. Juran, for example, advocates setting quality objectives and managing the quality plan according to these objectives. On the other hand, Deming is strongly opposed to management by objectives. He is also against the use of merit ratings and slogans to achieve objectives, while Peters and Crosby advocate the crucial importance of slogans and rewards in promoting excellence. Crosby recommends zero defects as a quality objective, whereas Juran and Deming oppose this notion because the inherent variability in all processes renders such an objective unrealistic (Chatterjee and Yilman, 1993).

Such contradictory advice stems from the fact that quality, rather than being a universal phenomenon, is a social and multifaceted phenomenon acquiring meaning through processes of intersubjective communication. Each guru tends to elevate one particular facet at the expense of the others. Hence, gurus' prescriptions should be viewed as attention-seeking devices rather than as universal theories of management. It is crucial for companies to develop organization-specific quality systems. It is impossible to simply lift an approach and try it out in the organization with the expectation that it will work unconditionally. Different companies have different priorities and must respond to different demands: therefore they need to tailor their quality approaches to fit their immediate circumstances and, in so doing, they may embrace some of the gurus' prescriptions but may reject others.

KEY CONCEPTS

Here are the key concepts covered in this chapter: measurement, inspection, feedback, precision, quality gurus.

QUESTIONS

At the end of this chapter you should be able to answer the following questions:

- To what extent is quality a universal concept?
- What are the most basic principles underlying the management of quality?
- What social and historical factors have influenced the development of quality management?
- What are the main differences between the models provided by individual gurus and to what extent can or should they be reconciled?

3 Quality in contemporary organizations

At the outset, quality was associated primarily with the operations function. This is not surprising given that the very first quality control techniques were developed by the manufacturing sector. More recently, however, its relevance to other organizational functions has become more apparent and recognized as crucial to the successful functioning of the organization as a whole. Numerous companies are currently pursuing quality management initiatives that cut across functions from design, marketing, strategy to human resources and accounting. Such an approach has been labelled *total* quality management (for a detailed discussion see Chapter 8). This chapter explores the relationship between the discipline and practice of quality management and other management disciplines and practices such as strategy, human resource management, marketing, accounting and design.

QUALITY AND STRATEGY

Quality programmes have a strong association with strategic change due to the fact that many companies adopt quality management programmes at times of crisis or due to institutional pressures from customers, competition, governmental regulations and so on. Such changes may or may not be revolutionary but they are strategic in that they typically require that the organization makes quality a long-term objective, allocates appropriate resources for its achievement and institutes control and evaluation procedures to review its progress. Consequently, quality management requires strategic management skills.

Strategic management is a process carried out at the top of the organization which provides guidance and direction for all aspects of operational management (Vinzant and Vinzant, 1996). This process has usually three broad steps:

1 Strategic planning, to determine the company's objectives.
2 Resource management, to configure and allocate resources among units within an organization to implement plans.
3 Control and evaluation, to ensure the implementation of strategies.

Strategic management emphazises organizational adaptation to environmental demands and opportunities via the dynamic and complex interaction between the behavioural aspects of organizations such as culture, learning and leadership; and technical aspects such as planning and budgeting. Quality management programmes are 'adaptation tools' for they typically aim to ensure a fit between the organization and the environment, by combining 'hard technologies' (the implementation of technical standards and processes of quality control) with soft ones (i.e., employee involvement, training, leadership and organizational culture).

One of the most useful techniques to pursue quality strategically is the strategic quality plan which has five steps:

1 The business plan is enlarged to include goals of quality.
2 These goals are deployed to lower levels in order to determine the resources needed, agree actions and fix responsibility for taking actions.
3 Measures are developed to permit evaluation of progress against goals.
4 Managers, including upper managers review progress regularly.
5 The reward system is revised to give appropriate weight to quality.

If the strategic nature of quality management programmes has been widely acknowledged in the literature, its role as a strategic resource (i.e., as providing organizations with sustainable competitive advantage) remains controversial. While in the 1980s, many writers argued that quality management was key to competitive advantage, by the 1990s quality was replaced by flexibility and quick response (traits usually labelled 'agility').

The link between pursuing quality management and organizational outcomes remains spurious. Studies carried out by Profit Impact Market Strategy Associates (PIMS) found significant correlations between quality and business results in over 3,000 businesses in North America and Europe. Yet other studies carried out by London Business School (1992), Durham University Business School (1992) and the Economist Intelligence Unit (1992) report significant degrees of cynicism over the impact of quality in the UK (all studies quoted in Wilkinson et al., 1998).

The 'resource based view' (Barney, 1991) provides a useful perspective on what makes firms successful: it could be quality, agility or neither. According to this theory, organizations consist of bundles of resources and capabilities that lead to competitive advantage. To do so, these resources should be valuable, unique and rare. Uniqueness is related to the concept of resource heterogeneity: that is, different firms hold different resource portfolios. It is these differences that lead to variability in performance across firms. Although firms may try to imitate successful ones, it is impossible to grasp the intangible and tacit resources of an organization (Barney, 1991).

Some of these resources may have been originally acquired under unique, non-replicable conditions and their operation may be too complex and/or ambiguous to be understood by managers from other firms. That is why quality management practices developed in Japan are thought to be non-transferrable to other cultures for they rely on cultural assumptions which are fundamentally incompatible with many Western assumptions (Young, 1992).

QUALITY AND MARKETING

If we adopt the user-based definition of quality (Garvin, 1984), it becomes clear that the relationship between the discipline and practice of quality management and marketing is a very close and important one. Marketing plays an important role in identifying customers' expectations and thus in setting the operational and strategic direction of the organization. Any preoccupation with quality must start with knowing what the customers want. Such wants must then be translated into an appropriate product/service which not only meets customer expectations but also matches the operational capabilities of the firm and allows it to make a profit. It is suggested that an important reason as to why more than 80 per cent of the new products fail is a lack of understanding of the whole experience of the customer from awareness to the disposal of a product. According to Berggren and Nacher (2000), marketing techniques could help organizations understand the complexity of the customer experience which will help them target the highest value customer segment and improve the relationships present in the value chain.

Improving relationships with important customers has led to the development of a new approach to marketing, one which rather than emphazising 'getting' new customers, concentrates on 'keeping' important customers. This approach, called relationship marketing, views the customer as a long-term annuity or stream of revenue receipts rather than as a single transaction with no strings attached. Building strong relationships with the customers can help reduce customer turnover rates and thereby increase profitability as retaining customers is significantly less costly than acquiring new customers. A loyal customer base is an asset composed of the discounted present value of the future stream of profits from a continuing relationship. The development of long-term relationships with customers and suppliers is also a fundamental principle of total quality management.

The philosophy of marketing has more recently turned inwards towards other functions/individuals within the organization, the so-called internal customers. On one level, the focus of internal marketing is on the fair treatment of employees and the satisfaction of their job-related needs with the view to enhance their customer-oriented performance and ensure external customer satisfaction. Internal marketing embraces the idea of 'getting everyone in the organization to practise marketing' (Berry, 1986); that is to be customer-focused and service-oriented in their internal interactions with other departments or individual employees. On another level, internal marketing views each function/department as an internal customer whose expectations must be known and met within the internal organizational value chain. In contingency theory terms, internal marketing ensures 'internal consistency' while relationship marketing ensures 'external congruency' with the larger environment.

QUALITY AND HUMAN RESOURCE MANAGEMENT

Aligning human resource practices with the philosophy of quality requires significant changes in the way organizations train, empower, evaluate and reward individuals and teams. The pursuit of quality alters significantly the way jobs are designed, requiring new behaviours, roles and responsibilities for all organizational members (Victor et al., 2000). However, work under a quality regime is dual in that it combines two distinct types of tasks: standardized tasks and continuous improvement tasks, in other words, execution and conception tasks. When confronted with the challenge of this dual role, some employees may experience a great amount of stress.

Most quality programmes rely on the use of HRM style policies to encourage employees to embrace both types of tasks and generate employee commitment (Rees, 1995). There are many definitions of commitment but in a nutshell a committed employee wants on his/her own what the organization wants. The rhetoric of the committed employee builds upon the imagery of total immersion in quality goals and supporting organizational practices. Here the individual is seen as a mature and committed self whose destiny is tightly coupled with the company (Kunda, 1992).

Building on Merton's (1957) work, it is suggested that there are five possible states of commitment, depending on whether the employee embraces organizational goals and/or institutionalized means for achieving them. These states are: identification, innovation, ritualism, resilience and rebellion (Merton, 1957).

1   Identification occurs when employees accept both the goal of quality and the organizational means for achieving it. The employees believe they are one with the company, embracing their organizational role with conviction.
2   Innovation occurs when employees may agree with organizational goals but reject the 'one best way' of doing things as enforced by top management. Thus, the goal of quality may be embraced by employees but the ways of achieving it are challenged on various counts.
3   Ritualism is that situation where employees conform to prescribed organizational routines but do not believe in organizational goals. Thus,

employees may not make quality a personal goal but conform to it for calculative reasons, out of comfort, or out of fear.

4 Resilience occurs when employees are against organizational goals and institutionalized means for achieving them. Resilient employees invoke rational or emotional reasons for rejecting the goal of quality and the organizational means for achieving them.

5 Rebellion takes place when employees want to replace organizational goals with something else and want to achieve that quite differently. Rebellion is an ideal state which cannot be sustained in practice as it leads either to the dismantling of the organization or to people quitting their work. In most cases, rebellion and resilience become redefined in terms of ritualism.

In reality, most employees feel at times both attachment to and detachment from the goal and means of achieving quality. Their responses are a matter of intersubjective definition and may change depending on the circumstances at hand. An extended critique of Merton's taxonomy is provided by Kelemen (2001).

Let us now review some of the HRM policies used to increase commitment to quality. Such policies attempt to establish a system of rewards and punishments that aligns itself with the ethos of quality management. Rewards refer to both monetary and non-monetary types, including the utility generated by participation in quality management activities (if any), the benefit of making one's job easier, safer, public recognition, pay rises, promotions, bonuses, profit sharing and equity ownership programmes.

1 *Participation and job improvement.* Quality management changes the nature of jobs and of the work itself, making tasks in some cases multifaceted and, therefore, more challenging. Many employees enjoy participating in quality processes that requires more of their knowledge and skills to solve problems. Although they typically receive the same (material) compensation, their job may become more desirable.

2 *Public recognition.* Various quality gurus view public recognition as contributing to increasing commitment to quality, see for example, Juran (1988) and Crosby (1979). Some organizations have campaigns such as 'employee of the month', 'employee of the year' whereby those employees who proved their commitment to their customers are being publicly recognized and given a diploma or insignia to certify to their achievement.

3 *Career advancement opportunities.* Under a quality management regime, career opportunities may also be enhanced, not in a traditional way, such as, by progressing more quickly from one hierarchical level to the next, but in a more lateral thinking way: thus one's area of responsibility and accountability may increase or one might be asked to take on board different sorts of projects.

4 *Appraisals.* Appraisal and self-appraisal systems are redesigned to account for quality-related tasks and knowledge. However, there is a

notoriously contradictory debate as to whether such quality related issues are to be rewarded materially or not.

5 *Quality-related pay.* Some organizations use pay for knowledge schemes to emphasize the importance of quality training and learning. Although the monetary rewards associated with such schemes are usually small, they could affect behaviour by breaking down the notion of seniority-based wages and emphazising the importance of learning. Gurus such as Ishikawa, Crosby and Deming are against quality-related pay arguing that money is a poor motivator and that numerical measures of perform-ance are flawed. Other gurus, such as, Juran and Mizuno argue that both material and symbolic rewards are valued by employees and should be used in combination. Providing that firms tie quality rewards to simple performance measures such as overall firm profitability (through profit sharing) or firm value (through employee equity ownership plans), there is more visibility and fairness which can lead to less conflict among the employees (Wruck and Jensen, 1994).

The problems of management in successfully generating employee com-mitment to quality through the use of HRM techniques are well documented. Management is trapped between two opposing ideologies: collectivism and individualism. On the one hand, managers attempt to develop a collective identity around practices of teamwork, on the other hand, they discriminate between individual employees through practices such as appraisal and performance related pay. Furthermore, employees may feel that an increase in their responsibilities is not coupled with appropriate decision-making power and the right level of rewards. For many, quality initiatives are synonymous with work intensification and the enhancement of exploitation (Delbridge and Turnbull, 1992).

Interestingly enough, the need for employee commitment and involve-ment to the goal of quality was not made explicit in the works of the quality gurus (see Chapter 2). For example, Deming's 14-point plan for introducing quality management (Deming, 1986) focuses on the changes management has to make with no mention of employee involvement or empowerment. Juran (1988) mentions employee involvement only superficially: his discus-sion of setting quality objectives and targets makes no reference to the role of employees. According to Wilkinson and colleagues (1997), the concept of employee commitment and involvement entered the discourse of quality via pop management writers such as Tom Peters (1987) and John Oakland (1989). While critical perspective on quality recognize the importance of the voice of the employee in defining what counts as quality, managerial defini-tions tend to concentrate only on the voice of the quality expert, the manager and the consumer.

Employee involvement is a multifaceted concept, the result of a number of factors among which the most important are (Wilkinson et al., 1997):

- *The educational factor.* Employees are involved in training activities that aim to increase customer awareness within the organization

- *Work reorganization.* This facilitates workers taking control of their work and consequently the removal of quality inspectors from the production line. Work is typically reorganized in cells, autonomous working groups and other teams that have the achievement of quality as a prime objective.
- *Problem-solving initiatives.* In the shape of workers' participation in quality circles, quality improvement teams and other less permanent quality initiatives.

A study of quality awards winners in America suggests that these firms have transformed their traditional command and control type human resources (HR) policies into policies supportive of a culture characterized by employee commitment, co-operation and involvement (Blackburn and Rosen, 1993). Collectively, these HRM policies aim to:

- communicate the importance of each employee contribution;
- stress quality-related synergies available through teamwork;
- empower employees to make a difference;
- reinforce individual and team commitment to quality with a wide range of rewards and enforcement.

The quality awards winners referred to above implemented a variety of systems to facilitate upward and downward communication such as round-table meetings, open-door policies and suggestion systems, employee attitude and satisfaction surveys. Within these companies, job design emphasized innovation, creativity and problem solving aimed at maximizing the quality and not the quantity of the output. These organizations had extensive training programmes: Xerox BP&S, for example, estimates that it had invested more than £75 million quality training. Based on two systematic studies, Motorola estimates that it earns £20 for every dollar invested in training. The integration of HRM and quality management practices in these companies has apparently lead to reduced costs, increased product reliability, greater customer satisfaction and shorter product development cycles (Blackburn and Rosen, 1993).

QUALITY AND DESIGN

The importance of design as part of continuously improving quality is widely recognized. Both manufacturing and value-based approaches to quality embrace this view. If the design is not right first time there will be problems during production. Therefore, quality must be designed into the product/service/process. A study of quality practices in 418 manufacturing plants from multiple industries demonstrated that both design and process management efforts have an equally positive effect on internal failure costs such as

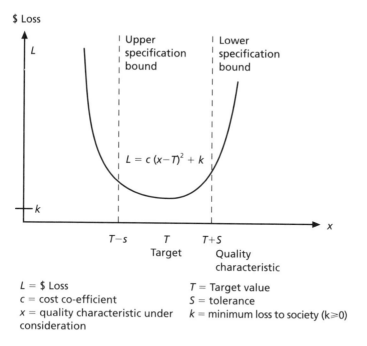

FIGURE 3.1
The quadratic
loss function
(adapted from
Taguchi, 1986)

L = \$ Loss
c = cost co-efficient
x = quality characteristic under consideration
T = Target value
S = tolerance
k = minimum loss to society (k⩾0)

scrap, rework, defects, and external failure costs such as complaints, warranty, litigation and market share (Ahire and Dreyfus, 2000).

One of the characteristics of most quality management systems in use today is their reliance on online controls: such controls take place when the product is already in the production stage. Although online controls are important, it is more crucial that one intervenes prior to the production process, in the design stage. Such offline controls are based on Taguchi's method. This method measures quality in accordance to the quadratic loss function (see Figure 3.1).

Quality, according to Taguchi, is the minimum loss imparted to society from the time the product is shipped (Taguchi, 1986). This includes customer dissatisfaction that leads to loss of reputation in addition to the usual costs such as scrap and rework. Loss (costs) increases exponentially as the parameter value moves away from the target and is at a minimum when the product/service is at the target value. Thus

$$L = c(x - T)^2 + k$$

Where L is the money loss, T is the target value, x is the quality characteristic under consideration, c is the cost coefficient, k is the minimum loss to society and S is tolerance. The loss function is continuous and indicates that making products within the traditional (upper and lower) control limits advocated by statistical process control (SPC) does not mean the product is of good quality (for a discussion of SPC see Chapter 8).

Taguchi's methodology is also named robust design. Its main aim is to identify factors which affect the quality characteristics of a product and minimize the deviation of quality characteristics from the target value. More specifically, it consists of three elements:

1 System design is typically achieved through the careful selection of parts, materials and equipment. Western companies are usually very good at coming up with excellent designs but they are less skilled at tightening parameters and tolerances.

2 Parameter design aims to determine the optimal levels for control factors by quantifying all likely interactions between variables with the view to producing a robust product/process which will remain close to the target value and will perform well under a range of variations in its production environment and a range of conditions in the end-use market.

3 Tolerance design aims to tighten the tolerance of those factors which have a large impact on variation in order to further reduce variation around the target value.

By building quality into the design process, Xerox Corporation, for example, claims to have captured 70 per cent of the market with its digitally controlled copier DC 256. Following the same approach, Hewlett-Packard developed the first oscilloscope that could be operated with a keyboard and a mouse. At Ford Motors, engineers have used three-dimensional computer design technology to learn on a screen whether people will have enough headroom in a new vehicle and whether parts near the gas tank will cause it to overheat. Other companies who use 'robust design' are Goodyear, Eastman Kodak, Chrysler and Boeing.

QUALITY AND ACCOUNTING

Accountants claim that only what is measurable can be controlled. Measurement is one of the oldest principles of quality control (see Chapter 2). All managerial approaches to quality embrace the view that quality must be rendered tangible via processes of measurement if it is to be controlled efficiently. Firms pursuing quality management programmes generally make major changes to their performance measurement systems, moving away from traditional accounting indicators (Wruck and Jensen, 1994). Traditional accounting measures emphasize the monitoring of operational efficiency via indicators such as manufacturing cycle time, product failure rates, late delivery rates, order lead times, new product development time, customer complaints, waste or scrap rates.

Quality management performance measures differ from traditional measures in a number of important ways:

1 They focus on measuring productivity and quality from the point of view of the customer.

2 They track day-to-day the progress of specific operations. Such measures supplement and sometimes even replace traditional accounting measures such as product cost, labour cost, labour rates, material and labour variances and profitability. Traditional accounting measures are viewed as providing weak direction to employees as they make daily decisions.

3 They are more disaggregate and are function or task specific compared with traditional measures, isolating the contribution of particular activities to performance. For example, employees easily understand how their actions affect cycle time or how they can reduce waste or scrap rates. However, it is more difficult to determine whether and how a particular employee action affects aggregate measures such as overall profitability or firm values.

In some of the firms embarked on quality management programmes, performance measurement has extended to areas such as employees' attitude, customer satisfaction, organizational climate and culture. British Telecom for example uses the following measurements:

- CARE (Communication and Attitude Survey for Employees): aimed to measure employees' attitudes.
- Line management index: aimed to measure how well people think they are being managed.
- Committed people index: a measure of how committed people feel to the company and what it is seeking to do.
- CARE Contracts: a measure used to benchmark BT against other blue chip companies so they can compare the way BT people think with similar results in other companies.
- Balanced scorecards: to asses company's success in terms of profit and meeting customers' expectations.
- Various customer satisfaction measures.

Although one can dispute whether these measurements are effective ways of capturing the human side of the organization, it is clear that more and more emphasis is put on rendering visible and therefore measurable what used to be seen as the private domain of the individual (be it the manager, employee or the customer). The quantification of intangible feelings and subjective perceptions has become the newly colonized terrain of accounting techniques.

SUMMARY

This chapter explores the ways in which the discipline and practice of quality management relates to other management practices. For example, it is argued that quality is not only a potential source of competitive advantage but also a managerial device that facilitates the effective implementation of strategy in an organization. The relationship between quality and marketing is also a close and important one, particularly if we adopt the user-based definition of quality. The implementation of quality management could trigger important changes in the way organizations train, motivate, assess and reward individuals. Thus the alignment of HRM ideas and practices with the demands of quality becomes paramount in achieving the goals of customer satisfaction and conformance to technical requirements. The manufacturing-based approach to quality signals the importance of robust designs of products and processes: design plays a crucial role in ensuring conformance to requirements. Finally, accounting techniques are also seen to be influenced by the implementation of quality: in turn, they play a large role in rendering visible what counts as quality or non-quality and in quantifying both the tangible and intangible aspects of quality.

KEY CONCEPTS

Here are the key concepts covered in this chapter: strategy, marketing, HRM, accounting, design.

QUESTIONS

At the end of this chapter you should be able to answer the following questions:

- Why do organizations view quality as a source of competitive advantage?
- To what extent can management ensure that employees are committed to the goals of quality?
- What is the relationship between internal marketing and quality management?
- Why does robust design play such a central part in the management of quality?
- To what extent can accounting techniques reflect and measure the efforts put into the achievement of and the effects of quality?

PART TWO

Practical approaches to quality

The management of quality in manufacturing, service and public sectors

The origins of quality management as a discipline and practice are usually traced back to the systematic efforts made by the manufacturing sector throughout the twentieth century. This may well explain why quality management is wider spread and more successful in the manufacturing sector than in services (Redman et al., 1995). However, there have long been customer-oriented initiatives in the service industry. The adoption of a user-based approach to quality (Garvin, 1984) in manufacturing has arisen from the perception that, unlike in services, customers' wants were not given full attention. In discussing the differences between manufacturing, service and public sector approaches to the management of quality, the chapter advances the view that there are potential synergies between these approaches.

QUALITY IN MANUFACTURING

The quality movement owes a great deal to manufacturing industries. It was in the manufacturing sector that quality inspection, quality control and quality assurance first took root. This is no surprise given that the Western world went first through a rapid phase of industrialization followed, only many decades later, by the growth of the service sector.

The distinction between goods and services, although difficult to maintain in practice, serves some useful analytical purposes. Goods are usually associated with the physical output of manufacturing processes, while services are seen to be the end result of the service sector. This distinction is socially constructed as there are no pure goods or services. Any product, whether the end result of the manufacturing process or service delivery, consists of a bundle of physical goods and services. For example, a washing machine (physical good) comes usually with a one-year warranty (a service).

Similarly, flying from London to New York is a service that relies on a number of tangibles (goods) such as: the aircraft, meals, newspapers, and so on.

Despite the blurred nature of the division, goods are characterized as:

- tangible;
- storable;
- standardized;
- physically enduring;
- consumed after their production.

David Garvin (1984) has identified eight dimensions of goods' quality:

1 Performance refers to the primary operating characteristics of a physical good: for a car, these would be traits such as acceleration, handling and speed levels. Such characteristics are clearly defined and quantifiable from a technical point of view: yet, they may mean different things to the consumer who although may equate quality with high levels of performance, may also view some of these operating characteristics not as contributing to quality but simply being part of the physical good.

2 Features are the added characteristics of a physical good: again taking the example of a car, features may include: side impacts, CD player, air bags, air conditioning. Such added characteristics do not contribute to the actual operation of the physical good but add more comfort to it. Their translation into quality differences depends to a considerable degree on individual preferences.

3 Reliability is the probability of a good failing within a specified period. The most important measurements of reliability are the mean time to first failure (MTFF) and the mean time between failures (MTBF). In the case of a car, reliability could be an important differentiator: Japanese and German cars, for example, are perceived as high quality cars due to their high level of reliability.

4 Conformance is the degree to which a good's design and its operating characteristics match pre-established standards. Conformance to specification is an objective measure of quality and is less likely to reflect individual preferences.

5 Durability is a measure of the good's life. Technically, durability is defined as the amount of use one gets from the good before it physically deteriorates and repairs become impossible. When the repair is possible, durability takes on an added dimension, of an economic nature. The consumer is faced with a number of choices every time a good fails and repair is possible: he/she must weigh the expected cost in money terms and personal inconvenience of the repair against the acquisition of a new good. Thus, even though durability is an objective measure, it is also shaped by the subjective preferences of the consumer.

6 Serviceability is the speed, courtesy and competence of the repair. Serviceability has two aspects: responsiveness and technical competence. The

former is measured via the mean time to repair (MTTR) and the latter is reflected in the incidence of multiple service calls required to correct a single problem. While these measures are objective, their importance varies with the preferences of the consumer: typically consumers associate rapid repair and reduced downtime with high quality.

7   Aesthetics refers to how the good looks, smells, feels, sounds like and it is a very subjective judgement. Indeed, for some consumers, the looks of the car may be more important than its reliability or price. For others, quite the opposite may be the case. Aesthetics is closely related to the last dimension of quality, namely perceived image.

8   Perceived image refers to the brand and reputation of a product. These aspects are difficult to measure objectively, yet in the consumerist age in which we live, they have become more and more suggestive. For many individuals, identity is closely linked with consumption practices: one is what one consumes. The brand gives away not only one's preferences and spending power but also his/her identity. Although it takes a long time to build up a brand image and a quality reputation, it takes no time to have them destroyed: in general accidents and failures which lead to loss of lives put an end to the reputation of the company.

It is clear from the above analysis that some dimensions of goods' quality rely to a great extent on subjective judgements, as is the case with the quality of services. Thus, the division between goods and services is more and more difficult to maintain, other than for analytical and heuristic purposes. Competing in the global economy requires that companies provide a bundle of goods and services in order not necessarily to differentiate themselves but simply to survive.

QUALITY IN THE SERVICE SECTOR

The widespread development of service industries in the last three decades, has lead to an approach to quality that shifted its emphasis away from technical conformance to specifications, to pleasing the customer by meeting and exceeding his/her expectations. It has taken a relatively short time for service quality to develop its own techniques and approaches to the management of quality. At the beginning of the 1990s, services were still seen to lag behind manufacturing in systematic quality efforts (Gummesson, 1991). The importance of the service sector is, however, ominous; in the Western world the service sector employs the vast majority of people. In the UK the manufacturing workforce has reduced from 45 per cent in 1954 to 22 per cent in 1998 (Millar, 1998). More recently it has been recognized that added services could provide opportunities for differentiation in the manufacturing sector.

Services cover an extremely wide range of activities. Haywood-Farmer (1987) argues that the diversity is so great that any global, all-encompassing approach to service management is naive. Despite this, numerous authors have attempted to provide classifications for services, some of which are discussed below.

Chase (1981), for example, positions various services along a continuum from high to low contact. Contact is defined as the duration of a customer's presence in the service system. For example, a bank will have a higher level of contact than a mail carrier or a remover service. However, within banking itself, there could be different degrees of customer contact, depending on the sort of service the customer needs and the way in which the bank is organized. This classification is seen to be problematic because contact does not account for the degree of real interaction of the customer with the service company. Maister and Lovelock (1982) attempt a more sophisticated classification of services based on two attributes, namely the degree of customer contact with the service process and the degree of process customization. The former is defined as the period of time the customer is in contact with the service provider and the latter as the degree to which the service is tailored to that particular customer.

Another categorization is proposed by Schmenner (1986) who suggests that services should be classified depending on the degree of labour intensity and the degree of customer interaction and customization. Here the degree of labour intensity is defined as the ratio of the labour cost incurred in the value of the plant and equipment.

Despite the current lack of consensus on defining and classifying services, there is a shared understanding that services differ from physical goods and, as a result, service managers face different challenges as compared with production managers. This, however, may not always be the case: in a low labour intensive service, service managers must pay attention to issues that are very similar to the concerns of manufacturing, namely capital decisions, technological advances, demand management and service delivery scheduling. In a high labour intensive business, service managers have to concentrate on hiring, training and development, employee welfare, and workforce scheduling.

It is also important to acknowledge the differences between the front office and the back office of a service. The back office (in financial services, for example) may display a low degree of service customization, being organized and managed for efficiency: many of the tasks could be automated or carried out in batches. At McDonalds and other fast food places, burgers are cooked in batches and assembled on a production line. Here the degree of labour intensity is relatively low as a result of the costly and sophisticated equipment. On the contrary, the front office may be characterized by increased customer contact and interaction, a higher degree of labour intensity, as well as a higher degree of customization. Given this situation, it is off-target to argue that a set of universalistic prescriptions could provide a complete solution to all the problems faced by services.

Service quality

Various authors discuss the special nature of services (Haywood-Farmer, 1987; Gummesson, 1991; Lovelock, 1992). It is argued that services differ significantly from goods for they are, generally speaking:

- intangible,
- heterogeneous,
- perishable,
- less controllable than the goods (i.e., the provider cannot entirely control the production and the delivery of services for there is a high degree of customer participation in both).

Service quality has become a topic on its own and various attempts have been made to highlight the importance and necessity for better and more sophisticated service quality models. It is widely accepted that achieving service quality presupposes the elimination of the gap between customers' expectations and perceptions. Gronroos (1983), for example, distinguishes between 'technical quality' (what is delivered) and 'functional quality' (how it is delivered) and argues that functional quality plays a significant role in the perceived service quality. Lehtinen and Lehtinen (1982) views service quality in terms of 'process quality' and 'output quality'. According to this perspective, the customer judges process quality during the service, while output quality is assessed after the service is performed. In my view, both process and output quality influence customers' perceptions. Think about someone who checks into the hospital for a kidney operation. She may be very happy with the 'process quality': the medical staff is nice, the room facilities very good, the waiting time between procedures very low, but may be less so if the surgeon removes the wrong kidney. The quality of the output is obviously way below the expectations of the patient. Similarly, imagine you are flying to Delhi via Dubai. The plane leaves on time, the food on the plane is pleasant, so are the entertainment and the stewards. Yet, when you are just about to change planes in Dubai you are told that your flight was cancelled due to technical difficulties and you have to wait for the next one which is in nine hours' time. The process quality may have been great but that was not sufficient to make your air experience a positive one.

Various authors have attempted to measure customers' perceptions of service quality using the survey method. Parasuraman, Zeithaml and Berry (1988) have developed a measurement scale called SERVQUAL that allowed them to distil five determinants of service quality (i.e. five dimensions based on which customers judge the quality of a service) as follows:

- tangibles, i.e., physical evidence;

FIGURE 4.1
The gap model
(adapted from
Parasuraman
et al., 1985)

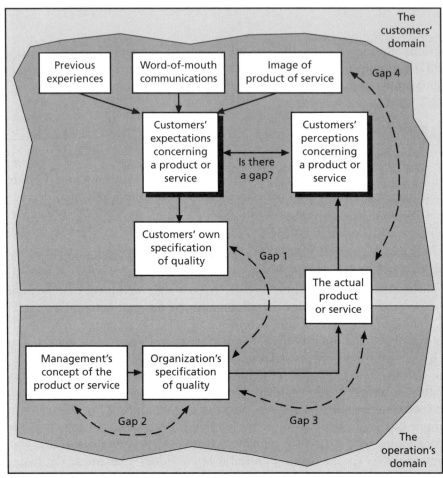

- reliability, i.e., accuracy and dependability;
- responsiveness, i.e., promptness and willingness;
- assurance, i.e., knowledge, trust and confidence;
- empathy, i.e., attention to customer.

If closing the gap between customers' expectations and perceptions is the main task of service managers, Parasuraman, Zeithaml and Berry (1985) argue that they must attend to the following five sub-gaps (see Figure 4.1).

1 the gap between customers' expectations and management's perceptions;
2 the gap between management perceptions and service quality specifications;
3 the gap between service quality specifications and service delivery;

4　the gap between service delivery and external communication to customers;
5　the gap between perceived service and expected service.

Despite its logical appeal and sheer sophistication, the sub-gap model is questionable for a number of reasons:

First, there is no objective window onto what customers expect. Each individual customer has a unique and particular basis of defining what counts as service quality. Therefore, such expectations cannot be generalized or indeed predicted. Management perceive a diverse and sometimes contradictory mass of views and opinions. In order to make it coherent, they impose order by squashing the messy data into manageable categories. This represents a unified but incomplete account that serves to establish service quality specifications. Thus, the sub-gap between customers' expectations and managers' perceptions cannot be totally eliminated.

Secondly, when translating their perceptions into service quality specifications, managers are forced to reduce ambiguity even further. Standards must be clear, concise and easy to interpret. Therefore, any contradiction they would have perceived is typically set aside as unimportant and only data that flows logically and linearly is marshalled together for purposes of standardization. Thus, the second sub-gap cannot be totally eliminated either.

Thirdly, despite the conscious attempts of top management to set clear and concise standards, employees may interpret the meaning of standards in different ways, according to individual circumstances and priorities. Furthermore, their interpretations do not translate into action in a linear way. Thus, they may perceive standards as too constraining and may try to subvert them or draw on them only when they are under direct control and observation (see Part 4, Case Study 6 for a critical analysis of how employees and managers respond to standards). Thus the third sub-gap is as problematic as the first two.

Finally, external communication may have a hard time reflecting objectively what is being delivered. Whose perceptions will form the basis for the judgement of service delivery? Is it management or is it the service employees themselves? What happens when there are contradictory views with regards to what is delivered? Will external communication try to cover up such disagreements in favour of a managerial perspective? The experience shows that this is usually the case.

It is for these reasons that Parasuraman and colleagues' model cannot provide an all-embracing, ultimate solution to the subtleties involved in bridging customers' expectations and perceptions. Nor can other models do that, either. Thus, we could conclude that there is no generally accepted operational definition of service quality, nor is there any generally accepted way of measuring service quality. Therefore, what is needed is locally negotiated models and definitions that account for as many voices as possible, and are shared by sufficient actors in order to be implemented democratically.

QUALITY IN THE PUBLIC SECTOR

Public services come in several broad categories depending on the relationship between the service provider and the public. Gaster (1995) proposes the following classification:

- Some services are provided to everyone (e.g. universal services such as street sweeping, rubbish collection).
- Some services are demand led (e.g. advice, information, primary health care).
- Some services are only available to those deemed eligible, according to legislation or locally determined rules (e.g. welfare benefits, council housing).
- Other services are rationed by resource availability or by decisions based on an assessment of 'need' (e.g. day nursery places, home help, most forms of health and social care).
- Some services are imposed through legislation aiming to benefit or protect individuals or society or both (e.g. primary and secondary education; some social services; probation services, mental health services, food standards and health and safety, police and prison).
- Some services are preventive aiming to help people and communities help themselves or to provide group support in order to pre-empt individual crises (e.g. community development).
- For some services there are no eligibility requirements: they are available for all to use as they wish, sometimes for a charge (e.g. leisure services, libraries, transport).

The public sector in the UK has undergone radical changes in the last two decades or so. Successive governments, irrespective of their left or right alignment, have viewed the market as the saviour of an outmoded and underperforming public system. The market was brought in via a variety of policy mechanisms including privatization and the creation of new institutional arrangements through which planning and purchasing of services were separated from their delivery. A rhetoric of quality improvement and consumer choice has typically accompanied such reforms (Pfeffer and Coote, 1991). Kirkpatrick and Lucio's (1995) edited collection sheds some light on the ways in which the imagery of quality has been used to legitimate intervention and change in public organizations, rather than to address the needs of the users and the providers of services. Rather than defining and managing quality according to the traditional ethos of the public sector (an ethos that draws on values such as trust, equality, fairness and professionalism), private sector tools and definitions have been imported. This reflects a general belief in the superiority of the commercial enterprise and the values and assumptions of private sector management (Keat and Abercrombie, 1991). Such a belief may in fact have little basis on which to substantiate itself: the privatization of British Railways has proven to have disastrous consequences for rail transport and has angered customers. On the other hand, Royal Mail continued to stay in the public sector and to deliver good quality services (despite some industrial relations problems which have from time to time confronted the organization).

Such was the tendency in the UK, particularly throughout the 1980s, when the Thatcherite drive for efficiency, for doing more with less and securing value for money was in bloom. More recently there has been a move away from such single-minded concerns towards a fusion between private and public sector management ideas. This so-called public service orientation takes some ideas from the private sector and applies them in a distinct fashion to the peculiarities of the public sector. At the heart of this model is a major concern for service quality and a clear understanding of the values and concerns of the users (rather than customers).

Indeed, there are relatively few public services where people are treated like *customers*, in other words, where people are paying for services and have a choice whether to use the service or not. The rather widespread use of the word 'customer' in the public sector suggests that individuals have either an 'exit option' and/or a 'voice option' which could be pursued when they are dissatisfied with the quality of a particular service. In reality, unless one can afford to use services provided by the private sector, exercising influence via the 'exit option', by withdrawing custom and going elsewhere is not normally possible. It is more possible for individuals to get together and make suggestions for improvement (the voice option) but the evidence suggests that the effects of such strategies are usually limited (Gaster, 1995).

It would be a relatively easy task to blame the UK government for the current state of affairs in the public sector. It would be just as easy to blame the public sector manager, the professional or the user of the services. The problem, however, stems in part from the fragmentation of the public sector, which makes it very difficult to see where and how the lines of public accountability are drawn and whether they involve a democratic dimension. For example, at the level of central government, ministers may avoid being questioned on the grounds that 'operational' matters are the responsibility of chief executives of the Next Step agencies. Locally, more and more services are being contracted to providers whose only answerability lies in the contract itself not to the public or its elected representatives (Gaster, 1995).

Notwithstanding accountability issues, public sector managers are also faced with a number of dilemmas among which the flexibility/standardization and co-operation/competition are the most significant ones. On the one hand, one must attempt to make services more consistent and reliable (see for example the Citizen's Charter which promotes rational standards and equal services to all; and performance tables which attempt to make transparent how successful schools, hospitals and universities are), while on the other hand, one must try to make services more flexible and responsive. While consideration for standardization and ensuring equity and equality must not be lost, the fight on the hands of public service managers in Britain may well be that of retaining the right to make decisions most suited to actual circumstances, rather than providing standard replies to non-standard problems.

Secondly, there is a real tension between, on the one hand, the forces that encourage divisiveness and competition, contracts and privatization, league tables and performance-related pay (which no doubt could have an effect on increasing choice for the user) and, on the other one, those factors deriving from collectivist ideologies that foreground public sector ethos and encourage working together and mutual support (and which again may have some impact on improving customer choice).

Such dilemmas are magnified rather than resolved by quality management initiatives. Furthermore, there is sufficient evidence to suggest that the introduction of quality management in the British public sector represented an attempt by the government to regain control over powerful professional groups leading in fact to the politicization of workplace and numerous institutional conflicts (Reed, 1995). Indeed, there is a noticeable gap between the rhetoric of quality and the various management led initiatives aimed to increase user voice and choice. This, again, points to the fact that quality is not a neutral, technical issue although it is presented as such in the various theories put forward by public sector gurus. The position and values of the various stakeholders (citizens, consumers, front line staff, managers, policy-makers, academics) influence the ways in which quality is defined and pursued in practice. Interests and values may at times coincide, but more often than not they will stand in opposition. For example, how can public service organizations pursue efficiency programmes while remaining true to public ethos? A critical review of these issues within the context of the British National Health Service is provided in Part 4, Case Study 1.

POTENTIAL SYNERGIES BETWEEN MANUFACTURING, SERVICES AND THE PUBLIC SECTOR

Some of the problems outlined above are by no means peculiar to the public sector. Manufacturing and service organizations within the private sector also face dilemmas of standardization/flexibility and competition/co-operation. Furthermore, the boundaries between public and private sector management are constantly being redrawn. Many public sector organizations (and those agencies providing public services through the contract process) now develop strategic objectives and business plans. Furthermore, values that are traditionally associated with the public sector (i.e., trust, professionalism, altruism, etc.) have been more recently appropriated by the private sector in an attempt to revamp their image. Thus, it makes little sense to view the public and the private sector as totally separate domains each facing distinct problems in the field of managing quality.

In so far as goods and services are concerned, there have been a number of steps taken to bring their respective approach to quality management closer together. Thus, in manufacturing, service quality has become part of product strategy and of overall business strategy. Added services ensure at times differentiation and therefore competitive advantage, while at other times they are a mere ingredient for organizational survival. For example, when Daewoo introduced a three-year comprehensive warranty policy on all their brand new cars in 1996 this acted as a differentiator from other competitors. This is now a common practice. Moreover, certain service organizational arrangements are adopted by manufacturing organizations in departments such as marketing, personnel, information technology (IT), research and development (R&D), and so on. Such departments are viewed as service providers rather than intrinsic to the manufacturing operation.

Vice versa, we have witnessed numerous developments in the service sector that build on manufacturing logic. Schonberger (1990) documents the formation of self-managed work cells, the adoption of a systematic data collection and statistical process control in service organizations. In fact the back office of numerous service organizations is organized according to manufacturing principles. In some cases, the mechanization and automation present in the service process makes it possible to run the entire organization like an assembly line (see, for example, fast food organizations, super-markets, large-sized cinemas). Such organizations are typically referred to as service factories, relying not on the work of professionals but on the work of low-skilled individuals who perform monotonous and repetitive tasks. The deprofessionalization of services is a trend that has been witnessed by other service industries, most notably the financial services, due to the advent of call centres and Internet banking. And finally, physical goods could be part of the service package and thus lead to service differentiation.

SUMMARY

Although the chapter has treated manufacturing and services, private and public sectors separately, it is important to remember that the boundaries between those are socially constructed and hence, slippery, and that there are numerous lessons to be learnt across these sectors. In fact, managing quality is equally challenging whether one talks about manufacturing goods or delivering services in the private or public environment. The important thing to remember is that no quality model will deliver instant success and that each company must decide for itself what is appropriate for its business and its customers. To do so, each organization must understand the needs of the market in which it operates and find ways to respond to such needs with improved bundles of goods and services. The models and theories presented in this chapter provide a useful starting point in helping companies construct their own version of product/service quality and deciding on the 'best' way in which this can be delivered within that particular context.

KEY CONCEPTS

Here are the key concepts covered in this chapter: manufacturing, services, public sector, service quality, service gap model, SERVQUAL.

QUESTIONS

At the end of this chapter you should be able to answer the following questions:

- To what extent is service quality more difficult to manage than product quality and why?
- What are the benefits and shortcomings of the service gap model?
- In what way do the aims and values of the public sector differ from those of the private sector? To what extent do they affect the management of quality?

Quality standards, certification and awards 5

An important way in which quality management is put into practice is through the implementation of quality standards. In the past two decades or so quality standards have become more and more widespread in both manufacturing and service organizations. Such organizations usually subscribe to a manufacturing-based approach to quality whereby conformance to specifications becomes the most important quality goal. Some organizations genuinely believe that quality standards are the first step towards creating a culture of excellence; others implement quality standards due to institutional pressure (from customers, governments or industry regulations) or as a marketing ploy to signal to potential customers that they can trust the quality of the product on the market. Given the importance of quality standards, this chapter provides a summary of the most important quality standards, namely the International Quality Standards ISO 9000 series (with their environmental variation: ISO 14000 series). The benefits and limitations of implementing quality standards are highlighted from the point of view of multiple stakeholders. The chapter then reviews two of the most important quality awards, namely the European Quality Award and the Baldrige Award (the equivalent North American award) and comments on the value of such awards to the organization and its customers.

QUALITY STANDARDS: A SYSTEMIC PERSPECTIVE

Quality standards subscribe to the manufacturing-based approach to quality. They are systems which enable 'conformance to requirements'. As systems, they consist of a number of components, namely the organizational structure, responsibilities, procedures, processes and resources necessary for implementing quality management. These components must work well together in order to achieve the main objective of the system, namely consistency in the ways in which products or services are designed, manufactured and/or delivered within the organization. A quality system usually relies on three levels of documentation (Dale, 1994):

- Level 1: company quality manual – this is the most important document which provides a summary of the company's quality strategy/policy, the ways in which it relates to company's objectives and mission as well as a synopsis of the existing quality system.
- Level 2: procedure manual – this document describes the quality system functions, structure and responsibilities in each department.
- Level 3: work instructions – these are specifications and detailed methods for performing work activities.

Companies usually have a database that comprises all other reference and supporting documents covering all facets of the organization from design, planning, purchasing, manufacturing, packaging, storage to delivery and service.

In order for a quality system to be effective, it has to be developed in relation to a benchmark or a point of reference. This point of reference is typically represented by a quality system standard or more simply put, a quality standard. The early quality standards were provided by major customers to their suppliers and therefore were customer or sector specific, having a strong bias towards inspection activities. This method of assessment is called second-party certification. Most of the current quality standards have evolved from military standards (e.g., Mil-Q-9858, American Military Standards and the NATO Allied Quality Assurance Publications). As early as 1938, Chester Barnard discussed the role of standards in ensuring technological, social and economic integration, viewing them as important elements in the executive/leadership process.

During the 1970s there was a plethora of quality system standards on the UK market. Such standards were produced by a variety of second- and third-party organizations. The British Government adopted in 1979 a national series of standards, entitled British Standards BS 5750, with the view to unify existing approaches and minimize the difficulties of comparing approaches to quality across industries and sectors. In 1985 it became compulsory for certification bodies to be accredited by a central agency, namely, the National Accreditation Council for Certification Bodies. The main task of the agency was to assess the independence, integrity and technical competence of leading certification bodies applying for governmental accreditation.

At the beginning of the 1980s, the British Standards Institute (BSI) proposed the formation of an international technical committee to develop international standards. More than 20 countries took part in the development of the first international quality standards, which were published in 1987 under the name of the ISO 9000 series. These standards were based on the 1979 version of BS 5750.

ISO 9000 SERIES STANDARD

Since it was originally devised in 1987, more than 250,000 companies across the world have registered to ISO 9000. ISO 9000 has recently been re-designed with the view to help companies respond in a more proactive way to the demands of their customers. The revised version, the ISO 9000:2000, is based on a process model that is applicable to any firm irrespective of size and any industry including services. All organizations that are ISO registered under the previous version (revised in 1994) have to update their current quality systems according to the new requirements if they want to retain their ISO certification.

ISO 9000:1994 and ISO 9000:2000 offer different models of quality. ISO 9000:1994 consists of five individual standards divided into four parts:

1   The first part comprises ISO 9000 and ISO 9004 which are intended as guidelines only on how to apply the standard.
2   The second part comprises ISO 9001 which provides specifications for design/development, production, installation and servicing.
3   The third part comprises ISO 9002 which provides specifications for production and installation.
4   The fourth part comprises ISO 9003 which provides specifications for final inspection and test.

ISO 9001 defines quality around 20 key elements a company uses to effectively and consistently produce products and/or deliver services. These are management responsibility, quality system, contract review, design control, document control, purchasing, purchaser supplied product, product identification and traceability, process control, inspection and testing, inspection, measuring and test equipment, inspection and test status, control of non-conforming product, corrective action, handling, storage and delivery of materials, quality records, internal quality audits, training, servicing, and finally statistical techniques.

The new ISO 9000:2000 standard is more generic and less prescriptive than the previous version and has three parts:

1   ISO 9000: lays out the fundamentals and the vocabulary of the new series.
2   ISO 9001: states the requirements of the system.
3   ISO 9004: provides guidelines for implementation and fleshes out the requirements of ISO 9001.

The new ISO 9001 is in fact replacing the old ISO 9001, ISO 9002 and ISO 9003 and has four major sections (and eight in total). The first four sections provide background and logistical information, while sections 5, 6, 7 and 8 lay out the requirements for the new ISO 9000 in the following areas:

Section 5: Management Responsibility
Section 6: Resource Management
Section 7: Product Realization
Section 8: Measurement Analysis and Improvement

According to Pearch and Kitka (2000), the new version of ISO 9000 is much improved compared with its previous version for it makes the voice of the customer a crucial part in how the standards operate: customer requirements drive input and customer satisfaction drives output. Organizations seeking certification need methods able to describe and monitor what each customer wants when they place an order, and processes to measure and analyse customer satisfaction. Moreover, the new version supports and reinforces continuous improvement: organizations are expected to be in a position to measure and improve internal processes. And finally, ISO 9000:2000 bestows on management greater responsibility. Management's role in the previous version was to establish and review quality policy, commit resources to it and appoint management representatives to supervize the process. In the new version, executive management plays a far more central role and can no longer delegate the process to quality professionals.

Companies who are already ISO registered have three years to complete the transition to the new version. Specialists argue that the costs involved in updating the documentation should be insignificant in companies well run but may be less so in companies which have sought ISO certification for marketing and public relation purposes only.

The old version of the ISO 9000 series has been described as cumbersome and unsystematic, and lacking structured methods for a unified business approach (Babicz, 2000). These standards were designed mainly for large corporations, in particular, manufacturing. The ISO series is based on the British standard, BS 5750 whose early predecessor was in fact the AQAP series of quality standards developed by the Ministry of Defence; thus the major purpose of the standard was to prevent non-conformity. While this was a reasonable expectation at the time, given that the main avenues for improving performance was by division of labour and specialization of work as well as financial control, in contemporary organizations, management's task has stopped being one of simply ensuring conformance and has become one of redesigning and improving processes (Seddon, 1994).

The advantages of the new ISO 9000:2000 series fall under three general categories. First, the standards aim at improving work relations through encouraging knowledge sharing and acting as an efficient interpersonal communication tool. Secondly, the standards could lead to cost savings by helping to identify and eliminate waste (despite the fact that first time registration ranges from $250,000 to $1 million depending on the size of the company, and the biannual audits cost $10,000). Thirdly, standards are argued to lead to improved customer satisfaction through a reduction of errors and customers' complaints and to improve the image and reputation of the company.

Despite such advantages, there are a number of limitations related to the bureaucracy involved in the documentation and accreditation and the time taken to write and update the procedures and the certification documentation. Costs could also be a factor, particularly in the case of small firms. Critics argue that standards stifle creativity, increasing pressure to conform to the prevailing rationality of the organization. Furthermore, they may fail to have a substantial impact on the quality of the product or service, particularly when they are perceived as an extra task rather than as intrinsic to the job, by the employees. Such disadvantages are typically viewed not as inherent in the conceptual framework of ISO 9000 but related to the way in which the series is implemented. Consequently, many authors have researched the ways in which the standards have been implemented with the view to highlighting best practices in the field. Dale's (1994) guidelines for ISO implementation are presented below:

- The implementation of ISO 9000 must be managed like a project with clear milestones and time deadlines.
- The organization must be clear on the reasons it seeks certification.
- ISO certification should not be confounded with TQM: it is merely the first step towards a TQM culture.
- Commitment from top management is an essential ingredient: the establishment of a steering committee comprising all heads of departments and chaired by the CEO should act as a major driving force.
- Training at all levels in the organization must ensure that people understand the standard's rationale, methodology and procedures.
- An internal quality audit should be performed prior to inviting the external assessor in order to identify weaknesses and remedy them on time.

More recently there has been a shift towards the application of standards to environmental concerns. The first environmental management standards, the ISO 14000 series, were published in September 1996. Their use has grown steadily, particularly in Europe and the Far East. According to a survey carried out by The International Organization for Standardization (ISO), there were 5,017 certificates in December 1997 worldwide, out of which only 79 were issued to US organizations. The ISO 14000 series is concerned with how an organization's activities affect the environment through the lifetime of the product. Such effects include among others pollution, waste generation, energy use, noise and depletion of natural resources (Hogarth, 1999).

For many organizations, the next step after ISO certification is the achievement of a quality award. A number of organizations give quality awards to their suppliers, such as, Chrysler, Eastman Kodak Co., Ford Motor Corp., General Electric, IBM, Texas Instruments, Xerox and Whirlpool. The most prestigious quality award in Europe, instituted in 1992, is the European Quality Award offered by the European Foundation of Quality Management (EFQM).

THE EUROPEAN QUALITY AWARD

The EFQM is an organization that promotes quality and excellence in Europe. In the UK, The British Quality Foundation has the same objective but targets only British companies. At the heart of the EFQM model lies the idea that customer satisfaction, people satisfaction and impact on society are achieved through a leadership that effectively drives policy and strategy, people management, resources and processes, leading ultimately to excellence in business results. The EFQM model was reviewed in April 1999 and re-titled the EFQM Excellence Model. This new version emphasizes the importance of partnerships and the need for continuous learning and innovation with a focus on management and sharing of knowledge (see Figure 5.1).

Winners of this quality award are rather diverse. In 2000 Nokia Mobile Phones, Europe and Africa (Finland) won in the category large businesses, The Inland Revenue, Account Office Cumbernauld (UK, Scotland) won in the category of public sector and Burton-Apta Refractory Manufacturing Ltd (Hungary) was the winner in the category of SMEs/subsidiaries of a large organization.

The EFQM model is a non-prescriptive framework that recognizes there are many approaches to achieving sustainable excellence. The building blocks of this approach are described below (for more details, see the official website of the EFQM: www.efqm.com):

1 *Results orientation.* Excellence is dependent upon balancing and satisfying the needs of all relevant stakeholders (this includes the employees, customers, suppliers and society in general as well as those parties with financial interests in the organization).

FIGURE 5.1
The EFQM excellence model (adapted from EFQM official website: www.efqm.com)

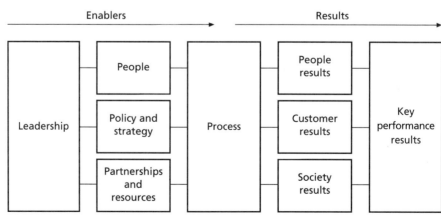

2 *Customer focus.* The customer is the final arbiter of product and service quality. Customer loyalty, retention and market share gain are best optimized through a clear focus on the needs of current and potential customers.

3 *Leadership and constancy of purpose.* The behaviour of on organization's leaders creates a clarity and unity of purpose within the organization and an environment in which the organization and its people can excel.

4 *Management by processes and facts.* Organizations perform more effectively when all interrelated activities are understood and systematically managed and decisions concerning current operations are planned. Improvements are made using reliable information that includes stakeholders' perceptions.

5 *People development and involvement.* The full potential of an organization's people is best released through shared values and a culture of trust and empowerment, which encourages the involvement of everyone.

6 *Continuous learning, innovation and improvement.* Organizational performance is maximized when it is based on the management and sharing of knowledge within a culture of continuous learning, innovation and improvement.

7 *Partnership development.* An organization works more effectively when it has mutually beneficial relationships, built on trust, sharing of knowledge and integration, with its partners.

8 *Public responsibility.* The long-term interests of the organization and its people are best served by adopting an ethical approach to management and exceeding the expectations and regulations of the community at large.

The EFQM Excellence Model can be used in four ways by organizations:

1 as a framework for developing organizational goals in a tangible, measurable way;

2 as a framework which helps organizations identify and understand the systemic nature of their business, key linkages and cause and effect relationships;

3 as a basis for applying for the European Quality Award;

4 as a diagnostic tool for assessing the current health of the organization.

Through this last process, also called self-assessment, an organization is better able to balance its priorities, allocate resources and generate realistic business plans. The EFQM is committed to researching and updating the model based on the results of tested good practices from thousands of organizations both within and outside of Europe. In this way it is ensured the model remains dynamic and in line with current management thinking (see the EFQM official website: www.efqm.com).

COMPARING ISO AND EFQM CRITERIA OF SUCCESS

Russell (2000) discusses the commonalities and differences between the EFQM Excellence Model and the new ISO 9000:2000 series suggesting that the latter is a necessary but not sufficient criterion for the achievement of excellence. Russell's analysis, which is outlined below, points to the fact that the EFQM model is wider in scope than the ISO series, accounting for the needs and interests of all organizational stakeholders. Russell's analysis follows closely the excellence model from Figure 5.1.

1 *Leadership*. Although the importance of top management action is clearly set out in ISO 9001:2000, requiring evidence of commitment to the development and improvement of the quality system, the scope of leadership under the excellence model is wider. The model views leadership as including the executive team, all other managers and those in team leadership positions. As far as leadership tasks are concerned, the model places an emphasis on external relationships beyond the customer and on ensuring the motivation and recognition of people.

2 *Policy and strategy*. While ISO 9001:2000 requires the organization to have a quality policy and to develop objectives and plans consistent with this policy, the EFQM model is concerned with wider organizational policies and strategy and seeks information from a wider range of sources to inform formulation.

3 *People*. Although the new ISO standard requires the organization to identify competences, provide training and evaluate effectiveness of that training, it stops short of addressing wider aspects of human resource planning, team working, the development of people (other than through training), involvement and empowerment, as well as issues regarding rewards and recognition, which are chief concerns on the EFQM agenda.

4 *Resources*. The ISO standard requires the identification, provision and maintenance of facilities needed to achieve conformity of product. It also has a number of requirements regarding information management. These concerns are mirrored by the EFQM Excellence Model, which also stipulates requirements regarding the use of knowledge, the development and cultivation of intellectual property and the creation of innovative thinking through knowledge sharing.

5 *Processes*. Although improvement of processes is part of the new ISO standard, it does not require the levels of innovation and involvement of employees, customers and partners expected by the EFQM model.

6 *Customer results*. ISO 9001: 2000 does require an organization to gather and analyse information on customer satisfaction/dissatisfaction; however, it leaves the organization to determine the research methodologies to be used. The EFQM's requirements are wider for they include concerns for market share and loyalty.

7 *Key performance.* ISO requires the measurement of processes, product and supplier performance but does not address any requirements regarding financial performance, whereas the excellence model sees financial performance as an important indicator.

The evidence to date suggests that the new ISO 9000 standard complements well the excellence model.

THE MALCOLM BALDRIGE NATIONAL QUALITY AWARD

This award was created in 1987 in the United States. Each year up to two companies can win the award in each of the four categories: manufacturing, service, small business (fewer than 500 employees) and non-profit organizations (this was introduced only in 1999). A study conducted by Tai and Przasnyski (1999) shows that Baldrige organizations have seen their shareholder value increased.

The Malcolm Baldrige National Quality Award core values are:

1 customer-driven quality;
2 leadership;
3 continuous improvement and learning;
4 valuing employees;
5 fast response;
6 design quality and prevention;
7 long-range view of the future;
8 management by facts;
9 partnership development;
10 public responsibility;
11 results focus.

The winners of this award are diverse: in 1999, BI, a company delivering performance improvement programmes to help customers achieve their business and Ritz Carlton Hotel won in the service division, STMicroelectronics Inc. won in the manufacturing division and Sunny Fresh Foods won in the small business sector category.

According to evidence collected by Hendricks and Singhal (1999), quality award-winning firms do better than other companies on a number of indicators, such as operating income, sales, total assets, employees, return on sales and return on assets. Nevertheless, there are examples that suggest that having a quality award does by no means guarantee a place in heaven. The Wallace Co., the first small service firm ever to receive the Malcolm Baldrige

National Quality Award in 1992 was, two years later, on the threshold of bankruptcy, acquired by Wilson Industries.

TECHNICAL, IDEOLOGICAL AND AESTHETIC CONSIDERATIONS REGARDING QUALITY STANDARDS

Numerous practitioners and academics see quality standards as the quintessence of scientific management in that they map out 'the one best way' for the organization. Such one best way is the result of applying scientific methods of design, planning and control to the activities performed in the organization with the view to optimize, rationalize and improve the overall efficiency and efficacy. Supporters argue that standards are 'not an impediment to the development of civilization, but on the contrary, one of its immediate pre-requisites' (Gropius, quoted in Guillen, 1997). Indeed, we all expect that the organizations with which we interact as customers have certain quality standards in place. Such standards inspire our trust: we trust that the brand new CD player will play music nicely and not explode in our face, that the train journey we are taking will deliver us safely to our destination and that the food we buy in supermarkets will provide nourishment rather than kill us. All the conveniences that we take for granted are to a great extent the end result of standardized approaches to quality.

This is not to say that quality standards do not have their own limitations. How many times have you been annoyed when you called a company and the operator read out an entire script that did not even deal with your own inquiry? How many of you have trusted reputable organizations and their quality standards, only to realize that they are just a marketing ploy and not a means to satisfy their customers? I have had many such negative experiences with reputable and allegedly customer-focused service organizations. As most of this book had been written during a sabbatical taken in the United States, I was in a position to 'experience' the American approach to quality standards and customer service and compare it with the British one. To my surprise and probably to the readers' surprise, I have found that the so-called customer-focused American approach to quality is in fact a myth. Most services, including banking, insurance, public transport, mobile phones, and so on, were overly standard driven but, in my experience, lacked customer focus. For example, Aetna Insurance took more than three months and two telephone conversations a week to rectify a mistake they made when updating my dental insurance record. This mistake made it impossible for me to have any approved dental treatment while they were updating my records. Our local bank would not add me on my husband's bank account without me holding a social security number. The only way to get a social security number, since I was not employed in the US, was to pass a driving test. Amtrack, the national rail company was on average three hours late on the trips I took from Philadelphia to State College and return. Verizon, the local telephone provider, put me on hold for up to 20 minutes each time, and when I would finally get an operator to talk to me, he or she would read to me a 'standard' script that did not answer my question. And the list could go on.

If standards can potentially lead to dissatisfied customers, what sort of effect do they have on the employees? While some employees may enjoy the routine of the one best way, others may feel frustrated with the rigidity of the standards and with the fact that they cannot use their own commonsense and experience to deal with a specific problem raised by a specific customer. Critics have been arguing for a long time that standards reflect the dominant managerial rationality and are not necessarily geared towards using employees' best abilities. Standards are seen by some to structure organizations in ways prescribed by management (both as a profession and as a body of knowledge) that ignore the needs of other organizational stakeholders (customers and employees, in particular). If standards are to be implemented effectively, their meaning has to be shared by those who are expected to put them into practice, namely, the employees. Instead of viewing standards as universal and objective 'entities' to be embraced regardless, we need to see them as processes whose constitution and effective working depends on wide intersubjective communication and participation among all organizational members.

While the technical and ideological aspects of standardization have been discussed at length in the literature, the aesthetic aspect of standardization remains relatively unexplored. According to Guillen (1997), standards may in fact contain an aesthetic message that emphasizes regularity, continuity and speed at the expense of commonsensical notions of beauty. The ideology and methods associated with scientific management and standardization captured the imagination of the so-called modernist architects and other artists in continental Europe at the beginning of the twentieth century who created houses, public buildings, factories and other artefacts and durable goods whose beauty did lie precisely in the routinized way in which they were conceived and produced. Such *avant-garde* modernism took standardization to heart because cost and efficiency were socially and politically desirable but they also formulated an aesthetics based on the efficiency of the machine, and the possibilities it offered for artistic expression that went beyond any economic consideration.

SUMMARY

Quality standards play an important part in the way many organizations from the manufacturing, service and public sectors orchestrate their efforts to manage quality. Although 'conformance to specifications' is not synonymous with 'meeting customers' expectations', many organizations believe that having standards in place is beneficial to the business as it generates trust in the products and services offered on the market. The chapter describes and analyses the benefits and limitations of most popular quality standard, the ISO 9000 series. ISO 9000 undertook significant alterations in 2000 in order to improve its applicability and enhance its benefits to other sectors outside manufacturing. The chapter also introduces two quality awards: The European Quality Award and the Baldrige Award, a North American quality award which follows closely the European model. Such awards help organizations to gain legitimacy in the eyes of the society and build trust in the eyes of the potential customers. While most of the literature on quality standards and awards adopts a managerial perspective on quality deeply rooted in systemic thinking, the chapter ends by looking at some of the ideological and aesthetics consequences of quality standards by suggesting that standards are more than systems. They are constituted through social and political processes and have unintended consequences upon a wide range of organizational stakeholders.

KEY CONCEPTS

Here are the key concepts covered in this chapter: quality standards, quality system, quality awards, certification, accreditation, ISO 9000, EFQM.

QUESTIONS

At the end of this chapter you should be able to answer the following questions:

- Why have quality standards become so widespread in organizations in recent years?
- What are the advantages of the new ISO 9000 standard adopted in 2000 compared with the 1994 version?
- What are the similarities between the ISO 9000:2000 standard and the 'excellence' model designed by the European Foundation of Quality Management?
- What is the relationship between quality standards and the concept of quality?
- What are the ideological and aesthetic aspects of quality standards?

Managerial definitions of quality (reviewed in Chapter 1) view quality as an objective entity that can be measured and controlled with the help of various tools and techniques. It is no surprise that considerable attention has been paid to the quantification of quality via the costs of quality. The quantification of quality serves multiple purposes, among which the identification of areas that need more effort and resources, budgeting, comparison between departments as well as motivational purposes. The drive behind quantifying quality is related to the view held by many senior managers that numbers can reduce the complex nature of quality to simpler and hence more manageable patterns. Speaking for the reality they are trying to capture, numbers, in the shape of costs of quality, could legitimize and enhance the role of quality because they speak a language widely understood and difficult to contest. While stressing the difficulty in collecting, analysing and reporting the costs associated with quality, the chapter outlines a number of quality costs models. The most widespread quality cost model splits the costs of quality into prevention costs, appraisal costs and failure costs and suggests that there is an economic cost of quality that could be objectively calculated. Other models take issue with the economic cost of quality arguing that the principles underlying such calculations do not fit with the 'zero defects' or the 'continuous improvement' practices promoted by Japanese organizations. But first, let us review some real life examples of costs of quality.

EXAMPLES OF QUALITY COSTS

In Chapter 1, I discussed the reasons behind the space shuttle *Challenger* accident: I will now highlight the costs associated with the accident. Not all of these costs could be quantified in an objective manner but their overall magnitude was staggering (Bank, 1992). Bank argues that such costs could be divided into: costs associated with loss of life (as seven astronauts lost their life) which amounted to several tens of million dollars; costs associated with the lost opportunities for NASA during the three years' downtime for the American space programme; costs of appraisal and prevention which were in the region of $2.4 billion; and costs associated with loss of image for NASA.

On 7 October, 1999, BMW ordered the recall of 3 million cars built between 1988 and 1994, worldwide because flawed radiator caps threatened to fill the passenger compartment with scalding steam. The total cost of recall was thought to be several million pounds but this figure did not account for the inconvenience caused to the customer and the time these had to waste on bringing the car to the garage (*The Guardian*, 8 October, 1999).

In 1999, Ford recalled the majority of its Focus cars sold in Europe to fix an electrical fault. The Focus was launched in the UK in October 1998 and soon replaced the Fiesta as the company's top selling model. More than 60,000 cars were recalled in the UK and 200,000 in Europe at a cost of more than £2 million (*The Guardian*, 17 July 1999). In the USA, Ford recalled more than 900,000 vehicles in 2000 (mainly the 1997 Ford F-150; F-250 pick ups) which were thought to have developed fuel leaks. Ford was also entangled in the Bridgestone/Firestone tyre scandal although the company had continuously maintained that the problem was exclusively related to Firestone. Bridgestone/Firestone recalled more than 6.5 million tyres in North America. Prior to the US recall, Ford had recalled tyres in at least ten countries, including Thailand, Malaysia, Oman, Qatar, Saudi Arabia, Venezuela and Ecuador. The US recall is estimated to be a long process and has already caused havoc for both Ford and Firestone due to fierce customer complaints (Ammons and Vujasinovic, 2000).

Other well-known manufacturers which, at one point or another, have recalled their cars are Porsche, Ferrari, Hyundai, Mitsubishi, Peugeot, Citroën, Jeep, Audi, Land Rover, Honda and Renault. In an unprecedented case, Mitsubishi publicly apologized for their long-term practice of keeping two sets of complaints books in an attempt to hide serious vehicle defects. One set of records kept track of non-safety mechanical defects which did not pose any environmental or safety hazards and for which there was no governmental pressure for product recall. These issues were always in the public eye and were dealt with successfully by customer satisfaction programmes. The second type of records listed defects that could affect vehicle safety and would have therefore triggered government investigation. These complaints were always resolved behind the scene, away from the public eye. The company kept the second type of records to itself until a whistleblower made it public: this led to the resignation of the company president and to a public apology (Brown, 2000).

CLASSIFYING QUALITY COSTS

Industrial and quality engineers, operation managers and accountants have approached the issue of 'quality costs' from a quasi-mathematical point of view. There are numerous classifications of quality costs (Feigenbaum, 1951; Juran, 1979; Crosby, 1983, 1984; Bank, 1992). General Electric was the first American company to introduce, in 1946, a quality cost management system. The most widely used classification of quality costs follows closely the General Electric model and is reflected in both ISO 9000 series and the British Standards BS 5750. In this traditional mode, quality costs are allocated under four headings:

1 *Prevention costs.* These are costs that aim to reduce the possibility of failure (either internal or external) costs occurring. Typical examples include: quality planning, training, supplier assurance, design verification, quality engineering.
2 *Appraisal costs.* These are costs associated with activities that aim to ensure the conformance of products and processes to pre-set requirements. Typical examples include: stock evaluation, inspection, machine testing, calibration, maintenance, inspection machinery, process control.
3 *Internal failure costs.* These are costs that occur when a product fails to meet the requirements, such failure being identified before delivery to the customer. Typical examples of internal failure are scrap, repair, troubleshooting, failure analysis, lost productive time and rework.
4 *External failure.* These costs occur when a product fails to meet the requirements after delivery to the customer. Typical examples are loss of sales, warranty claims, complaints, returned material repairs and recall costs.

According to Juran (1979), the total cost of quality (TCQ) is the sum of failure costs (internal and external/IFC and EFC) and defect control costs (DCC) composed of prevention costs (PC) and appraisal costs (AC). Thus:

$$TQC = PC + AC + IFC + EFC$$

PC and AC are costs relating to ensuring that the product conforms to specifications (conformance costs), while IFC and EFC are costs of nonconformance (Crosby, 1983). Bank (1992) extends this classification by adding to the costs of non-conformance, the costs of exceeding requirements. A third overall category is also added, namely, the costs of lost opportunity:

- costs of conformance (prevention costs + appraisal costs);
- costs of non-conformance (internal failure costs + external failure costs + costs of exceeding requirements);
- costs of lost opportunities.

Costs of exceeding requirements refer to those costs incurred as a result of providing information or services that are not necessary. They occur due to the fact that the customer specification is not clear. Examples include: redundant copies of documents that are not needed, management reports

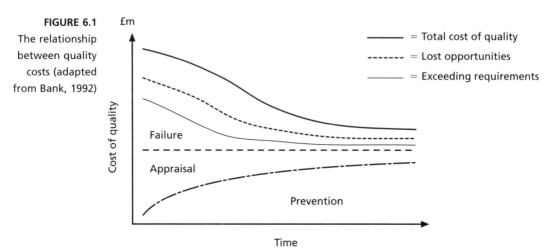

£m

——— = Total cost of quality

------- = Lost opportunities

——— = Exceeding requirements

Cost of quality

Failure

Appraisal

Prevention

Time

which are too extensive and therefore unusable for quick decision-making, detailed analytical effort when a simple estimate would have been enough (Bank, 1992).

Cost of lost opportunity is the most difficult one to quantify. Some classifications regard this cost as an external failure cost but it is important to single it out in order to highlight what losses the company could incur, for example, as a result of losing its current customers due to failure to deliver products on time and/or unavailability of products when needed most on the market. Examples of such costs include cancellations by customers due to inadequate service response time, ordering competitors' products because the company's products were not available, and the intangible cost of demoralized workforce. The relationship between these various types of costs is presented in Figure 6.1.

Other, more recent, contributions to the quality cost concept (cf. Giakatis and Rooney, 2000) are Baston's (1988) structured flow dynamic system that takes into account customers' complaints and managerial pressure; Coulson's (1993) which introduces the economic ratio of income/cost incurred as a result of marketing innovation and improvement activities; Merino's (1988) model which details the economic and technical aspects of quality costing and Dahlgaard and colleagues' (1994) model which proposes a method for estimating total quality costs which accounts for the long-term/strategic nature of quality. Giakatis and colleagues (2001) argue that it is important to differentiate between quality costs and quality losses. One cannot simply assume that prevention and appraisal costs are quality costs while failure costs are losses, for there can be a percentage of quality loss even in the prevention/appraisal activities, particularly when those are not very successful. If these activities are successful, the organization saves money, but if the reverse is the case, the organization not only loses the invested money but also encounters further losses.

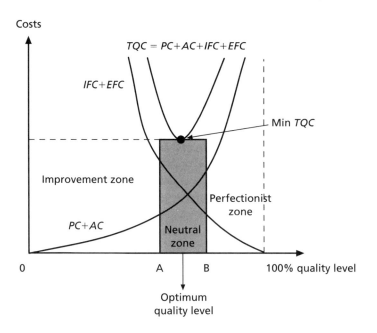

FIGURE 6.2
Traditional
model/optimum
quality (adapted
from Olaru,
1999)

Dale's (1994) cost model challenges directly the traditional prevention/appraisal/failure model which dominates much of the thinking in the area. For Dale there are three categories of quality costs:

1   Costs incurred in designing, implementing, operating and maintaining quality management systems.
2   Costs of introducing and sustaining a process of continuous and company-wide improvement.
3   Costs incurred due to the failures of the systems, products or services.

According to the above model, costs alone must not be used to determine an optimum level of quality as suggested by traditional 'economic cost of quality' models (see Figure 6.2).

In Figure 6.2, there is a point on the TQC curve where the total cost is minimum and to which it corresponds an optimum level of quality (see the area between A and B, also named the neutral zone). In the neutral zone, failure costs equal appraisal and prevention costs. To the left of the neutral zone is the so-called, improvement zone. Here, the weight of the failure costs is much higher that the weight of the appraisal and prevention costs. Therefore, a small increase in the investment for appraisal and prevention could lead to significant reduction in waste and therefore in failure costs. To the right of the neutral zone, in the so-called, perfectionist zone, failure costs amount to less than appraisal and prevention costs. In this zone, one needs to make huge investments in quality in order to achieve a relatively small reduction in failures and waste. According to the traditional model, the most economically advantageous zone is the neutral zone (Olaru, 1999).

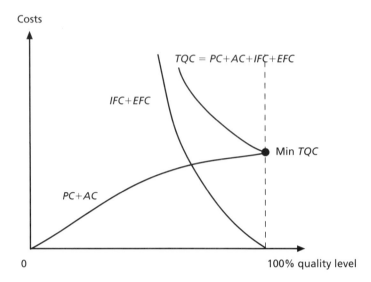

FIGURE 6.3
The 'zero defects' cost regime (adapted from Olaru, 1999)

The model, although well-intentioned in warning against spending unnecessary money on pursuing quality, does not account for management practices such as zero defects and continuous improvement. It also stands in opposition to the principle of 'excellence' which presupposes that one can pursue maximum quality with minimum costs. Schonberger (1988) challenge the idea that the achievement of higher quality presupposes infinite investment. Their model recognize that there is a minimum point on the TQC curve but this point does not correspond to an optimum level of quality but to a maximum one (see Figures 6.3 and 6.4). They argue that it is possible to increase levels of quality while at the same time reduce both failure and appraisal and prevention costs under a 'zero defect' and/or 'continuous improvement' regime.

Strengths and limitations of the traditional model

The main advantage of the traditional model is that it provides an organization-wide view of quality costs. The model enjoys more or less universal acceptance among practitioners and academics due to the fact that it provides clear criteria based on which to decide whether costs are quality-related or basic work and allows top management to keep the focus on long-term targets.

On the other hand, this model provides little insight into the micro-level picture and does not give any direction as to how individual processes could be improved. The model embraces a conventional approach to production, assuming the existence of standardized, repetitive, well-defined manufacturing and inspection steps. Thus, it fails to follow each process and document how costs are actually incurred. Existing accounting systems cannot readily yield information about quality costs as they are presently defined and

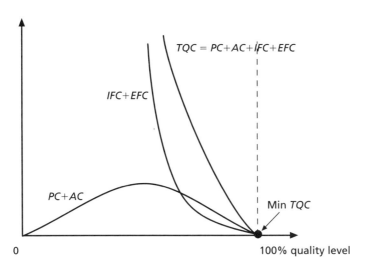

FIGURE 6.4
The 'continuous
improvement'
cost regime
(adapted from
Olaru, 1999)

categorized. The traditional categorization usually serves the purpose of post-collection exercises which seem to be of interest only to quality department employees.

Moreover, there are a number of assumptions underlying the traditional model that need revisiting:

- The model emphasizes the idea of optimization rather than zero defects or continuous improvement.
- The definition of a defective unit or product belongs to the engineers and designers and has therefore an internal focus which implies that the producer has the capability to determine what features of a product are desired by the customer.
- Little attention is given to the definition and measurement of external failure costs. Failure is usually defined as the inability of a product to continue functioning in the role anticipated by the supplier/designer. External failure cost is thought to be the cost associated with repair or replacement of the product and does not include cost borne by the customer.

The model fails to acknowledge that, ultimately, it is the customers who determine what quality is and what counts as a failure. Customers' satisfaction is not an engineering concept but a behavioural construct that must be addressed satisfactorily if a firm is to succeed in the long run and earn maximum returns. Managers need to be able to conceptualize the role of quality in the marketplace in terms of price, demand, profitability and market share. Thus viewing quality enhancements as a cost-causing exercise to be optimized as implied in the traditional quality cost literature ignores the long-term 'revenue-causing' implications of quality enhancement assumed in marketing and economics (Jacobs and Kamm, 1998).

COLLECTING AND REPORTING QUALITY COSTS

It is difficult to decide what should be included in quality costs. Are market research costs a marketing cost or a quality cost, given that they add value by teasing out customer expectations? Are costs associated with training on customer awareness, personnel costs or quality costs? This questioning could go on endlessly but the main issue remains that it is hard to allocate certain expenditures only to quality and not to design, engineering, purchasing, personnel, marketing and sales. According to Crosby's definition, if such expenditures help to get things right they are quality costs. However, this definition is too loose to be of any significant use in practice.

Various surveys carried out in the UK, USA, Japan, Australia and India (cf. Shah and Fitaroy, 1998), suggest that very few companies collect quality-related costs due to the difficulties in setting up procedures that fit with existing accounting systems. Consequently, it is easier to set up a quality cost collection procedure in greenfield sites rather than existing organizations due to the inflexible nature of accounting systems already existing in companies (Dale, 1994).

When setting up a cost collection procedure, a teamwork approach is necessary. Quality and accounting departments must work together to examine and carefully analyse existing processes and construct a procedure of cost collection that is sound, relevant to existing processes and user friendly. Collecting quality costs may be a necessary step but not a sufficient one: to make proper use of costs, organizations have to have an effective system of reporting and acting on quality costs. Reporting quality costs is not a widespread practice in organizations. Quality may be on managers' agenda in terms of its technical or behavioural aspects but its financial reflection (costs) is seldom an item of discussion. Reporting quality costs is a delicate matter: different reports may be needed at different levels in the organization. Not accounting for the needs of these various parties could lead to information overload or insufficiency. For example, weekly reports of costs of scrap and rework may be very useful to supervisors and their teams who could then analyse causes of poor quality and take remedial action. Monthly reports of total costs highlighting progress on quality improvement projects (or problems) may be of great benefit to middle managers, while top managers may be interested in overall costs and costs on which they have to act immediately.

While the majority of quality gurus agree on the importance of quality cost reporting, Schonberger (1990) advocates eliminating all cost accounting and variance reporting. In their place, he suggests a yearly ABC (activity-based-costing) audit in which the cost of all activities is calculated merely for budgeting and resource allocation. In an activity-based accounting system each activity of the organization is analysed in terms of customers' needs. Workers document, control and display their own process and assess whether or not their services are needed by the customer. Once this is done, the activities related to cost reporting would become redundant.

USES OF QUALITY COSTS

Giving a numerical shape to the elusive concept of quality can serve useful purposes. For example, it could help quality professionals secure support from top management. Quality costs highlight the importance of quality to top managers by showing them the impact of quality-related activities on key business criteria such a profit, sales and reputation. Quality costs could also facilitate comparisons of performance between departments and organizations, providing that a common definition of quality cost is enforced and the cost collecting procedure is similar. They could help identify opportunities for improvement by departments and teams and to establish bases for budgets with a view to exercising budgetary control over the whole quality operation. Quality costs also facilitate motivation by singling out individuals and teams whose contribution to the quality effort is outstanding as well as individuals/departments and teams which lag behind.

Thus measuring the costs of quality is thought to have positive effects on the organization on the whole, as well as those individuals and teams that demonstrate their commitment to the cause of quality. Critics warn that an over-concern with quantifying quality costs could lead to mindless bureaucracy and may distract attention from the actual task of improving quality. But, if such an endeavour does not have the back up of the accounting department, conflicts could arise between quality professionals and accountants which could lead to quality costs not being reported and acted upon.

It could be concluded that quality costs are useful in directing attention to a particular way of thinking and managing quality. Such costs are by no means objective reflections of what is going on in the organization with respect to quality. They help structure the organizational reality in ways that make certain activities and individuals more visible and therefore more central to the quality effort.

SUMMARY

This chapter sheds light on some of the existing quality costs models. In so doing, it implicitly subscribes to the managerial view that quality is an objectifiable, measurable and controllable entity. As such the costs of quality are usually associated with prevention activities, appraisal activities and failures occurring within or outside organizations, all of which can to a lesser or higher degree be measured. The traditional model of quality costs assumes that there is an optimum level of quality for which the total cost of quality is the minimum: hence organizations must strive to achieve this optimum. Having reviewed this model, the chapter moves on to outline its flaws and propose other ways of quantifying the costs of quality. While collecting quality costs is a difficult process, the use of quality costs can potentially serve a number of useful purposes among which are budgeting, comparison between departments, motivational purposes as well as the identification of problem or successful areas.

KEY CONCEPTS

Here are the key concepts covered in this chapter: quality costs, prevention costs, appraisal costs, failure costs, optimum quality.

QUESTIONS

At the end of this chapter you should be able to answer the following questions:

- To what extent is the traditional model of quality costs a useful device for the managers of an organization?
- What are the limitations of the traditional model of optimum quality and how can they be overcome?
- What are the difficulties involved in collecting, analysing and reporting quality costs?
- What purposes do the costs of quality serve?

Quality control and assurance

Chapter 6 subscribed to the view that quality can be measured, controlled and predicted with the help of scientific techniques. The current chapter expands this view by introducing two popular techniques of quality control: Statistical Process Control (SPC) and Acceptance Sampling (AS). Quality control is a crucial element of quality assurance, a process which consists of all those planned and systematic actions necessary to provide adequate confidence that a product or a service will satisfy the given requirements for quality.

Quality control comprises the measurement of certain characteristics and the use of this data to assess the quality of production or service provisions in order to provide an indication of whether any changes should be made to processes, materials, and people working in the organization. Many forms of quality control exist but two forms in particular have been extensively used to ensure conformance to standards, namely SPC and AS. This chapter is structured around Slack and colleagues' (1995) model of quality control, which consists of six steps (see Figure 7.1).

STEP 1: DEFINING QUALITY CHARACTERISTICS

As discussed in Chapter 1, there are various ways to define quality. Managerial definitions (product-based, value-based, manufacturing based, user-based) subscribe to the view that quality is an entity that can be controlled and adjusted with the help of scientific techniques. In line with such managerial definitions, Garvin's (1984) research identified eight dimensions of product quality (performance, features, conformance, reliability, durability, serviceability, aesthetics and image) while Parasuraman and colleagues' (1988) research highlighted five dimensions of service quality (tangibles, assurance, reliability, responsiveness and empathy). The way in which one defines quality and its characteristics has significant consequences for the ways in which quality is to be measured and controlled.

FIGURE 7.1

Model of quality
control (adapted
from Slack et al.,
1995)

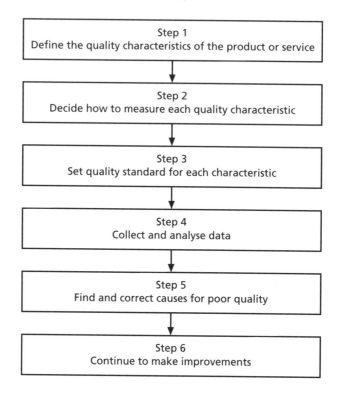

Step 1
Define the quality characteristics of the product or service

Step 2
Decide how to measure each quality characteristic

Step 3
Set quality standard for each characteristic

Step 4
Collect and analyse data

Step 5
Find and correct causes for poor quality

Step 6
Continue to make improvements

STEP 2: MEASURING QUALITY

When quality can be measured on a continuous variable scale we consider the measurement as done by *variables*. The measurement could refer to product characteristics (weight, diameter, length, arrival time and so on) or to process parameters (speed, pressure, temperature, chemical analysis). Measurement by *attributes*, on the other hand, is the result of assessing quality using dichotomous judgement such as go/no go gauges or pass/fail, accept/reject criteria. It is important to minimize subjectivity by clearly defining boundaries of acceptance and rejection according to the quality standards in use.

STEP 3: SET QUALITY STANDARDS FOR EACH CHARACTERISTIC

Whereas traditional quality standards focus mainly on mean overall perform-ance (for example, the average or overall percentage of products without defects or the average unit product cost), newer standards are expressed in terms of both mean and variance. The objective is not only to achieve a mean level of performance but also to improve predictability through reductions in process variations.

STEP 4: COLLECT AND ANALYSE DATA

It is very important to get a good overall picture of how the process/product performs. In order to pursue this objective successfully, one needs to decide whether data is to be collected as variable or attribute, the size of the sample/subgroup and number of the samples/subgroups to be taken, the exact ways in which the check is to be performed and the frequency of the collection. Depending on whether one deals with a process or a product, one needs to decide where in the operation to check that the process is conforming to the standards (start, during, end) or whether every product is to be checked or only a sample.

STEP 5: CONTROL THE QUALITY OF THE PROCESS/PRODUCT/SERVICE

There are two major types of quality control: statistical process control (SPC), which is most often associated with sampling a process during the production of goods or delivery of services; and acceptance sampling (AS) which is usually performed to assess samples of incoming or outgoing goods and services.

Statistical process control

SPC has been widely credited as being one of the critical ingredients of success in manufacturing (Robinson and Kimod, 2000). SPC relies on the use of statistical methods to monitor and improve the quality and productivity of manufacturing and service operations (Stoumbos et al., 2000). It involves the implementation of control charts to detect any change in a process that may affect the quality of the output. The method was born in the late 1920s at the Bell Laboratories and is typically associated with W.A. Shewhart's work (see Figure 7.2).

SPC has been widely used by Japanese companies since the Second World War but was ignored in the West until the early 1980s. In the interim, Western industry resorted to the very worst way to control quality: the inspection of products and processes by professional inspectors. In the past two decades the use of control charts has extended beyond manufacturing to environmental science, biology, medicine, finance, law enforcement and athletics. In Rao's words:

FIGURE 7.2
Shewhart's
concept of
statistical
control:
(a) processes
under control;
(b) processes not
under control
(adapted from
Bank, 1992)

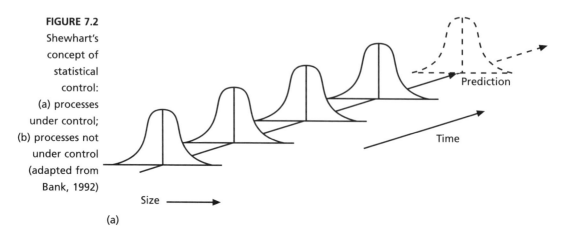

(a)

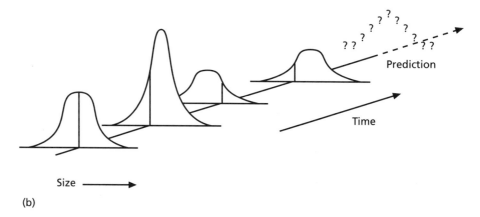

(b)

It is not surprising that a recent book on modern inventions lists statistical quality control as one of the technological inventions of the past century. Indeed, there has rarely been a technological invention like statistical quality control, which is so wide in its application, yet so simple in theory, which is so effective in its results yet so easy to adopt and which yields so high a return yet needs so low an investment. (1989: 992)

SPC relies on the use of statistical tools such as flow charts, check charts, histograms, Pareto analyses, cause and effect diagrams, scatter diagrams and control charts (see Chapter 2 for a detailed description of such tools). Such techniques are used to verify the suitability of measurement systems, machinery, production equipment and assess the capability of the process. Given that the responsibility for quality in the transformation process lies with the operators of that process, these tools are useful in allowing them to assess whether the process for which they are responsible is capable of meeting preset requirements, whether the process is meeting the requirements at any point in time, and identify and adjust the process or its outputs when the requirements are not being met.

Process control charting presupposes the frequent sampling of the process and plotting the results on statistical control charts. All processes need monitoring because in time something may change and possibly cause deterioration in the process quality. Products manufactured under the same conditions and to the same specification are seldom identical and will vary in certain respects. Variation is the result of either special (assignable) causes or common (unassignable) causes.

Special causes occur intermittently and reveal themselves as unusual patterns of variation. They could be removed by operators providing they have the technical knowledge and are empowered to do so. Examples of such special causes are: change in raw materials, change in machine setting, broken tools, failure to clean equipment, poor lighting, keying in the incorrect data, equipment malfunction.

Common causes lead to so-called natural (or random) patterns of variation being observed in the data when they are free of special causes. If only common causes (inherent to the process) are present, the process is thought to be stable and hence predictable. Examples of common causes include: inappropriate work instructions and standards, poor supervision, inappropriate facilities layout, poor design and so on. These causes require the attention of management but according to Deming and Juran cannot be eliminated completely.

SPC can be subdivided in three distinct steps. The first step presupposes the examination of the 'state of control' of the process by the operators. This will help them understand the process and its performance by providing answers to the following questions:

- Can we do the job correctly?
- Are we doing the job correctly?
- Have we done the job correctly?
- Could we do the job more consistently and on target?

The second step, 'the process capability study', shows the magnitude of the random variations (due to common causes) compared with the specified requirements and whether the process will generate products or services that match the specified requirements

The third step refers to the actual process control by using charts (one could imagine the control chart operating as a traffic signal, the operation of which is based on evidence from samples taken during the process):

- green light indicates that the process should be allowed to run without adjustment;
- amber light: trouble is possibly imminent and more information is required;
- red light: there is no doubt that assignable or special causes of variation have been introduced so the process must stop.

Control charts are pictures of what is happening in the process at a particular time and are based on taking samples from the process and observing the values of a particular quality characteristic, named x. They could be constructed based on either variable and attribute data. Attribute data, however, lends itself better to the method of acceptance sampling that will be discussed later in the chapter. All control charts start with computing very simple statistics, namely, measures of central tendency such as mean, median and mode, and measures of dispersion such as standard deviation and range.

The mean is determined by adding all the values together and dividing that amount by the number of values. If $x_1, x_2 \ldots x_{n-1}, x_n$ are the values observed, the mean is:

$$X = \frac{\sum_{i=1}^{n} x_i}{n}$$

The median is the middle value in a group of measurements when they are arranged from the lowest to the highest, while the mode is the most commonly occurring value.

Measures of dispersion quantify the amount of variability or spread that is found in the data. The range, R, is that difference between the smallest and the largest values within the data to be analysed. Thus,

$$R = x_{largest} - x_{smallest}$$

The standard deviation is a measure which conveys by how much, on average, each value differs from the mean. Thus:

$$\sigma = \sqrt{\frac{\sum_{i=1}^{n} (x_i - X)^2}{n - 1}}$$

Variable data control charts could be based on:

- mean and range;
- mean and standard deviation;
- median and range;
- moving average and moving range;
- individual value and moving range.

Let us illustrate the process of constructing a mean and range control chart.

In the first instance let us suppose that we have decided to use ten samples. For each sample, we calculate the sample average (x) and the range value (r). We then calculate the process average (X) as the mean of all sample means, and the process mean range (R) as the average of all sample ranges (we plot those lines as full lines). We then calculate and plot on the chart the control limits (as a dotted line) using the following formulae:

The upper control limit for the mean is $UCL_x = x + A_2R$
The lower control limit for the mean is $LCL_x = X - A_2R$

Where A_2 is a constant derived from statistical tables and is dependent on the sample size.

For the range control chart we calculate the upper control limit $UCL_r = D_4R$ and the lower control limit $LCL_r = D_3R$ where D_3 and D_4 are constants derived from statistical tables and are dependent on the sample size.

The distance between the control limit and the process mean is a measure of the inherent variability of the process. High variability as measured by R will give wide control limits and low variability will result in narrow limits. These control limits are usually set at 3 standard deviations, a measure based on the experience of American firms.

Interpreting the control chart from Figure 2.8 (see page 34) is the most challenging part of the process. The following clues may be useful:

1 If the sample average is outside the control limits, a special cause has been introduced: we must stop the process and investigate.
2 If all the data fall inside the limit but we see curious patterns, such as more than seven sample averages point in a particular direction, constantly increasing or decreasing, we must stop to investigate the process.
3 Another curious pattern to watch out for is when we see a run of more than seven consecutives points on one side of the reference.
4 We should also stop when two-thirds of the points lie within the mid third of the chart.

Control charts could also be constructed with attribute data. Here the subgroup/sample size must be larger and more subgroups sampled. The collection and organization of data are almost identical with that for variables except that for each sample the number (percentage, fraction) of non-conforming items are recorded.

In a nutshell, SPC has four main uses (Dale and Shaw, 1994):

- controls process variation by eliminating special causes;
- reduces the variation by continually improving the process and eliminating some of the common causes;
- helps assess the performance of a process;
- provides information to assist management with decision-making.

Assessing the success of SPC

Despite general interest in SPC by both practitioners and academics, companies are dissatisfied with its implementation. Various reasons have been invoked (Robinson and Kimod, 2000):

- Lack of managerial commitment: managers tend to have a limited understanding of SPC as a mere inspection and control tool. They tend to resist SPC because the process seems too complicated and expensive to implement.

- Numerous organizations impose the adoption of SPC on unwilling suppliers: these may comply mechanistically in order to retain their customer base but very often they do not understand how SPC could improve their operation.
- Lack of training and/or responsibility: the people who understand how to draw control charts are not in a position to fix the processes and those who can fix the process may not understand how the chart works. It is inconsistent to create processes that can be run by a low-cost unskilled labour force and then expect the same people to get involved in under-taking complicated statistics.

Control charts may not be appropriate in all situations and on their own they cannot solve problems: they simply record the dynamics of the process which may simply confirm that there is a problem. However, by listening to the language of SPC, operators and managers can take better decisions regarding how to direct process improvement efforts and investments. The spread of SPC to industries outside the manufacturing sector has been slow and there is little research into the benefits or limitations this approach may have when applied to services: Duthika Perera's case study on the use of SPC in the British National Health Service (see Part 4, Case Study 1) is among the few studies that provide a hands-on analysis of the social dynamics of SPC in the service sector.

Acceptance sampling

While SPC is usually the preferred method of controlling quality, it is not always the most appropriate method. Sometimes, entire batches of products or services need to be inspected before the actual process of production can commence. Acceptance sampling is usually carried out on attributes and not variables, using the proportion of wrongs to rights. The purpose of acceptance sampling is to decide whether, on the basis of a sample, to accept or reject the whole batch (Slack et al., 1995).

Given the following that n is size of the sample, c is the acceptance number of defects in the sample and x is the actual number of defects in the sample:

if $x < c$, accept batch
if $x > c$, reject batch

There are, however, risks involved in this approach: for example, one may well reject the whole batch when in fact the batch is of good quality. This is the so-called producer's risk or Type I risk. On the contrary, if the batch is not acceptable and yet it is accepted, the consumer will bear the risk (Type II risk).

Unlike SPC, organizations do not need to draw up their own acceptance sampling plans. The Dodge-Romig Sampling Inspection Tables provide values for n and c, given a set of risks. Four factors must be decided upon, namely:

- Type I error: the usual value used for the producer's risk is set with a probability of 0.05. This means that management is willing to take a 5 per cent chance that a batch of good quality will be rejected when in fact it is actually acceptable.
- Type II error: the value for the consumer's risk is often set with a probability of 0.1. Thus management is willing to take a 10 per cent chance that a batch of poor quality will be accepted.
- AQL: the acceptable quality level is the actual percentage of defectives in a batch which the organization is willing to mistakenly reject 5 per cent of the time (assuming a 0.05 Type I risk) when the batch is actually acceptable.
- LTPD: the lot tolerance percentage defective is the actual percentage of defects in a batch that the management is willing to mistakenly accept 10 per cent of the time assuming a 0.1 Type II risk.

It is beyond the purpose of the chapter to describe the mechanics of acceptance sampling. Suffice to say that this technique has been heavily criticized by both academics and practitioners for subscribing to the idea that a certain percentage of defectives is acceptable.

Challenging statistical process control and acceptance sampling

Both SPC and acceptance sampling assume that a certain percentage of failure is acceptable to the organization whereas a 'right first time' attitude and a zero defects policy should be the fundamentals of any organization.

Statistical process control is based on process charts which are far from optimal and may in fact be inappropriate. At the outset, they were designed to make it relatively easy for employees without too much statistical training to set up, apply and interpret a process using only pen and paper for calculation. Although it is not often explicitly stated, these charts are based on the assumption that the distribution function of a quality characteristic is one of the few standard distributions (normal, binomial or Poisson) and that successive observations of the quality characteristics are independent. In reality, this may not be the case. Furthermore, the design of the Shewhart's charts are traditionally based on simple heuristics such as using samples of four or five observations at suitable sampling intervals and using 3 standard deviations as the control limit. Such parameters make it difficult to spot any variations in the operating conditions other than the largest ones. To counteract such limitations Motorola developed a methodology that requires that variance be low enough that 6 standard deviations from the mean is still within pre-set control limits: this is the Six Sigma approach.

Six Sigma is a version of control charts that aims to systematically identify and eliminate defects and waste in all processes through the use of advanced assessment and statistical tools. The Greek letter sigma indicates the standard deviation from the average in a bell curve of any process or procedure. The common measurement index for the Six Sigma approach is 'defect per million units'. Thus, three-sigma means 66,807 defects per million, four-sigma 6,210 defects per million and six-sigma 3.4 defects per million.

The main idea underlying the Six Sigma approach is that the quality of a product is determined in large part by the quality of its components. Even relatively simple products have numerous components each consisting of characteristics that determine their quality. These characteristics are sometimes referred to as opportunities for defects (OFD). It can be shown mathematically (using the binomial formula) that a product with 1,000 OFDs, each with a defect rate of 0.1 per cent, per opportunity will be defect free only 36.7 per cent of the time. Conversely to reach a goal of 99 per cent defect-free products, the defect rate per opportunity must be 0.001 per cent (or 10 defects per million). Thus for a product to have acceptable quality, the quality of components must maintain exceptional levels. The formula below quantifies the defects per million units.

$$Q = \frac{D}{N}OFD$$

where Q is defect per million units, D is the number of defects found during inspection, N is the number of units/products inspected and OFD represents opportunities for defects. For example if one found 4 defects during inspection while inspecting 500 products, each having 50 components, then the number of defective parts per million is 160, not a very good result by Motorola standards (expressed as a fraction this would be 0.00016 and as a percentage 0.016 per cent). The six-sigma approach goal is 3.4 defects per million opportunities or a 99.99997 per cent error free performance. Motorola was the first company in the USA to embark on the Six Sigma journey in 1987, but it was not until 1995 that the company actually achieved the 3.4 'defects per million' benchmark.

Much theoretical research on improving control charts has been done over the past five decades but the diffusion of this research to practical applications has been very slow. Stoumbos and colleagues (2000) review a number of such theoretical developments, in particular 'the exponentially weighted moving average of current and past samples' (EWMA) which allows for the detection of small and moderate shifts in the control statistic, and 'the cumulative sum' (CUSUM) which allows for accumulating information across current and past samples. Automatic process control (APC) can also be used in situations in which there is auto-correlation in the data and a mechanism is available to adjust the process when it appears to be deviating from the desired state. The idea behind this method is to forecast the next observations and then use the adjustment mechanism to change the process so that the observation will be closer to the desired state. The basic philosophy of APC is to compensate for undesirable process changes rather than detect and remove them as in SPC.

These forms of quality control form the core of the so-called managerial approach to quality. As suggested earlier, quality is not simply the outcome of the efficient application of statistically driven methods of management, but a complex process with significant cultural and political ramifications. It is to these aspects that we turn in the next couple of chapters.

STEP 6: CONTINUOUSLY IMPROVE THE PROCESS

While recognizing that common causes cannot be totally eliminated, SPC attempts to remove all special causes and as many as possible common causes. Once the process is rendered stable and predictable, via the elimination of all special causes, the capability of the process can be assessed. The next step is to reduce as much as possible common causes of variation so that the output from the process is centred on a nominal or target value. This process is called continuous improvement and is one of the pillars of Total Quality Management, a holistic approach to the management of quality that we discuss in more detail in the following chapter.

SUMMARY

This chapter provides an overview of Slack's model of quality control. In particular, two methods of quality control are presented: Statistical Process Control and Acceptance Sampling, along with their benefits and limitations. Motorola's Six Sigma approach which holds the '3.4 defects per million opportunities' limit as the benchmark for quality control, is argued to be more suitable than SPC in today's competitive environment. The chapter concludes by suggesting that quality control should be part of a continuous improvement approach, a principle that lies at the heart of Total Quality Management (see Chapter 8).

KEY CONCEPTS

Here are the key concepts covered in this chapter: quality control, six sigma approach, continuous improvement, statistical process control, acceptance sampling.

QUESTIONS

At the end of this chapter you should be able to answer the following questions:

- What are the steps necessary for implementing statistical process control and acceptance sampling?
- How useful are statistical process control and acceptance sampling techniques under a 'zero defects' regime?
- What are the barriers hindering the successful implementation of statistical process control?
- What is the main difference between SPC and the six sigma approach?

Total quality management 8

Total Quality Management (TQM) is a philosophy and practice of management which aims to satisfy the customers by means of employee involvement, consistent leadership and continuous improvement. In so doing, it brings together a number of hard and soft technologies of quality management. This chapter examines the fundamental principles of TQM and the contribution made by the various gurus to its development. It then introduces five metaphorical lenses for analysing TQM (Morgan, 1986). Some of these metaphorical lenses embrace a managerial approach to quality (for example, the machine and the organic metaphor), while others (i.e., the cultural, the change and the political metaphor) view quality as a process and shed light on the social constitution of TQM practice and the contradictions that exist at the heart of the TQM concept.

DEFINING TQM

The origins of total quality management are usually ascribed to Japan's search for quality improvements in the 1950s and its success in moulding ideas on quality into a coherent operating philosophy. Much of the miraculous turn around of the Japanese industry is associated with the introduction of statistical quality control in Japan by three American quality gurus in the early 1950s. These were W.E. Deming, J.M. Juran, and A.V. Feigenbaum. Both Deming and Juran argued that quality control should be conducted as an integral part of management control systems. This developed into the notion that prevention not detection was the key to success and this idea was heralded as a managerial breakthrough. The development of quality control into a holistic concept is attributed to Feigenbaum. Feigenbaum broadened the concept of quality control to include all aspects of the business. Thus, the idea that every function within the organization is responsible for quality was developed and led to the notion of total quality control (TQC) (Bendell, 1991).

During the latter part of the 1980s TQC became known as total quality management (TQM). One of the problems in the discussion of TQM is the apparent lack of a generally accepted description of what it actually consists of. Wilkinson and colleagues (1992) argue that there is confusion as to what different writers mean when they discuss TQM. Spencer (1994) provides a thorough review of the extant TQM literature arguing that different quality experts emphasize different aspects of it. For example TQM is described as a new way of thinking about the management of organizations (Chorn, 1991), a comprehensive way to improve total organizational performance and quality (Hunt, 1993), a systematic approach to the practice of management (Olian and Rynes, 1991), an alternative to management by control (Price, 1989) and as a paradigm shift (Broedling in Spencer, 1994). We can conclude that despite thousands of articles and books written on it, TQM remains a highly ambiguous concept.

Zbaracki (1998) provides insights into how a reasonably well-defined technical intervention like TQM could become an ambiguous and sometimes dubious intervention. Quite often TQM invokes the socially legitimate goal of improving quality without adopting a well-defined routine for accomplishing it. Institutional theory (Selznick, 1957, 1965) emphasizes the importance of values, norms and intentions in understanding why organizations change, in this case, why organizations adopt TQM. Institutions are defined as social structures and processes which provide stability and meaning to social behaviour and allowing individuals and organizations to come to accept certain values and norms as legitimate. Thus, to institutionalize is to infuse with values beyond the technical requirement of the task at hand (Selznick, 1965). When TQM gains institutional value, and becomes the accepted way to conduct business, its symbolic value may supplant its technical efficiency. Thus, TQM may provide an organization with little technical benefit but the claim to use TQM may confer legitimacy to the organization.

Despite existing controversies over the meaning of TQM, there are two broad approaches to TQM:

1   The hard approach emphasizes continuous improvement by the use of statistical methods (see Chapter 7). This approach is associated with early gurus' work, its aim being to improve productivity and profits.
2   The soft approach focuses on leadership, employee involvement and cultural change. The approach was popularized by the late wave of American gurus and its aim is to create a strong organizational culture aligned to the demands of the customer (see Chapter 10).

One of the most accepted definitions of TQM, proposed by Hill (1991) incorporates both hard and soft elements; accordingly, TQM is a business discipline and philosophy of management which institutionalizes company-wide planned and continuous business improvement through employee participation and involvement with the purpose of satisfying the customers in the marketplace. According to most TQM approaches, top management commitment, continuous improvement through scientific knowledge and employee involvement constitute the three fundamental pillars of TQM.

TOP MANAGEMENT COMMITMENT

Most of the literature views top management's commitment to TQM as the most important factor in ensuring the successful implementation of TQM (Coulson-Thomas, 1991; Doyle, 1992). Top managers are seen to be engineers of a culture that respects the individual and fosters creativity. In this capacity, their most important tasks are to provide employees with an understanding of why quality is important, help them conceive of quality in strategic terms, set achievable quality standards and provide training on quality. Without a significant financial and time investment and faith in the long-term future of the business, TQM is argued to have few chances to succeed. Critics, however, warn that top managers make little difference to the success of a TQM programme (Samuelson et al., 1985; Hall, 1991). Other factors, of a macroeconomic and social nature, play a more significant role in deciding the fate of TQM programmes. Nevertheless, the notion of success/failure is highly controversial for there is no agreement as to what criteria are most appropriate for judging it and whose point of view is to be considered the most valid.

Continuous improvement through scientific knowledge

Continuous improvement usually relies on the generation of objective data (i.e., facts that are perceived to be true) that can be used systematically to improve work processes and products. Continuous improvement sits at the heart of Juran's 'quality spiral' (see Figure 8.1) which views quality as a never-ending process unfolding systematically and continuously throughout the organization.

Prevention (as opposed to detection) plays a significant part in any process of continuous improvement. Prevention presupposes predictability; thus, detailed figures are needed at all stages in order ensure the removal of special causes. Statistical tools and techniques are considered to be important means by which processes could be understood, controlled and continuously improved by both managers and employees. They help individuals single out causes and effects in order to alter the relationship between them. Continuous improvement does not simply have to be a mechanistic act of pursuing statistical routines: it can also be about pursuing enhanced learning,

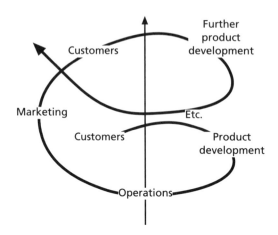

experimenting with new ideas and challenging commonsense in an imaginative way.

Employee involvement

At the core of TQM lies also the idea that all individuals are to play a substantial role in quality improvement. TQM emphasizes open communication between individuals and departments as well as teamwork. TQM claims to offer individuals the opportunity to fulfil personal goals and aspirations while pursuing the objectives of the corporation. The assumptions behind such claims are that individuals search for meaning in work (rather than outside work) and their sense of achievement in life is closely connected to the act of production (rather than the act of consumption). This, of course, may be a far cry from what is in fact the case. Some employees may be quite happy to perform mindless tasks without having to think about ways for improving their work. For others, work may be only a means to an end: the means for survival or well-being via consumption practices.

TQM: A MULTI-METAPHOR ANALYSIS

Given the multifaceted nature of TQM, this chapter proposes to analyse it from a number of metaphorical perspectives. In so doing, the chapter draws on Gareth Morgan's (1986) book, *Images of Organization*, in which the author invites us to view organizations, among others, as machines, organisms, cultures, flux and transformation and as political games. Metaphors are substitutions of one element of language for another which allow individuals 'to conceive the world in a fresh dynamics of potentiality' (Eco, 1979: 59). The metaphor is a central sense-making mechanism by which 'humans forge their experience and knowledge of the world in which they live' (Morgan, 1986: 610).

This chapter invites the reader to view TQM from five distinct metaphorical perspectives:

- TQM and the machine metaphor;
- TQM and the organic metaphor;
- TQM and the culture metaphor;
- TQM and the change and transformation metaphor;
- TQM and the political metaphor.

The first two metaphors subscribe to a managerial approach to quality, while the last three metaphors take a more critical view on quality.

TQM and the machine metaphor

The machine metaphor sees organizations as displaying the characteristics and behaviour of machines. Organizations are imagined to be systems of interlocking parts intended to achieve a particular purpose, for example, speed and efficiency. The behaviour of organizations is thought to be predictable, controllable and knowable at a distance, usually with the help of scientific data and models. One of such scientific models is TQM, which is viewed here from a hard perspective. This perspective emphasizes a managerial definition of quality, as well as the importance of measurement, statistical control and quality standard systems such as BS 5750 or the ISO 9000 series in successfully managing quality. As such, TQM seeks to control the behaviour of processes and people by removing special causes and ensuring that individuals behave uniformly and in accordance with the requirements of the process. TQM's final goal is thus to increase profits through conformance to technical requirements. This over-reliance on technical controls and standardization made some critics argue that TQM is just another form of Taylorism, for it expects people to behave like the components of a machine, thus stifling creativity and personal growth. Viewing TQM from the machine lens is a useful project but a very incomplete one, too. TQM is more complex than the analysis above might have suggested: conformance to standards is only part of the story; employee involvement and empowerment is yet another part (as the organic metaphor suggests).

TQM and the organic metaphor

The organic metaphor sees organizations as displaying the characteristics and the behaviour of organisms. Organizations are born, grow, mature, peak and die according to the human life cycle. They are not closed systems that regulate themselves according to some internal logic: rather they are influenced by and influence the environment in which they are embedded in very complex ways. The organization is an open system that has to adjust itself to the environment in order to survive. Contingency theory postulates that for an organization to survive, it must display both 'internal consistency' (i.e., all internal components must work well together) as well as 'external congruency' (i.e., there must be a fit with the environment).

TQM could be seen to facilitate both processes of internal consistency and external congruency, for, on the one hand, TQM works to improve communication between the company's departments and between individual employees via empowerment programmes and better communication (internal consistency), while on the other hand, TQM acts as the buffer between the company and its external environment in both technical and symbolic ways (external congruency). Some organizations adopt TQM in order to be in a better position to respond to customers' demands, in other words, for technical reasons. Others implement TQM due to institutional pressures coming from competitors, customers and the public: such organizations may not necessarily seek to improve quality (although this may automatically happen) but aim to gain legitimacy in the eyes of their most important stakeholders.

TQM and the culture metaphor

The culture metaphor sees organizations as networks of shared values, beliefs and attitudes. Smircich (1983) suggests that there are two approaches to culture: on the one hand, culture can be seen as a variable, something an organization acquires, changes and manages according to some grand plan. On the other hand, culture can be seen as a root metaphor, something the organization is, and cannot be easily changed. Many TQM advocates take the former view, arguing that TQM acts as the unifying culture of an organization by making explicit those behaviours and attitudes the organization values and rewards, as well as those that are to be disregarded and/or marginalized. Top managers are seen to play a crucial role in enacting, maintaining or changing a particular version of TQM culture via the management of meaning. By constructing those individuals who oppose TQM as irrational and irresponsible, top managers can turn individual stories of organizational failure into organizational stories of individual failure to take on board the spirit of TQM and comport themselves accordingly (Kelemen, 2001). TQM is seen to be a culturally enacted phenomenon, negotiated and maintained through the use of rituals, myths, stories and taken-for-granted language. As such the TQM culture does not merely reflect commonalities between people: it also imposes them. Such imposition is not a mechanistic process that unfolds linearly and top down, but one which is met with resistance and challenged at times.

TQM and the change and transformation metaphor

If most theories of organizations emphasize stability, this metaphor suggests that organizations are in constant flux and transformation. Change is an inherent part of organizational and individual life and must be a fundamental ingredient of our explanations of any organizational phenomena. Thus, TQM could be seen as a change programme. The prescriptive approach to change views TQM as a string of clear steps and milestones to be worked upon (with the help of consultants). Implementing TQM in such fashion is common practice and may encompass both technical change (the implementation of new standards, the rationalization of the organizational structure) as well as cultural change (via training programmes, a new style of leadership and the emphasis on teamwork). A useful model to understanding TQM is Pettigrew's (1985) model of change management developed inductively from empirical data collected over a long period of time at ICI. The model has three elements: context, process and content. The context refers to the external or internal factors that may drive the adoption of TQM, the process refers to the ways in which TQM is implemented (with the help of internal or external consultants, the time frame and so on) while the content refers to what it is that is changing: technical requirements (i.e., standards) or behavioural ones (i.e., attitudes and behaviours etc). Most models of change management assume that change can be managed at a distance, as an apolitical process: the political metaphor challenges this perspective.

TQM and the political metaphor

The political metaphor views organization as coalitions of actors with different interests and aspirations. Such interests are not unitary but pluralistic and occasionally antagonistic. Thus, TQM could be viewed as a political game which serves certain interests while suppressing others. TQM may serve to enhance the already dominant meanings in the organization (held by managers and quality professionals) and may push to the margin other voices. This is not to say that managerial ideologies reign comfortably *ad infinitum*: resistances are always mounted by individual employees and/or trade unions, as well as customers and/or the public at large. This metaphor draws our attention to the fact that TQM is not a managerial, technical achievement, but one that needs to be constantly worked upon and negotiated; one that emerges at the confluence of diverse overt and covert agendas and whose constitution requires political action. Power and politics are natural, inherent features of organizational life and TQM practices are no exception: they are interwoven with power relations in complex and unpredictable ways. The power metaphor is useful in allowing us to go beyond TQM's rational façade and inquire into the consequences TQM may have upon managers, employees and other organizational stakeholders. This metaphor will be unpacked further in Chapter 12 by drawing on the work of the French philosopher, Michel Foucault (1977, 1980).

Each of these metaphors sensitizes us to particular aspects of TQM: as such, they contradict each other at times. Rather than suppress some and elevate others, it is more important to accept them as partial accounts capturing the workings of TQM and its diverse consequences on the experiences of various organizational stakeholders.

TQM: SUCCESS OR FAILURE?

To understand the widespread nature of TQM, one needs to carefully analyse the conditions that facilitate its adoption. Certain macro-social factors are thought to play a significant role in explaining the emergence of TQM as a common organization pattern. In institutionalized environments, normative pressures contribute to isomorphisms (processes by which organizations imitate one another), and the emergence of common organizational practices over time (Westphal et al., 1997). Westphal's study found that the later the date of TQM adoption the greater the level of conformity to the normative pattern of quality practices already introduced by other organizations. Thus, in the early stages of TQM institutionalization, organizations may adopt customized versions and derive mainly technical benefits from its adoption (improved quality, improved organizational performance etc.). As TQM becomes more and more institutionalized as the way to conduct business, organizations start to adopt versions of TQM which are the norm (they conform rather than customize) and the main benefits to the organization are symbolic, namely, gaining organizational legitimacy in the eyes of the main stakeholders. While the findings of Westphal and colleagues' study show a transition from customization to conformity in implementing TQM, as TQM becomes institutionalized over time, there may be further phases of institutionalization. One possibility is that TQM may become deinstitutionalized as poor performance of later adopters reduces its legitimacy, thus allowing organizations to get rid of their programmes. Alternatively, institutional pressures may persist but performance problems may lead organizations to resist TQM implementation openly. Perhaps the most likely scenario is that the nature of conformance will evolve over time from complete acquiesce to institutional pressures to a more complex form of conformity where organizations formally adopt normative TQM programmes but also customize their informal practices to the unique needs of their contexts (Westphal et al., 1997).

TQM advocates argue that irrespective of the form of TQM adopted, the approach has positive consequences on the bottom line performance (Garvin, 1987; Dean and Snell, 1991). Hendricks and Singhal (1999), for example, suggest that implementing an effective TQM programme will increase revenues, improve the profitability of the firm and reduce costs.

However, evidence quoted by Choi and Behling (1997) suggests that the 1990s have not been too good for TQM programmes. For example, a survey of 500 executives in US manufacturing and services firms indicated that only one-third believed that TQM made their company more competitive. A survey of 100 British firms that had implemented quality programmes found that only a fifth believed that their programmes had a significant impact on the organization. McKinsey and colleagues found that two-thirds of the TQM programmes they examined had ground to a halt because they failed to produce expected results. Furthermore, widely acclaimed TQM programmes began to stumble. Florida Power and Light, winner of the Deming Prize for Quality Management, slashed its quality department staff from 85 to 3 after the chairman found that the quality improvement process was perceived by the workforce to be a tyrannical bureaucracy.

Such failures should not be quietly swept under the carpet but carefully analysed in order to draw lessons and insights into what can go wrong with TQM programmes. Most explanations regarding TQM failure emphasize problems with its implementation (Redman and Grieves, 1999) rather than any inherent theoretical weaknesses of the TQM model. Such implementation issues are discussed below:

1   Lack of integration between total quality management and everyday business practices. TQM practices are viewed by many as an add-on to what is already going on in the organization, rather than as fundamentally changing or challenging taken-for-granted ways of thinking and doing. As such, they are seen to inconvenience rather than facilitate work in the organization.
2   Lack of management commitment has been blamed by many to be the most crucial reason behind TQM failure (Peters and Austin, 1985; Coulson-Thomas, 1991; Doyle, 1992). Such studies suggest that managers may utter words of commitment but their behaviour does not reflect such commitment and when times get tough they forget the soft language of quality and embark on the tough language of volume, outputs and production levels.
3   Problems of adapting HRM practices to support TQM. As discussed in Chapter 3, it is important that HR practices are aligned with the quality management ethos. Critics suggest that such alignment is a lost cause from the very beginning because TQM emphasizes standardized behaviours while the main role of HRM is to unleash creative potential and enrich the daily work routines of the employees. The sceptics argue that in fact TQM and HRM go hand in hand as they both attempt to institutionalize disciplinary regimes that render individuals more observable and therefore more controllable (Townley, 1994; Kelemen, 2001; for a more detailed account see Chapter 12).
4   The controversial relation between TQM and downsizing. An often-found explanation of TQM failure rests on the difficulty of maintaining or implementing it at a time of job insecurity and redundancy (McCabe and Wilkinson, 1998). At the other end of the spectrum lie those who suggest that TQM does in fact soften the redundancy blow by improving the morale of the people who remain in the organization.
5   Too many quality initiatives: in many cases, TQM is one of the very many quality initiatives present in the organization. Occasionally, issues of

incompatibly may arise between such initiatives (i.e., BPR, performance management, delayering) and TQM. More often, however, TQM complements such initiatives but lacks an overall strategic direction to the extent that people find its message confusing and unhelpful.

Reger and colleagues (1994) suggest that the implementation of TQM often fails because top management does not frame it appropriately. TQM is argued to represent a fundamental shift in values, attitudes and behaviours: as such it may be a dramatic departure from current organizational practices and culture. Organizational culture provides a set of constructs individuals can use to describe what is central, distinctive and enduring about their organization (Albert and Wetten, 1985). As such it can constrain or enhance individuals' understanding and support of new initiatives such as TQM. Thus, establishing cognitive connections between core organizational culture constructs and TQM constructs will increase the probability of members' acceptance of fundamental change (Reger et al., 1994).

There are also significant fundamental theoretical contradictions at the heart of TQM (but perhaps this is true for any normative strategy imposed by management): on the one hand, it advocates the commitment and co-operation of all employees, on the other, it strengthens the centrality of management and its control prerogatives over the workforce. Secondly, TQM comprises two fundamentally different goals: control and learning. Organizational efficiency hinges on the capacity to balance the conflicting goals of stability and reliability (which require controls) and of exploration and innovation (which require learning). At times of low task, product and process uncertainty, practices associated with control will be more appropriate while when uncertainty is high, the organization needs to concentrate on learning and innovation. These dualities are clearly expressed in the opposing positions adopted by the advocates and the critics of TQM. The advocates view TQM as a benign and beneficial initiative that leads to competitive advantage while at the same time empowering the workforce. Critics view TQM as yet another development in the capitalist labour process intended to buttress managerial control and intensify work (Sewell and Wilkinson, 1992).

SUMMARY

This chapter charts the development of Total Quality Management. The three pillars of TQM: top management commitment, continuous improvement and employee involvement are analysed and five metaphorical lenses are introduced to shed light on the complex workings of TQM. The chapter also assesses the extent to which TQM has been successfully implemented to date and ways in which TQM implementation could be improved. It concludes that there are fundamental theoretical contradictions at the heart of the TQM concept and, as such, no implementation model can provide a total guarantee of success.

KEY CONCEPTS

Here are the key concepts covered in this chapter: TQM, metaphor, commitment, continuous improvement, employee involvement, success, failure.

QUESTIONS

At the end of this chapter you should be able to answer the following questions:

- How would you define TQM? What are the three pillars of TQM?
- To what extent is it useful to view TQM through a number of metaphorical lenses? What can you learn from each of them?
- What are the obstacles to successful TQM implementation? Can they be entirely eliminated?
- What are the theoretical contradictions at the heart of the TQM concept?

Conc.

TQM can not succeed without commitment by top mngment.

9 Business process re-engineering

The emphasis on long-term continuous improvement as propagated by TQM has recently been challenged by a new approach to improving quality: Business Process Re-engineering (BPR). BPR pursues not only the goal of quality improvement but many other goals which are to be achieved concomitantly and in a short period of time. The chapter provides insights into the conceptual underpinnings of BPR as well as a snapshot of its implementation practice. The chapter also compares and contrasts BPR with TQM on a number of analytical dimensions including reasons for implementation, approach to change, role of employees, scope and objectives, nature of leadership, the role of IT and so on. It is suggested that most companies implement BPR as an add-on to their TQM programmes that have run out of steam and that rather than viewing these approaches as incompatible we should regard them as bedfellows. Finally, a critique of BPR is being mounted: its violent nature and the dehumanizing effects it has upon work relationships are further discussed.

DEFINING BUSINESS PROCESS RE-ENGINEERING

The genesis of BPR can be traced back to 1983, when the Massachusetts Institute of Technology (MIT) conducted a research programme into the likely impact of information technology on organizations in the 1990s. Since then, BPR has received considerable media and professional attention.

Despite its popularity, there is relatively little consensus as to what process re-engineering means. The most widely used definition of re-engineering belongs to Hammer (1990) who defines it as the fundamental rethinking and radical redesign of business processes to achieve dramatic

This chapter builds on material published by the author and her colleagues, Paul Forrester and John Hassard in the edited collection *The Re-engineering Revolution: Critical Studies of Corporate Change* (2000), D. Knights and H. Willmott (eds) London: Sage.

improvements in critical contemporary measures of performance such as cost, quality, service and speed. The core concept of this definition is the notion of process. Hammer and Champy define a process as a 'set of activities that, taken together, produces a result of value to the customer' (1993: 35). In an equally influential work, Davenport defines a process as a 'structuring measured set of activities designed to produce a specified output for a particular customer or market' (1993: 12). In an earlier article by Davenport and Short (1990) a business process is defined as 'a set of logically related tasks performed to achieve a defined business outcome'. In a similar vein, Earl defines a process as 'a lateral or horizontal form that encapsulates the interdependence of tasks, roles, people, departments and functions required to provide a customer with a product or service' (1994: 13).

The popularization of re-engineering is typically credited to Hammer and Champy who at the beginning of the 1990s packaged this approach in an attractive form for managers. According to Hammer and Champy, BPR inverts the logic of the Industrial Revolution, breaking free from the long established principle of the division of labour. BPR is heralded as a radical departure from conventional change management programmes and as the most important managerial innovation in the last two centuries. It is claimed, for example, that the renewal of the American economy in the 1990s has much (if not everything) to do with the fact that organizations learnt how to re-engineer their processes and focused only on value added activities. The central idea is that, rather than trying to evolve business operations gradually over time, the organizational designer takes a blank sheet of paper and starts from scratch. In so doing, the designer (usually the manager) devises a radical new system that ignores completely what went on before and embraces a totally new and dramatically different way of organizing the business.

Much of the logic encapsulated in BPR stems from the consumerist discourse that pledges to elevate customers' needs to a supreme status. But BPR proponents are also clear on the fact that BPR will deliver shareholder value. According to Hammer and Stanton (1999), re-engineering allows the managers to see through the surface structure of their organizations and focus on customer satisfaction in a way that creates profit for shareholders.

Academics have been keen to jump on the trendy bandwagon of BPR to either critique or support its approach. Although the original formulation of BPR has been largely operational and pragmatic, which may well explain some of its appeal to management audiences (Conti and Warner, 1994), more recently, we have seen sustained efforts by researchers to construct, what is perceived as, the missing theoretical foundations of BPR.

The novelty of BPR is called into question by many critics: BPR is viewed as mainly drawing together, synthesizing and providing an articulation for ideas and practices that have been floating around in the business world without a catchy label or a champion for quite some time. Its recent popularity is due not to its uniqueness or inherent rationality but to the way in which it is packaged to provide a perceptual bridge between existing business challenges, the history and the traditions of the American nation

and the current zeitgeist (i.e., spirit of the time) (Grint, 1994). Grint (1994:
182) suggests that re-engineering can be reduced to ten generic organizational practices:

1   a switch from functional departments to process teams;
2   a move from simple tasks to multidimensional work;
3   a reversal of the power relations: from superordinate to subordinate
    empowerment;
4   a shift from training to education;
5   the development of reward systems that drop payment for attendance in
    favour for payment for value added;
6   a bifurcation of the link between reward for current performance and
    advancement through assessment for ability;
7   the overturning of employee focus: from concern for the boss to concern
    for the customer;
8   changes in management behaviour: from supervisors to coaches;
9   the flattening of hierarchies;
10 changes in executive behaviour: from 'scorekeepers' to leaders.

In contesting the originality and novelty of each of these ideas, Grint
(1994) examines why this ensemble of ideas, marketed as business process re-
engineering, has become so popular in the USA. None of the above ideas are
innovations as they have been around in one shape or another for a number
of decades: for example, process teams such as cells and autonomous
working groups have been around since the early 1970s (see, for example,
the non-functional team-based approaches adopted by Volvo in 1974). The
idea of multidimensional work was the basis of job rotation and job
enrichment programmes, in operation since the early 1970s. The concept of
empowerment is not new or particular to re-engineering or indeed to the
contemporary business organization: Grint (1994) suggests that many hierarchical organizations, such as the armed forces have had technical autonomy for group leaders on the ground, while collective forms of
organizations (i.e., producer cooperatives and anarchic communes) have
always devolved responsibility to their members. The shift from training to
education, and the move from traditional payment systems to payment for
value added are HRM practices not essentially connected with re-engineering. Furthermore, the claim to overturn the employee focus away from a
concern for the boss to concern for the customer was previously made by
total quality management. Changes in management behaviour and changes
from hierarchical control to self-control, two other BPR practices, could be
traced back to the culture management movement of the 1980s.

If it is not the novelty of these practices that makes re-engineering such
a popular management programme, it may be the packaging and the selling
of the package that makes re-engineering different and therefore appealing.
Grint (1994: 192) goes on to suggest that re-engineering is popular because it
is able to generate a resonance with popular opinion about related events.
First, re-engineering provides a new discourse with which contemporary

developments can be simultaneously explained and controlled. Secondly, in juxtaposing the old and the new, re-engineering reminds its audiences that any novelty element has to be historically rooted in the culture of a nation. Thus, success is to be achieved not through a break with American tradition but through a radical return to it.

IMPLEMENTING BPR

According to Hammer and Champy (1993), the implementation of BPR programmes requires a number of steps, as described in the following paragraphs.

Stage 1: First, the organization must be clear as to why re-engineering is needed. In some cases, BPR may be called upon in order to solve a well-known problem that no other management programme was able to work through. In others, BPR acts as a convenient anchor for TQM programmes that have run out of steam. Quite frequently, IT departments drive the adoption of BPR, using it as a new banner under which to relaunch failed IT programmes. BPR could also be adopted in a proactive manner to, for example, identify the potential for outsourcing, or as a prerequisite to ABC. Having clarified and communicated the need for re-engineering, the organization must embark on the development of a broad strategic vision into which the process redesign fits. The organization could set a particular target for pre-tax profit increase to be achieved as a result of cost reduction and/or revenue increase measured across the business unit as a whole.

Stage 2: Like most managerial innovations, BPR's chances of success improve if top management is committed to it. Obtaining business unit (BU) leaders' commitment is thus a necessary ingredient, without which the process of implementation cannot proceed further. BU leaders must grasp the business vision and refine it by challenging the assumptions and principles on which the businesses are currently run. It is expected that companies will commit 20–50 per cent of the business unit leaders' time to the project.

Stage 3: At this stage, the company moves on to identifying the processes that need to be redesigned. There are two approaches one could take: the exhaustive approach attempts to identify all processes within an organization and then prioritize them according to some urgency/importance criteria. Secondly, the high-impact approach attempts to identify only the most important processes or those most in conflict with the business vision. In order to define processes appropriately, one needs sound information from varied sources such as customer interviews and visits, competitor benchmarking, the analysis of best practices in other industries and economic modelling of the business. A process has a number of components: beginning and end points, contents, interfaces and the organizational units involved (see Figures 9.1, 9.2, 9.3 and 9.4).

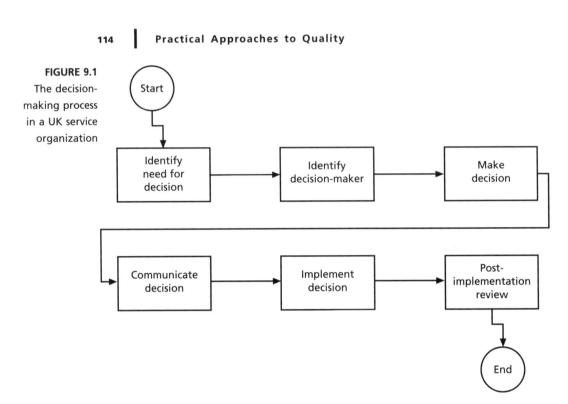

FIGURE 9.1
The decision-
making process
in a UK service
organization

Stage 4: Having identified each process, it is important to be able to measure how well they perform and what is their current contribution to the bottom line. Measurement can serve as a means to understand current processes and as a basis for future improvement and/or change. Measurement may also serve purposes of justification for the costs of the proposed changes, allowing for financial comparisons of the merits of design alternatives.

Stage 5: Armed with information about the existing processes, management can start to design new processes with the help of IT. In so doing, managers must learn to recognize and build upon the new and unfamiliar capabilities of the new technology. The role of IT as an agent of change in the organization has been heavily emphasized in the BPR literature. The idea of aligning the design of organizational processes with the associated infrastructure has been one of the major driving forces for the development of BPR. CASE (computer-aided system engineering), for example, allows managers to draw models rapidly and make changes suggested by process owners. To satisfy the needs and requirements of all possible users, a process model should be able to integrate and represent many forms of information. There are at least four different perspectives on process models (Curtis et al., 1992):

- The functional perspective which concerns itself with what processes are to be performed and what flows of information entities are relevant to these process elements.

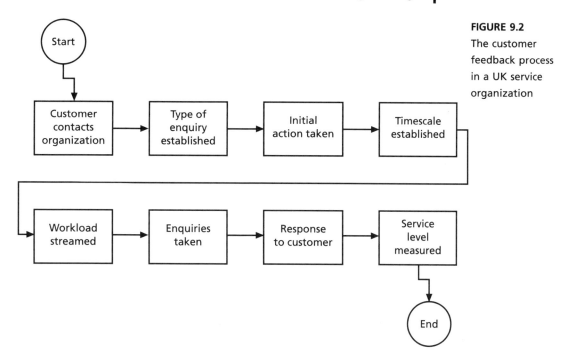

FIGURE 9.2
The customer feedback process in a UK service organization

- The behavioural perspective takes into account timing issues of when process elements are being performed and how well they are performed given existing policies and constraint.
- The organizational perspective focuses on where and whom in the organization performs processes.
- The informational perspective concerns itself with those informational entities that are produced or manipulated by a process.

These perspectives need combining in order to create a model that is more realistic and will meet the aim and goals of re-engineering. One of the major problems that contribute to a high failure rate in real-life re-engineering projects is the lack of tools for evaluating the effects of design solutions before their implementation. Business process simulation (BPS) could meet this challenge providing its inputs (in the form of data gathered across and beyond the organization) are comprehensive and sound. BPS could provide a quick return on investment through improved decision quality. It is also cheaper than computer programming, spreadsheet analysis, opinion modelling and trial and error implementation (Paul et al., 1999).

Stage 6: Having redesigned existing processes, top management must specify the technical and social solutions needed to implement the new processes. Managers must start planning for the new technology, standards, staffing, education and training needs by balancing the costs and benefits of the various scenarios. In some cases, existing technology and standards will be obsolete and require fundamental transformation. In most cases, staffing

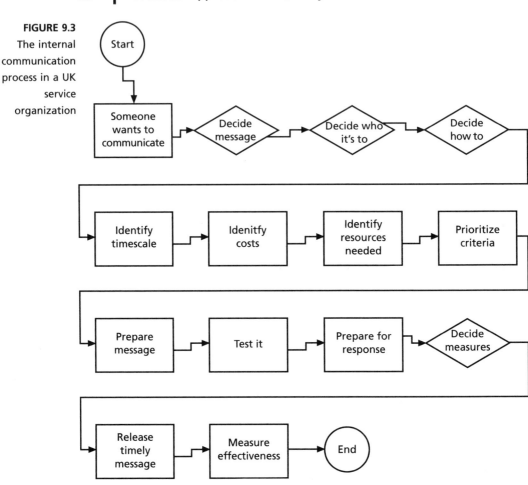

FIGURE 9.3
The internal communication process in a UK service organization

needs to be reduced and those involved in non-value adding activities made redundant. The consequences of such planning extend beyond financial considerations to social and emotional factors which may be harder to quantify in financial terms.

Stage 7: Having planned for the resources necessary to transform existing processes, managers could start implementing their plans. The management of the transition between the organization's functional state to its process-oriented state is one of the most difficult tasks ahead of management. Hammer and Champy advocate a tough, almost dictatorial style of management in the initial implementation stage. Only after the new processes are in place and the non-value adding activities cut out, could managers afford to involve and empower their employees. Research suggests that in the initial stage of BPR implementation morale is usually very low due to the fact that individuals feel threatened by the process and typically resent the new style of management which they perceive as dictatorial. Overcoming

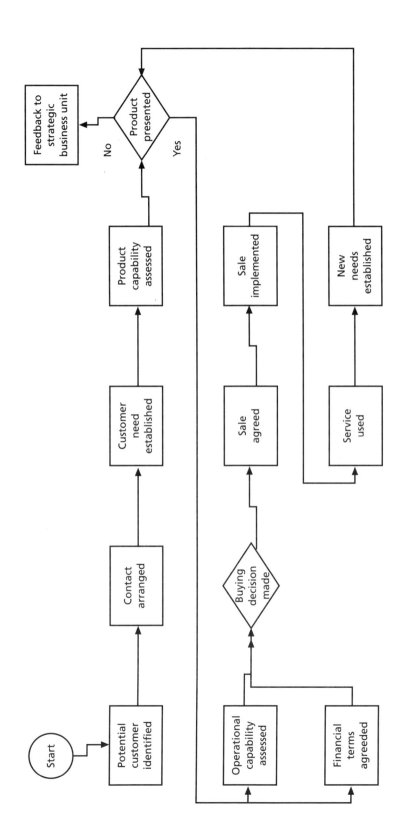

FIGURE 9.4 The sales process in a UK service organization

resistance to the management of change becomes one of the most important challenges of managers in this stage.

Stage 8: However appropriate the new processes may be, they have to be continuously improved. Continuous improvement does not require fundamental shifts but gradual, incremental changes brought about constantly in order to keep the processes under control. The appeal to the logic of continuous improvement which is core to the TQM philosophy suggests that the two approaches are not contradictory but in fact complementary.

BPR AND TQM COMPARED

Proponents of BPR suggest that BPR and TQM represent fundamentally different philosophies of organization (Hammer and Champy, 1993). Empirical evidence shows that in practice, the boundaries between BPR and TQM are more porous and that, BPR programmes can in fact build upon the foundations of TQM programmes that have either lost momentum or are in need of a new 'vision'. There appears to be little in the literature that describes the way BPR and TQM can interrelate and coexist (Dixon et al., 1994). Table 9.1 provides a summary of key analytical dimensions of BPR and TQM. The framework is by no means exhaustive; it is merely a heuristic device for contrasting the conceptual foundations of BPR and TQM, from evidence in the literature. While this taxonomy highlights some areas of potential overlap between BPR and TQM (such as objectives, reasons for implementation, measurement, rate of success and criticisms), it is often the case that BPR and TQM practices overlap much more substantially than the literature suggests.

Origins

The origins of total quality management are ascribed to Japan's search for quality improvements in the 1950s. Three American quality gurus, namely, W.E. Deming, J.M. Juran and A.V. Feigenbaum went to Japan in the 1950s to teach quality control to middle and senior managers. The Japanese adopted, developed and adapted some of these and by the late 1950s, Japan had begun to develop clearly distinctive approaches more suitable to its own culture (i.e. quality circles and team work, Pareto and fishbone diagrams, quality built in at the product design stage, and so forth). While the roots of TQM are a hybrid of American and Japanese ideas, BPR is depicted by its proponents as purely American. Accordingly, at the heart of re-engineering lie characteristics that have supposedly made Americans great business innovators: individualism, self-reliance and risk-taking (Hammer and Champy, 1993). The proponents of BPR argue that business success can be achieved not through breaks with tradition, but through a radical return to

Dimension	BPR	TQM
Origins	American	Japanese/American
Objectives	improvements in cost, quality, service, speed, organizational transformation around processes	improvements in quality
Reasons for implementation	institutional pressure/technical reasons	institutional pressure/technical reasons
Approach to change	revolutionary/fast	continuous/slow
Style of leadership	aggressive, autocratic	visionary, transformational
Role of employees	important at a later stage in the exercise	crucial from the beginning
Implementation	top down	top down and bottom up
Measurement	rational/objective	rational/objective
Language	violent/blunt platitudes	caring platitudes
IT	crucial	secondary
Focus	processes	processes and functions
Rate of success	20–30 per cent	20–30 per cent
Criticisms	managerial fad, revamped Taylorism work intensification and exploitation mixed, difficult to predict outcomes	managerial fad, revamped Taylorism work intensification and exploitation mixed, difficult to predict outcome

TABLE 9.1
A comparison of BPR and TQM on key analytical dimensions emphasized in the literature (Kelemen et al., 2000)

traditional American values (Grint, 1994). Grint and Case argue, however, that BPR can be seen as a form of inverse colonization in which American managerial discourse experiences cognitive dissonance in face of the growing influence of Japan: 'BPR literature has responded to the ascent of Japanese thinking and practice by both assimilating some of its features and xeno-phobically revolting against them' (1998: 575).

Objectives

The objectives of BPR and TQM programmes are usually identified a the outset, being rarely redefined in the process of implementation. While BPR pursues multifaceted improvement objectives that may include quality, cost, flexibility, speed and accuracy concurrently (Hammer and Champy, 1993), TQM focuses on fewer goals. For example, BPR programmes may attempt to pursue concomitantly goals such as: '100 percent improvement in cycle time', 'big leap in technology', 'cut cost by 75 percent', 'decrease head counts by 75 percent' (quoted in Dixon et al., 1994: 101). According to Ligus: 'The following changes are possible: 30–35 percent reduction in the cost of sales;

75–80 percent reduction in delivery time; 60–80 percent reduction in inventories; 65–70 percent reduction in the cost of quality; and unpredictable but substantial increase in market share' (1993: 58). In the case of TQM the stated primary objective is to improve quality, but it is recognized that such a goal will usually have a cascading effect upon other facets of the organization. Crosby (1979), for example, advocates the goal of quality improvement to reduce scrap, rework and inspection and ultimately to increase profits. Similarly, Hill (1995) suggests that improved quality leads to gains in productivity, responsiveness and competitiveness.

Reasons for implementation

External pressures, in particular the market, are seen to play a significant role in explaining why organizations opt for BPR or TQM programmes. In a survey carried out by Southern (1994), 80 per cent of the organizations examined were engaged in a BPR exercize in response to changes in the external environment. However, Dixon and colleagues (1994) argue that re-engineering is not necessarily a reactive response triggered by changes in the environment. On the contrary, BPR may be a proactive step, fuelled by internal concerns. TQM initiatives are also seen to be motivated to a significant extent by market pressure. organizations may embrace TQM in order to imitate the actions of market leaders, gain support from stakeholders or embrace new sources of competitive advantage (Reitsperger and Daniel, 1991). This view is supported by research carried out by Redman and colleagues (1995), which asserts that 91 per cent of the managers surveyed invoked the logic of the market as the reason for TQM implementation.

Approach to change

BPR is depicted as seeking radical performance breakthroughs, that are discontinuous rather than incremental improvements (Davenport, 1993; Ascari et al., 1995). In so doing, the BPR approach to change reflects a mechanistic model that emphasizes outcomes, precision, speed and a 'one best way' philosophy. TQM, on the other hand, embraces a philosophy of step-by-step improvement in which the process is consistently and continuously monitored in order to eliminate deviations from the prescribed trajectories. The TQM approach to change is inscribed in an organic model of change which emphasizes 'logical incrementalism' (Quinn, 1978), long termism as well as the importance of constantly re-negotiating the meanings surrounding processes of change.

Style of leadership

BPR's approach to leadership is a controversial one. In the implementation stage, a dictatorial style is advocated. Leaders must be tough, bold and determined to perform organizational lobotomy. Their leadership style must be autocratic and aggressive, in line with the unpopular, almost violent, decisions that have to be made (Hammer and Champy, 1993). Leaders must also be highly committed to BPR for it to succeed. This commitment is usually reflected in the amount of time leaders spend on BPR projects, typically between 20–50 per cent for successful programmes (Hall et al., 1993). Hall and colleagues (1993) suggest that, at a later stage in the process, top managers must act as consensus seekers and role models for employees. TQM writers also stress the importance of an active commitment from top management. Indeed, a survey of 80 organizations employing 1.6 million people reveals that top management commitment is overwhelmingly the most important factor in achieving TQM (Coulson-Thomas, 1991). As for the style of leadership, at least ideologically, TQM is aligned with a more caring, empowering style which can bring out the best in every employee and sets the scene for a culture in which each individual's contribution is recognized.

Role of employees

Supporters of BPR argue that re-engineering results in workers being given more responsibility in their jobs, such as on the spot problem solving and quality checks. In Hammer and Champy's words, 'people who once did as they were instructed, now make choices and decisions on their own' (1993: 65). Empowerment is not seen as a mere residue of re-engineering but as an essential condition for its success (Hammer and Champy, 1993). Critics, however, challenge these optimistic views on empowerment. Grey and Mitev (1995) and Willmott (1995) argue that re-engineering leads to work intensification and that empowerment is no more than another form of managerial control. Other critics (Knights and McCabe, 1998a) suggest that employees who remain in employment after re-engineering experience more stressful and intensive working conditions. According to Horsted and Doherty (1994), however, whether individuals stay with or leave a re-engineered organization, they generally experience subsequently feelings of psychological 'trauma' rather than empowerment.

Most of the TQM literature emphasizes the central role employees have in the quality process. Oakland (1989), for example, argues that there is no need to coerce employees to embrace quality as they, themselves, want to embrace it in order to achieve a sense of self-fulfilment. TQM's concern with employee involvement resonates with the neo-human relations notion of self-actualization (through empowerment) as key to human motivation. Some researchers, however, question the basis and the nature of such empowerment, as it merely confines employees within the systems designed by management. Empowerment within TQM regimes has been discussed by some of the critical management literature in terms of exploitation, work intensification and team surveillance (McArdle et al., 1995; Kelemen, 1998; Sewell, 1998).

Implementation

BPR is heralded as a top-down exercize (Hammer and Champy, 1993). Since business processes are usually cross-functional and cross-organizational, changes must be authorized at a sufficiently high level in the company. Frequently, the CEO or business unit head is the sponsor of the BPR project and drives it through the organization. Proponents of TQM suggest that TQM can be a top-down exercize, but since most ideas for improvement come from the shopfloor, it can also be implemented in a bottom-up fashion by 'reversing the pyramid' (Heller, 1993). However, it would be unusual for a shopfloor employee or even a middle manager to be TQM's main driver or 'champion' – far more likely the chief executive or the managing director will be the major sponsor of the TQM programme.

Measurement

BPR and TQM are premised upon assumptions that change can be rationally measured, and evidence can be provided in order to judge the quality and progress of change. In BPR's case, cost-benefit and time-based analyses, among others, form the basis of this rationality (Remeny and Whittaker, 1994). Dixon and colleagues (1994) argue that some of the measures may also be non-financial (e.g., team effectiveness), as long as they are consistent with, and reinforce, the goals of re-engineering. TQM also involves extensive data collection, analysis and feedback systems with the view to identifying problems and directing employees' attention towards them (Sitkin, 1995). According to a survey carried out in Britain, the main TQM indicators are, customer feedback, complaints, delivery performance and reject rates (Redman et al., 1995). Organizational concern for measuring quality is also reflected in the number of organizations registered for BS 5750 which, according to Hegarty (1993), amounted to 16,000 in 1992.

Language

Language is the main medium through which top managers provide accounts of their decisions (Boden, 1994) and attempt to justify and legitimize their actions (Davis and Luthans, 1980), including the reasons for adopting BPR or TQM. The language of BPR and TQM as constructed by the 'gurus', has been appropriated by a large number of managers and deployed in order to effect organizational change. BPR programmes are typically associated with blunt, colourful and violent language which frequently draws on a military repertoire (Willmott, 1995; Grint and Case, 1998). Hammer and Champy (1993) talk about axes, machine guns, lobotomy and shooting as devices to facilitate change in the organization. On the contrary, TQM programmes are locked into 'caring' platitudes about the customer, the market and the employee. 'Customer first', 'customer is king', 'people make the difference', 'right first time', to name but a few, are phrases which aim to strike a responsive chord in the employees. Phrases of this type bring the logic of the market to the organization and invite consensus over issues (such as quality) that otherwize may prove to be controversial.

I T

Re-engineering represents a significant break with previous performance improvement approaches in requiring a high level of state of the art information technology (Guimares and Bond, 1996). According to Davenport and Short (1990), IT is critical to the successful operation of new or redesigned business processes. However, Dixon and colleagues (1994) found that there is little evidence that the rapid evolution of IT is driving organizations towards re-engineering, although reengineered processes incorporate improvements in IT. While the emphasis on IT-enabled change distinguishes BPR form other managerial innovations (Conti and Warner, 1994), proponents of TQM do not regard IT as a fundamental pillar or driving force of TQM. Indeed, the role of IT is much less apparent in the implementation and operation of TQM programmes.

Focus

Most BPR and TQM literature suggests that, to be successful, the organization should be reconfigured as a set of horizontal processes that begin with the supplier and end with the customer. Knights and McCabe (1998a), for example, suggest that BPR re-engineers the structures and functions of the organization around the processes that link production to final consumption. In the TQM arena, however, there is growing evidence that most organizations remain highly bureaucratic with departments acting individually and building even more walls to guard their own space (Johansson et al., 1993). On the other hand, BPR cannot be conceived outside of the notion of processes which cross-functional boundaries. Depending upon the mandate from the sponsor, BPR projects can be either highly focused, or broad in scope. In the latter case, it is advocated that the BPR team include a cross-section of the various functions in the company. Even in the case of a highly focused project, it is necessary that the team broadly represent all the relevant constituencies. As a minimum, the team should include both people who are familiar with the core process(es) and those who are not familiar. The role of the former is to bring knowledge of the way things are done at that time; the role of the latter is to bring a sense of creative naiveté to the project.

Rate of success

Consultants and mainstream academics alike have portrayed TQM and BPR in the best possible light. Thus, Heller (1993) argues that the turnaround of many Western organizations was due to their TQM approach, while Guimares and Bond (1996) champion BPR for promoting similar organizational successes. These accounts are challenged, however, by evidence suggesting that TQM did not catch on in the West to the extent it did in Japan, its rate of success being less than 30 per cent (*The Economist*, 1992; *Wall Street Journal*, 1992; Schmidt et al., 1992). Similarly, 70–80 per cent of BPR programmes are seen to fail (in terms of not meeting the initial expectations of management), according to Rothschild (1992) and a survey carried out for *Personnel Today* (1994).

Criticisms of the approach

There are numerous criticisms levelled at BPR and TQM. Some critics see them as merely managerial fads (Blair et al., 1998; Gill and Whittle, 1993) or else as revamped Taylorism (Blair et al., 1998; Conti and Warner, 1994; Olian and Rynes, 1991). Blair and colleagues (1998) argue that despite its stated departure from Taylorism, BPR reinforces the development of organizational control systems to ensure compliance. Referring to TQM, Olian and Rynes (1991) suggest that even though TQM may provide more human freedom than scientific management, it may also reduce it by institutionally enlisting employees into preferred ways of solving problems.

Some researchers offer vehement critiques on BPR and TQM (Knights and McCabe, 1998a). BPR is seen to lead to work intensification and job redundancies (Grey and Mitev, 1994; Willmott, 1995). Willmott for example, challenges the possibilities for empowerment in a BPR regime by arguing that here empowerment 'legitimizes a process of *managerial colonisation* in which employees are represented as willing receptacles of the new, avowedly empowering, post-bureaucratic organizing principles' (1995: 92). In a similar vein, Dawson and Webb (1989) suggest that TQM serves capital in its search for more efficient exploitation of labour, while Tuckman (1995) argues that TQM is an ideology directed at making employees identify with the logic of the market.

Other researchers adopt a BPR perspective that draws on poststructuralist ideas of power, knowledge and resistance. Some (e.g., Grint, 1994; Grint and Willcocks, 1995) are concerned with the politics of information technology (mis)management, suggesting that the outcomes of BPR are mixed (both positive and negative) and difficult to know or predict in advance. Other researchers (Knights and McCabe, 1998a, 1998b; Blair et al., 1998; Kelemen, 2000) reinforce the highly political nature of BPR and TQM and call for empirically informed studies of BPR to explore the subjective experiences of employees during its introduction and operation. Lastly, there are those who view TQM and BPR as mere stories of organizing (de Cock, 1998; Lawrence and Phillips, 1998), which offer alternatives to the totalizing managerialist discourses surrounding them.

Empirical evidence suggests that TQM and BPR do in fact coexist in organizations (Kelemen et al., 2000). Both are programmes of management and as such are socially constructed phenomena arising in the contested, political and historical organizational arena. Therefore, the boundaries between them in practice are more permeable than the above theoretical taxonomy might have suggested.

IS THERE A FUTURE FOR RE-ENGINEERING?

So is BPR a mere fashion as some critics argue? Abrahamson (1996) defines a management fashion as the relatively transitory collective beliefs disseminated by management knowledge entrepreneurs (consultants, gurus, academics) that a particular management technique is at the forefront of rational management progress. Such collective beliefs stem from the rational view held by most managers that certain components of the organization can and must be controlled using progressive and rational techniques designed explicitly to manage these components (Abrahamson and Fairchild, 1999). BPR, for example, purports to control and dramatically improve organizational processes: given that no prior technique was able to deliver the expected improvements in process performance (see for example, continuous improvement, and total quality management), room had been created for a new fashion which could potentially fill the gap left open by the relative failure of prior fashions. The rapid and wide dissemination of BPR across sectors and industry was made possible due to the belief that organizations are similar in ways which would cause them to benefit equally from adopting the same managerial technique. Although the resource-based view denies the possibility of perfect imitation, companies in the West initially and then across the rest of the globe have been keen to try out this 'new' technique.

Whether BPR will survive or not in this new decade remains to be seen. Certainly, a newer development in re-engineering could be seen to take hold in the virtual space, the so-called e-engineering. The concept signals the central role of the Internet in helping companies re-invent the way they do business. The Internet is seen to help organizations change the way they distribute goods, collaborate inside the company and deal with suppliers and customers. Companies such as Intel and Dell have been first to seize on the Net to overhaul their operation. At Intel-Corp, for example, web-based automation has apparently 'liberated' 200 sales clerks from tedious order entering. As a result, they can concentrate on analysing sales trends and pampering the customers (Hamm and Stepanek, 1999). E-engineering is allegedly a more refined version of business re-engineering that heightens the primordial role of the customer and in so doing, releases the creative potential of both technology and people. As there is relatively little empirical evidence on e-engineering it is difficult to assess whether it is more successful that traditional re-engineering and what chances it may have in the future in being adopted more widely.

SUMMARY

The chapter unpacks the conceptual foundations of Business Process Re-engineering as a quality management initiative that aims to achieve a multitude of goals (such as quality, service, speed) concomitantly and in a short period of time. In so doing, it argues that BPR is by no means a novel and original technique of management but one that draws together ideas that had been floating around for a number of decades, without a catchy label or a champion. BPR promises a high degree of individual autonomy at work by inviting individuals to make choices rather than imposing them on them. For in order for BPR to be effective, organizational members must internalize its routines and procedures to a significant extent and behave according to requirements. In reality, BPR works by imposing bureaucratic and disciplinary controls over employees and managers alike rather than by increasing autonomy levels in the workplace. The chapter compares and contrasts BPR and TQM on a number of analytical dimensions and argues that the two may be bedfellows rather than competing approaches to improving quality.

KEY CONCEPTS

Here are the key concepts covered in this chapter: re-engineering, process, IT, e-engineering

QUESTIONS

At the end of this chapter you should be able to answer the following questions:

- To what extent can one argue that BPR is a novel approach to the management of organizations?
- How would you go about implementing BPR in an organization?
- Are the theoretical foundations of BPR fundamentally different from those of TQM?
- What are the most important criticisms levied at BPR?

Leadership, teamwork and organizational culture 10

This chapter reviews soft approaches to managing quality with an emphasis on culture, leadership and teamwork. So-called hard approaches had been reviewed in Chapters 5, 6 and 7 (i.e., quality standards, quality costs and quality control), whereas Chapters 8 and 9 introduced two holistic approaches to the management of quality (i.e., TQM and BPR) which rely on a mixture of hard and soft quality techniques. This chapter reviews approaches that argue that the success of quality management lies not in the presence of quality standards or quality controls but in creating a shared organizational culture that emphasizes teamwork and the importance of the customer. The concept of organizational culture is examined from three distinct yet related perspectives: the integration, the differentiation and the ambiguity perspective on culture (Meyerson and Martin, 1987). A critique of culture and its role in managing quality is articulated around a framework suggested by Willmott (1993). The chapter moves on to question the role played by leadership in creating a quality culture. In so doing, it reviews key approaches to leadership and evaluates the extent to which leaders can make a difference to organizational outcomes. The chapter concludes with a critical examination of the role played by teamwork in creating and maintaining a quality culture.

ORGANIZATIONAL CULTURE AND 'QUALITY CULTURE'

Proponents of soft approaches to the management of quality argue that having quality systems in place does not guarantee the satisfaction of customers. In order for these systems to work for the customers, organizational members must be able to relate to them and derive some meaning from their involvement with such systems. Only when employees take on board the message of quality and behave accordingly, can one talk about a quality culture. The project of building organizational cultures around the goals of quality has been explicitly promoted by TQM exponents (Crosby, 1984; Wilkinson, 1992). According to culture management gurus (Deal and Kennedy, 1982; Peters and Waterman, 1982), strong organizational cultures united around common goals and objectives are able to secure greater commitment from the employees and in so doing are more successful at achieving organizational goals. Strong cultures systematically reward employees (materially and symbolically) for internalizing organizational goals and acting according to espoused organizational values; this tends to lead to improved quality and productivity (for a review and critique of this position, see Willmott, 1993). This stance relies on unitarism, a position that suggests that the interests of individuals and the organization are not too disparate and can be reconciled, if the right mechanisms (i.e., culture) are put in place.

The following analysis of culture relies on a framework developed by Meyerson and Martin (1987): three lenses are employed to understand the concept of culture and its consequences upon the quality effort. The integrative view of culture depicts culture as something that is shared by the members of an organization and is therefore unique to a given organization or group. Thus, culture is the glue that holds together potentially diverse individuals and/or groups of organizational members. This perspective focuses on leaders as culture creators (Pettigrew, 1979; Schein, 1983); leaders are expected to provide meaning and direction for the rest of the organization. Cultural artefacts and manifestations that reflect the leader's own personal value systems tend to be emphasized: leaders' way of thinking and doing tends to be institutionalized, conferring on them a form of organizational immortality (Bennis, 1983). Cultural harmony is seen to lead to organizational effectiveness: thus, successful quality programmes must always start with a leader who understands and is committed to quality. The leader's way of thinking and behaviour could then be adopted by the rest of the organization via processes of cultural change. Such processes are organization wide and rely heavily on cognitive processes which emphasize the role of individual learning in accomplishing the task.

If the integration perspective on culture emphasizes consensus and denies ambiguity, the differentiation perspective on culture (Meyerson and Martin, 1987) shifts attention to inconsistencies and non-leader sources of cultural change. Thus, culture is seen to arize at the intersection between factors internal and external to the organization. Culture is viewed as a collection of manifestations, some of which may be contradictory. In fact, espoused values may be inconsistent with actual practices and words may carry different meanings in different contexts. Thus, what is unique to an organization is the specific combination of cultures that meet within an organization's boundary. This view of culture emphasizes external factors as important agents for change: thus, an organization may adopt TQM because its competitors have already done so or because customers demand it. The adoption of TQM has a localized (and not an organization-wide) impact on organizational functioning, as some departments/individuals may be more receptive than others to the new philosophy of quality. Such localized changes tend to be loosely coupled with each other and are frequently neither planned nor under the total control of leadership.

The third view of culture, the ambiguity view (Meyerson and Martin, 1987) suggests that the relationships among cultural manifestations are characterized by a lack of clarity, as well as paradox and ambiguity. Thus, culture is neither fully integrated, nor fully differentiated: at times, individuals may agree on certain quality issues, at other times they may be indifferent, ignorant or in total opposition. When a particular issue becomes salient, one particular pattern of connections becomes relevant. This view stresses individual adjustment to environmental fluctuations, including patterns of attention and adaptation. It follows, that leaders cannot fully control the fate and trajectories of their own words and that they cannot be engineers of a quality culture. Ambiguity gets in the way: a more detailed discussion of the role of ambiguity in the enactment of a quality culture is presented in Chapter 12.

Each view on culture is useful in directing attention to a particular way of understanding and managing quality. In practice, the most widely accepted perspective is the integration one which stresses commonalities among individuals and their commitment to the quality effort. Having a strong/integrated culture is seen to be key to the effective management of quality. The central argument of this position, which is usually referred to as corporate culturalism, is that through loyalty to their organization, individuals not only contribute to achieving organizational goals but also accomplish a sense of self-fulfilment. Strong cultures encourage employees to devote themselves to the organization's values and products and to assess their own worth with respect to those. Such cultures imprint upon the employees a certain way of being and acting: those who internalize it are rewarded, while those who challenge or disobey it are marginalized. The benefits of participating in such a culture are usually portrayed in terms of respect for individuality and the chance of the individual to become a winner.

Such benefits are considered to be welcomed by the individual who, with the help of corporate values, is able to simultaneously achieve individual autonomy and contribute to enhanced organizational performance. Corporate culturalism is not, however, a neutral, apolitical phenomenon, for, far from lessening management control, it refines and extends it through the design of value systems and the management of symbolic and emotional aspects of the organization (Willmott, 1993). Instead of providing intellectual and cultural resources to help individuals reflect upon and choose from the myriad of possibilities and opportunities that may exist, corporate culturalism circumscribes individual choice to the authority of corporate values (Willmott, 1993) by giving the impression that personal autonomy is respected and enhanced.

Having highlighted the potentially enlightening as well as the dark side of organizational culture, the chapter now turns to discussing the extent to which leadership can contribute to the enactment of a quality culture. For, if leadership shapes and is shaped by the organization of belief and meaning

(Smircich and Morgan, 1982), unpacking the relationship between culture and leadership becomes paramount in understanding the ways in which quality is being constructed and managed in organizations.

THE ROLE OF LEADERSHIP IN CREATING A QUALITY CULTURE

Research on leadership is vast and full of controversies. After a comprehensive review of the literature, Stogdill concluded that: 'There are as many definitions of leadership as there are persons who have attempted to define the concept' (1974: 259). One of the major controversies in the leadership literature is whether leadership is a collective process shared among the members of an organization or whether it is about a person who carries out a leadership function that cannot be shared without jeopardizing the success of the group's mission (Yukl, 1989). This section outlines briefly the most popular approaches to leadership: the trait approach, the style approach, the contingency approach, the charismatic and the transformational approach as well as the interpretative approach. It is eventually concluded that leadership is a socially constructed phenomenon which exists only in the eyes of the followers/believers.

The trait approach

The trait approach stresses the personal qualities of leaders, suggesting that leaders are born rather than made. There are three broad factors addressed by the literature. First there are physical factors such as physique, weight, height, appearance, age. The second type of factors concerns ability characteristics such as: intelligence, scholarship, knowledge, fluency of speech. The third type of factors concerns personality features such as: self-confidence, emotional control, introversion–extraversion, and so on. Leaders are seen to display a certain assemblage of traits which are largely innate and, therefore, not amenable to change. The implication of this approach is that leaders are born not made, since training cannot essentially alter their capacities. The trait approach has been questioned by a number of leading authors who have argued that personal factors associated with leadership are situation specific (cf. Kirkpatrick and Locke, in Bryman, 1992) and, in other words, there are no universal leadership traits.

The style approach

The style approach stands in opposition to the previous approach, although the focus is still on the individual. The style approach emphasizes what leaders do and considers that once the behaviour that makes effective leaders is known, individuals can be trained to exhibit that behaviour. Adair (in Bass, 1990) suggests that 'leadership is learnt quality and that nothing could be more effective than learning from success and failure'. The major line of research on leadership style has sought to identify behaviours associated with effective leadership by examining the differences in behaviour patterns between effective and ineffective leaders.

Both the trait and the style approach to leadership have found resonance in the TQM literature. Tenner and DeToro (1992), for example, highlight the skills and behaviours associated with TQM leadership: namely, visioning, aligning, empowering, coaching and caring. For Price (1989), TQM leadership is about personal integrity, listening to the others, a strong belief in team play, as well as the willingness to take risks and not fear failure.

The contingency approach

The contingency approach purports that the effectiveness of a leader is situationally contingent. This means that there are no universally appropriate styles of leadership and a particular pattern of behaviour will be effective in some circumstances but not the others. This approach emphasizes the importance of contextual factors such as the nature of the work performed by the subordinates, the attributes of the subordinates, the nature of the external environment. By doing so, it signals the importance of followers in judging whether someone is a leader or not. Role theory, for example, suggests that the role set (a role set is composed of one's expectations of one's role and other people's expectations of that role) is important in shaping leaders' behaviours (Kahn, 1964), whereas attribution theory employs cognitive arguments to explain how leaders and followers attach meaning to various situations. The contingency approach views leadership as a collective process and accords followers and leaders equally important roles. If leadership is contingent, different TQM programmes require different leadership styles/traits for their success. Some of these traits/behaviours may trigger followership, others may not.

Charismatic leadership

Charismatic leadership Kirkpatrick and Locke (in Bryman, 1992) conceptualize charisma as a personal trait whereas other authors examine charisma in terms of how the leader is perceived by his or her followers: thus, charisma is seen to be an attributional phenomenon. Followers attribute charismatic qualities to a leader based on their observations of the leader's behaviour and outcomes associated with it (cf. Conger and Kanugo in Yukl, 1989). There is however, little evidence to back up the view that charismatic leaders achieve greater successes than others. Nevertheless, the charismatic leader is often portrayed as key in ensuring the successful implementation of TQM.

Transformational leadership

Transformational leadership refers to the process of influencing major changes in the attitudes and assumptions of organizational members. Bass (1990) considers charisma a necessary but not sufficient condition of transformational leadership. Transformational leadership seeks to empower and elevate followers whereas in charismatic leadership the opposite sometimes occurs. Burns (1978) describes transformational leadership as a process of evolving interrelations in which leaders influence followers and are influenced in turn to modify their behaviour as they meet responsiveness or resistance. TQM literature dwells considerably on the importance of transformational leadership in creating and maintaining a quality culture.

The interpretative approach

The interpretative approach asserts that leadership concepts and theories are subjective efforts by social scientists to interpret ambiguous events in a meaningful way, not precize definitions of immutable natural laws (Yukl, 1989). Leadership may be a label used to explain events which otherwize may seem inexplicable. The role of leadership is less one of determining the course of events and more one of justifying collective activity that leads to such outcomes (Tolstoy, 1957). Thus, it may be convenient to blame leadership for the failure of TQM programmes: conversely, leadership may be elevated as the most important cause, when TQM is successful.

It becomes obvious from the literature review that there is a wide and contradictory variety of leadership definitions. In light of this, it is important to shift our analytical lens to the social and political mechanisms by which certain definitions are elevated and others are played down. Leadership is inherently a matter of social and political interdependence, being achieved through the social coordination of actions around specific definitions, in particular those disseminated by the leaders themselves. In order to resist accounts that may seek to delegitimize leadership's central position, pro-leader accounts must be constantly reproduced by the leaders themselves or important followers (Grint, 1997). It has been acknowledged a long time ago that the functions of leadership are essentially discursive (Barnard, 1938). Leaders manage the available language conventions to achieve an accepted sense of organizational rationality. But the 'rational sayings' available to the individual leader are of indeterminate meaning. The rationality, wisdom and objectivity of leaders' sayings depend on their followers who supply the interpretations of the sayings. Leaders cannot control the fate of their expressions; they are empowered only through the accounts of others.

In the TQM context effective leadership depends on the extent to which leaders' definitions of quality serve as a basis for action for others. The key challenge for a leader is to create and manage meaning in such a way that individuals can orient themselves towards the achievement of quality. Bridging the individual and organizational agendas with a quality discourse becomes the most challenging task of leadership. The evidence regarding the role of leadership in achieving TQM is, however, sparse. There does not seem to be a consensus as to whether leadership makes a difference to organizational outcomes. This state of affairs is typically blamed on the lack of rigorous evidence: most studies on leadership and its relation to organizational outcomes are unsystematic, use methodologies which are difficult to replicate and have considerable difficulty in defining the concepts.

Quality cultures are often associated with effective teamwork. In the next section, we look at the positive and negative aspects of teamworking and discuss three types of teams that are usually relied upon in the management of quality.

TEAMWORK AND QUALITY CULTURES

Teams have played an important role in organizational life for the past 200 years (Grint, 1994). They are by no means an invention of the late twentieth century. In the nineteenth century, for example, German, American and Japanese shipyards were organized around process-driven teams characterized by relatively little specialization and a low division of labour. What is interesting to note, however, is the fervour with which teams have been advocated by the quality management literature.

Proponents of TQM are united in arguing that teamworking leads to improved levels of quality. Generally speaking, teamworking is viewed as a method of management which ensures the efficient use of human resources. If managerialist discourses are quick to elevate the benefits of teamworking, critics have been more inclined to point to the normalization effects of teamworking and the negative effects this may have upon the experience of the team member. Advocates of teamworking argue that teams are better than individuals on complex tasks which require more work than a person can put in and more knowledge than a person can possess. Such complex tasks usually require a variety of skills and roles which can only be performed by groups (Schein, 1980). Critics on the other hand, argue that teams are sites of conflicts and very often underachieve. They stifle individual creativity and run the risk of 'groupthink' (Janis, 1972), that is, the risk of going along with the opinions of the group despite having personal doubts over certain issues. Sewell (1998) goes further by suggesting that teams are a control mechanism: such controls have a disciplinary nature. Team-surveillance works by inviting members to internalize the goals and means of the team and act according to those in the pursuit of personal identity.

A more balanced approach to teamworking is adopted by Knights (2000) whose research explores what teamworking means for the employees of a manufacturing company based in the UK. His research broadly identifies three responses to the concept of teamwork: first, there are some employees who internalize the values and agendas of teamworking. Secondly, there are employees who appear disturbed and upset by this new form of work which they see as intruding into their personal sphere. Thirdly, there are those who are 'bewildered' by teamworking due to the fact that it challenges the established ways of working in the organization. Such responses (or variations of those) are probably typical within other organizational and sectorial contexts as well as with regard to other managerial innovations. There are many forms of teamworking pursued in the achievement of quality: this chapter reviews project teams, quality circles and quality improvement teams.

Project teams are usually organized around one-off projects (Dale and Boaden, 1994). Such projects are typically identified by top management and are concerned with key improvement issues, usually of a strategic nature. Top management identify the project owner who then selects a team of employees to work on the issue. The owner (typically a senior manager) can either lead the team in a hands-on fashion, or act as a mentor to the team. Such one-off projects dissolve once the issue has been resolved and certain deliverables have been achieved. Membership is compulsory in that the project owner requests certain employees to join in the project. The scope of project teams tends to be cross-functional for improvement issues usually require diverse skills and talents from various functions and departments. The most important advantage of such teams is that they bring together top managers and employees on issues of strategic importance to the organization. Given that only a limited number of people can participate in such teams, they are not a broad participative vehicle (Dale, 1994).

Quality circles are a parallel structure which attempt to get employees involved in problem-solving (Ishikawa, 1985). A parallel structure is a structure separate and distinct from an organization's regular ongoing activities: as such it operates in a special way and not according to the formal rules laid down by the organization. Such structures have numerous strengths:

- They allow organizations to deal with issues that otherwise may not be discussed and/or approached within the more formal structure.
- Their set up does not require too much effort and thus they cause little if any disruption to the formal organization.
- They permit problem-solving by individuals who might otherwise not have the opportunity to become involved.
- In some organizations, they may be the only participative mechanism that top managers are prepared to accept.
- They lead to increased information sharing among participants.

Among their limitations, one can mention:

- They are viewed at times as an auxiliary task and can be subject to cancellation.

- Their power is limited as they only make recommendations but have no prerogative to implement them.
- They may lead to an 'in and out' situation whereby individuals who do not belong to a circle may feel left out, unimportant and demotivated.
- They recommend improvements regarding changes in work methods and procedures but do not concern themselves with issues of a more strategic importance.

Research on quality circles shows that they go through a series of predictable phases (Lawler, 1986):

1 The honeymoon stage: a small number of circles are formed, they are strongly motivated to produce good ideas for improvement.
2 The expansion stage: more circles are being set up and their philosophy spreads across the organization.
3 The disillusionment stage: the costs start to mount, the recommendations made are not seen through, middle managers start to put up resistance.

Organizations can move beyond the stage of disillusionment by expanding the kinds of decisions made by quality circles to the realm of strategy and design.

Quality improvement teams are a cross breed between project teams and quality circles, in that they consist of members of a single department, a number of departments and/or customers and suppliers. Their membership could be voluntary or mandatory and can comprise a mixture of employees from various hierarchical levels. Such projects which have as a main goal the improvement of quality and productivity are formed either as a top management initiative or in response to the need to undertake some corrective action within the organization. This sort of team is more permanent than the project team and less so than the quality circle. It is also self-contained in that it can take the necessary action to put things right without asking for top management approval. After the objectives have been met the team usually dissolves.

Quality circles, project teams and quality improvement teams have been widely used by contemporary organizations. However, their contribution to the overall quality effort remains highly contested. Teamwork advocates view teams as crucial to creating and maintaining a strong organizational culture united around the prerogatives of quality. Critics, on the other hand, warn of the disciplinary effects teamwork had upon members and regard teams as control mechanisms rather than as empowering.

SUMMARY

This chapter advocates the importance of soft technologies of quality management such as culture, leadership and teamwork. It is suggested that in order for quality to succeed, employees must make quality a personal goal and align their individual agendas with the organizational one. No quality system can be successful unless employees are willing to get involved in it and secure a sense of personal identity in relation to that system. The creation of a strong organization culture united around the goal of quality and customer satisfaction is seen to be key to securing employee commitment and involvement in quality matters. However, the chapter questions the extent to which such cultures can exist in practice and whether leadership plays a significant role in engineering them. The chapter ends with a review of quality teams and the extent to which teamwork can be regarded as empowering or as a control mechanism.

KEY CONCEPTS

Here are the key concepts covered in this chapter: organizational culture, teamwork, leadership, control, quality circles, project teams.

QUESTIONS

At the end of this chapter you should be able to answer the following questions:

- What is a quality culture and to what extent is this a concept that can be achieved in practice?
- Does leadership make a difference to organizational outcomes?
- What are the advantages and disadvantages of quality circles and to what extent have they been successful in the West?
- To what extent do culture and teamwork act as control mechanisms? How effective do you think they are?

PART THREE

Consequences of quality

The morality and ethics of quality

The organizational pursuit of quality has wide ramifications and therefore must not be seen as a mere technical, apolitical process. Quality shapes and is shaped by current social and power relations: any examination of quality requires an understanding of the latter. That is why quality should be approached with a 'moral' lens which allows us to question its consequences on the experiences of various organizational stakeholders. The following questions become paramount in studying quality: is a 'quality culture' more ethical than other types of organizational cultures? Who decides the morality of a quality programme? Can and does a quality code of conduct bridge personal and organizational agendas? Is product integrity enough for a company to survive? Why is the morality of quality important? None of these questions have easy answers that can be applied uniformly across a variety of contexts. It is only through the active and democratic engagement of all concerned parties (managers, employees, consumers, shareholders, suppliers, the society at large) that such issues will find a suitable, however, partial and temporal, resolution.

In recent decades, quality has become part of the mainstream corporate language, signalling the importance of the market and the consumer in the organization of production and distribution processes. Quality, accountability and consumerism represent the new triumvirate trespassing on the life of the individual. For example, quality considerations play an important role in processes of accountability, that is, processes by which organizational members account for their actions to themselves and the others (their bosses, subordinates, shareholders, customers, etc). Moreover, the discourse of quality brought with it a whole repertoire of rights and duties attached to the individual as a consumer. At work, individuals are internal customers, who have the right to receive from the next person in line the level of service they themselves have the duty to perform for the person upstream. Outside work, the rights of the external customer reign with unquestionable supremacy: customer satisfaction is supposedly what drives the well-being of the society. The language and practice of quality are thus seen to be inherently moral.

The chapter starts by defining three interrelated terms: morality, ethics and integrity. Although used interchangeably in some of the literature there are reasons to suggest that morality is a wider term that is inclusive of ethics and integrity.

DEFINING MORALITY

The theory of morality is as old as philosophy itself. It basically tries to answer the question: what ought I to do? The response has most of the time come in the shape of universal principles: if followed, such principles would alleviate fear and provide reassurance that one is pursuing the right path in life. The Ten Commandments represent an enduring instance of such generalized codes of behaviour. Codes of behaviour came and went by but, generally speaking, they failed to improve relationships between people. A short excursion into the human disasters of the twentieth century would suffice to uphold the view that the modern world is not necessarily more moral than the pre-modern one. Perhaps the difficulty with such codes of behaviour was that rather than acknowledging that moral experience is a deeply individual project filled with trial and error, suffering and elation, pain and happiness, most codes of behaviour held onto a highly reified and deterministic view of the individual.

Given that both our production and consumption experiences are highly organized, that is, they take place in organizations, it is important to analyse the impact organizational codes of behaviour have upon individual and group morality. Quality management programmes attempt to institute, through the symbolic management of meaning, a regime of values and behaviours to be emulated by all organizational members (such values are typically construed around a customer satisfaction repertoire). Quality programmes tell the individual what to do in a subtle way, while at the same time, giving the impression that one is free to choose what is right and wrong. Such regimes may give the illusion of practical autonomy for the employees, but in fact they may heighten managerial control in an insidious and potentially dangerous fashion. In the latter case, quality cannot be considered a moral project for it does not concern itself with providing the employees with the necessary material and symbolic resources to make informed choices: on the contrary, it demands loyalty and commitment from them and attachment to the customer satisfaction cause, promising in exchange self-fulfilment and the achievement of personal goals (as long as these emulate organizational goals). This chapter inquires into the possibility of reconfiguring organizations in such a way that they become moral towards not only the customers but also towards their employees and the society at large.

Morality has interested social scientists and philosophers for quite some time. There seems to be a widespread belief that earlier forms of social organization were more moral than contemporary social arrangements. A sharp contrast is typically posited between 'community' defined as a naturally developed association which has intrinsic, moral values, and 'organization', a deliberately formed association whose foundations lie in rational logic (Tönnies, 1963). A number of dualisms accompany this split namely, affective/rational, non-instrumental/instrumental, homogeneity/heterogeneity and, most recently, following the work of Zygmunt Bauman (1995), moral/immoral.

It would be mistaken, however, to suggest that communal forms of organization are entirely affective, moral and non-instrumental, while contemporary forms of organization are purely instrumental and immoral (Parker, 1997). Communal forms of social organization are not always characterized by complete affective harmony and lack of instrumentality and rationality. In fact, some communities may pursue goals in a pragmatic fashion (including the goal of survival), in which case division of labour is absolutely necessary and conflict may occur (Parker, 1997). The Ephrata community, a small community set up by Conrad Beissel in eighteenth-century Pennsylvania is an intriguing illustration of how the 'Brothers' and 'Sisters' were united in their quest for God (through celibacy and hard work) and at the same time divided by the internal hierarchy, professional skills and their gender (Ephrata Cloister brochure, 2001). Similarly, contemporary forms of organization cannot be entirely summed up in terms of instrumental relations, as they could also be experienced through random (affective) experiences that are not necessarily aimed at a particular goal or finality. Thus, to confound morality with community and deny its place in contemporary organizations is to entirely miss the point.

The renewed interest in morality and in particular in how morality operates (or doesn't) in contemporary organizations needs to be understood with respect to the broader context in which organizations operate and the changes that have taken place in contemporary modes of knowledge. The environment in which organizations operate has changed dramatically in the last decades. Organizations inhabit a so-called post-industrial world (White and Jaques, 1995) where new forms of production and distribution have come into being. For example, the network organization, the process-driven organization or the virtual organization co-exist with, and in some cases have surpassed, the bureaucratic organization. Fordist technologies of mass production and distribution exist in parallel with post-Fordist technologies that allow for agility, flexible specialization and niche distribution (Piore and Sabel, 1984). These new organizational realities point to the importance of the market and the consumer in organizing both production and distribution. In this post-industrial era, the market is heralded as the 'Authority', an authority capable of deciding the best course of action and the most appropriate behaviour for the organization and its members. Therefore, the organization and the individual must entrust their hopes to the market.

While the workings of the market may be indeed the most efficient and may point the individual to the 'right track' with regards to achieving organizational goals, it is less obvious why 'the right track' should also be the moral one (one that accounts for the needs and interests of multiple stakeholders). Indeed, the conceptualization of morality along the logic of the market puts 'efficiency' and 'customer satisfaction' on a pedestal at the expense of other perspectives, such as, employee satisfaction, environmental protection, and so on.

Current profound dissatisfaction with the ways in which the market affects and is affected by morality is not surprising. According to Bauman (1995), neither the market nor the state can decide morality, for morality is primarily a personal pursuit which implies taking responsibility for the other. This means that the Other is not treated like an abstract category any more (in the way in which the market or the state treats it), but like an individual, with sympathy and emotion. The Other becomes the self's responsibility and this is where morality begins. But to be responsible for the Other is also to have power over him/her and be free *vis-à-vis* him/her. Taking responsibility for the Other presupposes safeguarding the uniqueness of the Other. Bauman coins this sort of relation as 'being for the other' and suggests it can only exist as a project, on its way to being completed but never quite accomplished. For him, this is a lonely and disturbing project as there are no rules by which to judge whether our acts will have positive consequences upon others or not. The occurrence of the state of 'being for the other' cannot be predicted in any deterministic or probabilistic way, as it has nothing to do with reason, but with passion, sentiment and emotion (Bauman, 1995). It is only through trial and error that the individual could pursue his/her moral project. While inspiring, Bauman's position may be difficult to attain within the realm of organization: if there are no criteria by which to judge values, conduct and behaviour, there is no way of knowing if the interests of all stakeholders have been accounted for and pursued within a particular quality management programme, for example.

But it is not just the nature of the organizational reality that has changed: new forms of knowing, that is, epistemologies, have accompanied such organizational changes (Burrell, 1996). Under the new regime of knowledge, researchers study not only the efficiency of forms of production and organization, but also the conditions that made them possible in the first place and the role they may have in reproducing these conditions (Hassard and Parker, 1993; Chia, 1996). Hence, the relationship between knowledge/truth, reality and power becomes of paramount importance, for knowledge/truth cannot escape the regime of power that makes it possible in the first place. Thus, researchers' accounts of quality, rather than being objective and ultimate representations of a reality out there, are in fact contextual and tentative, being inscribed in a certain set of social and power relations and having significant consequences on the process of reality construction.

Post-industrial realities and the new regime of knowledge have pushed morality to the front of organization theory and practice. But despite the burgeoning amount of writing on the topic, there is indeed little consensus as to what morality is: its meaning appears to be shifting with the position of social scientists and according to what is valued in cultural or economic terms at a particular point in time. In the current economic climate, morality is usually juxtaposed with ethics, being equated with codes of behaviour that organizations should pursue in order to conduct socially responsible business.

DEFINING ETHICS IN BUSINESS

A great deal has been written about ethics in organizations in the past decade or so. A search on the Internet, using the Altavista search engine, has identified more than 8 million web pages and 1,154 books on business ethics (25 June 2001). Business ethics is a field which has grown in response to the apparent decline in ethical standards in business (Trevino, 1986) and as a recognition that economic relations have their own morality which needs protecting. Aside of business ethicists, there have been attempts to theorize ethics from a wide range of other perspectives, inter alia, sociology, law, economics, philosophy and theology (White, 1993; Rae and Wong, 1996; Wilber, 1998; Bowie, 1999).

While it is beyond the purpose of this chapter to present a detailed review of the conceptual work and empirical research carried out in the field of business ethics (for thorough reviews see: Pearson, 1995; Vallance, 1995), the chapter does highlight the multitude and variety of topics which make up the field, for example, ethical decision-making, equal opportunities, corporate social responsibility, whistle blowing, green management, to name only a few. It is commonly accepted that two distinct positions can be found among writers of business ethics: some adopt a normative/utilitarian perspective on ethics (stressing consequences), others embrace a deontological approach (stressing intention). Following the former position, Fritsche and Becker's (1984) research explored how individual managers thought about ethical dilemmas at work. The research found that most managers evaluated behaviour in terms of social consequences. However, there are difficulties with the utilitarian approach over the boundaries and criteria of defining what counts as best consequences.

Other writers on business ethics adopt the second position, subscribing to the idea that the moral worth of an action is dependent on the intentions of the person taking action and not on the consequences. For example, some authors suggest that ethical decisions are those based on a consistent pattern of moral values (Smedes, 1991) while others suggest that individuals' decision of what is right and what is wrong is influenced by their level of cognitive moral development (Trevino, 1986). These Kantian reverberations suffer, however, from a number of shortcomings: first, moral principles are viewed as general rules, which apply universally and impartially to all individuals. Secondly, the individual is seen to possess the ability to decide what is right and what is wrong by the application of reason. Finally, the goal of ethics is to recognize and maximize each individual's absolute freedom, a practically unworkable formula (Pearson, 1995).

Both utilitarian and deontological ideas have found resonance in the quality management literature. The utilitarian approach transpires in studies which directly or indirectly suggest that TQM is an ethical approach, for it leads to the best consequences for the greatest number of stakeholders: suppliers, employees, customers, shareholders, managers and society at large. Indeed, TQM builds on the ideas of long-term partnerships with trusted suppliers, the empowerment of the employees, meeting and exceeding customers' expectations, improved financial performance and a better social and natural environment.

Those who view leadership as central to the achievement of TQM embrace a deontological position which posits that it is the intention of leaders and quality professionals that counts, since they are the main drivers of TQM programmes. Thus, leaders are viewed to be in a position to create cultures which mimic their personal value system. Such cultures lay down implicitly or explicitly those behaviours which are expected and valued by the leaders (and thus by the organization) and those which are to be discarded or marginalized. By emphasizing the importance of the customer and the central role of leadership, these cultures become codes of behaviour to guide the individual through the moral maze of organizational life. When such codes of behaviour are internalized by most of the employees, the organizational culture is strong and homogeneous. But this is not always the case: such codes of behaviour are usually challenged and resisted by some of the employees and it is often the case that more than one code of ethics exists in the organization. According to many business ethicists, it is important that the organization records its code of behaviour and makes explicit (in the shape of standards and procedures) the preferred way to go about doing its business. Such explicitness, it is argued, will ensure the integrity of an operation, product and/or service (Pearson and Parker, 2001).

DEFINING INTEGRITY IN BUSINESS

According to Pearson and Parker (2001), integrity is synonymous with predictable behaviour because doing what you said you will do is more likely to generate trust than unpredictable behaviour. Integrity is typically thought to be a technical term related to the achievement of understood performance standards. Some of these standards lead themselves to being written down in manuals, others are more intangible, but nevertheless understood by organizational members (Pearson and Parker, 2001).

The integrity of organizational effort is typically reflected in the integrity of the product, for the product is the embodiment of perhaps the most fundamental transaction a business fulfils. Product integrity is usually achieved through adherence to formal procedure standards, resulting at the intersection between product design, product materials, the manufacturing process, the delivery process and the aftersales use of the product.

A product design that lacks integrity is one that is not well thought out and does not deliver the expected output. It is not easy to spot problems in the design stage and yet some of these could lead to fatal accidents. One of the most interesting cases was Ford's introduction on the American market of the Pinto, a small and relatively cheap car to compete against European and Japanese ones, in 1970 (Gioia, 1992, 1999). Due to the toughness of the market, Ford had to design and produce the car in 25 months, almost half of the average inception–product time in the industry. Because of this short timeframe, some of the activities were not done sequentially but in parallel. Thus, tooling was well under way (thus, freezing the basic design) when routine crash testing revealed that the Pinto's fuel tank often ruptured when struck from the rear at relatively low speed. Reports revealed later that the fuel tank failures were the result of some rather marginal design features and it would only cost $11 per car to improve the design. Yet, a decision was taken against improving the design. Such a decision was justified on three counts:

- A widespread industry belief that all small cars were more unsafe than the larger cars.
- Ford had tried earlier to introduce the safety theme as part of their sales campaign but this had not materialized in bottom line improvements.
- A cost-benefit analysis was carried out, showing that it would be cheaper for the company to compensate for deaths, injuries and accidents than to implement the $11 design improvement.

Dennis Gioia, the author of the case study, was product recall coordinator at the time: he describes himself as a person with a strong moral basis, an activist in his youth and someone who truly wanted to do a good job (knowing him personally, I believe that this is indeed the case). So, what happened? Why did he vote against product recall when the evidence suggested that there was something wrong with the car? The author's personal reflections on the case (Gioia, 1999) give us a clue. First, despite the tragic nature of the accidents they did not fit an existing pattern and could not be traced to any particular problem or component failure. Even when a failure mode suggesting a design flaw was identified, the cars did not perform significantly worse in crash test when compared with the competition. Secondly, the author wanted to do a good job but also what was right. The synthesis between the two was influenced by the corporate context: thus, he came to accept the idea that it was not feasible to fix everything that someone may construe as a problem. Instead, he tried to do the greatest good for the greatest number. Thirdly, he could not let himself be ruled by emotions (seeing one of these crashed cars in the courtyard triggered powerful emotions), for taking the right decision was a matter of rationally informed judgement.

In retrospect, he argues that his decisions were legal and ethical (for they conformed to existing legislation and the code of conduct of Ford), yet, they may not have been moral: his deep impulses signalled to him that something should be done about the car and yet no action was taken. But did his decision have integrity? Yes: as product recall coordinator he followed closely the existing procedures for recall. However, the design of the car lacked integrity: the designers knew that there were problems with the car, knew how to fix the problem, but failed to inform the recall office until very late in the process. The Pinto case is an important case in historical terms for it set a precedent: in 1973 a grand jury took the unheard of step of indicting Ford on charges of reckless homicide. Ford was the first company to be tried for alleged criminal behaviour.

The manufacturing process could also lead to the product lacking integrity. The manufacturing-based approach to quality (Garvin, 1984) stresses the importance of conformance to standards and specifications. Typical examples of products lacking integrity due to manufacturing faults include products which are left misassembled, or are produced with flawed materials or on defective machinery and with unskilled workforce. The final product does not conform to the intended specifications and the defect/non-conformance is not picked up in the final inspection stage but is passed on to the customer.

Using inappropriate materials to manufacture a product or deliver a service can also lead to lack of product integrity. The product-based approach to quality (Garvin, 1984) defines quality in terms of desired ingredients or attributes of a particular product. If such desired ingredients are missing or are not present in the required quantities, the product lacks integrity.

How a product or service is being delivered could also affect integrity. If we take the case of heart surgery, for example, one expects the surgeon to follow established rules and procedures rather than be innovative and experiment on the patient: conversely, if one goes to a jazz concert, one might be quite thrilled to see the musicians improvising (for aesthetic reasons and not performative ones). The existence of procedures which documents the delivery of a service or product builds trust for the customer: he or she knows that the organization has thought through every small detail and taken necessary steps to prevent things from going wrong.

The aftersales use of a product can also influence the level of product integrity. The manufacturer has a duty to inform the user if the intended or foreseeable use of a product may expose the user to danger if not used correctly or if used at all. Thus, a washing machine would be accompanied by an operating manual, a piece of furniture that needs assembling would have instructions as to how to proceed, drugs would be accompanied by warnings such as not to operate machinery when taking this drug, not to exceed the stated dose, and so on. If such instructions are missing, the customer is said to be put in a situation of danger and thus the product is thought to lack integrity. However, there is a fine line between what constitutes a reasonable and well-known risk and what is not. For example, do tobacco companies have to warn their customers of the diseases associated with smoking? Critics suggest that such warning is paramount. Furthermore, tobacco companies should not be allowed to use images of a healthy and prosperous life style when the consequences of smoking could be a far cry from it. The industry, on the other hand, argues that customers understand the risks they are taking and there is no need to play on negative imagery to magnify the probability of the occurrence of such risk.

The cost of a product is also a factor that affects the integrity of a product: a product/service must be sold at a price that is perceived as reasonable by the customers: not too high, for the customer will feel ripped off and not too small, for the customer may think the product on offer is shoddy.

Ensuring technical integrity is an important part of ensuring product/service liability. Farnworth (1994) defines product/service liability as the liability of a manufacturer or service provider for personal injuries or property damage suffered by any person as a result of a product which is unsafe and defective or a service that is inappropriate. Liability is concerned with products/services that fail to meet safety standards that the user may reasonably expect. In most European countries, important legislation has been adopted to bring the concept of strict liability into force. The objective of this legislation is to improve the position of the user by extending his/her legal rights that were previously enjoyed only by a purchaser in a contractual relationship with the vendor. As a result of this legislation (adopted in Britain in 1987), the consumer does not have to prove that the manufacturer has been negligent as the attention is shifted to the product. A product is seldom defective in an absolute sense and therefore its defective state is judged in reference to other factors such as current industry standards. This legislation attempts to provide a more balanced legal framework for the user to secure compensation for injuries suffered as a result of defective products or services. It also places responsibility with the producers or service deliverers who are expected by law to supply safe products and services on the marketplace. Improving safety leads directly to improved product integrity and quality.

SOCIAL INTEGRITY

Many commentators view product integrity to be mainly a technical issue for it focuses on the relationship between the company and the customer as mediated by the product/service. There may, however, be other ways in which the company could establish a relationship of trust with its customers or the public at large. Such ways, which are not directly mediated by the product/service on offer, lead to what has been called social integrity. If a company has a high level of social integrity, its products may be perceived to have technical integrity, but the reverse may not necessarily be the case (Pearson and Parker, 2001).

To achieve social integrity, the company must be seen to be engaged in socially responsible behaviour, such as: green management, community involvement, equal opportunities, and so on. Such endeavours are publicized through various PR and advertising campaigns: when the message sent to the public is challenged by the reality, the reputation of the company is partially or totally ruined. Recall Shell's problems with the Brent Spar and the consequences this had on the company's sales and profits. It is only recently that the company was able to shake off some of the negative feelings associated with Brent Spar. The case of Gerald Ratner's, a British jewellery entrepreneur, also sends an alarm signal to all those corporations which do not appreciate the powerful role played by their customers. In his speech at the Institute of Directors' Conference in London, on 23 April 1991, he talked about the company's approach to customer satisfaction, telling an audience of 600 executives that they could also get through a recession by selling junk and bad taste products as he does in his shops. As his message was publicized by the mass media the next day, the customers of this massively successful operation reacted angrily to the point where the company could not sustain its losses and went bankrupt (Bank, 1992).

In most cases, technical integrity on its own can lead to financial success: the company does what it says and this results in constantly meeting customers' expectations. But product integrity cannot always guarantee legitimacy in broader social terms. In the same way, some socially responsible companies have a hard time in getting their product integrity right. It follows that the recipe for success is pursuing both technical and social integrity: TQM has been heralded as providing the foundations for both types of integrity. The synthesis between the hard and the soft elements of TQM could theoretically ensure the achievement of both technical and social integrity: quality standards, on the one hand, could ensure the existence of documented, effective procedures for getting the work done, continuous improvement could ensure that such standards are constantly monitored and improved, the focus on the customer could ensure that their requirements are translated in operational terms and delivered according to the needs and requirements of the customer. Furthermore, TQM emphasis on close relationships with a trusted base of suppliers, the empowerment of the workforce, and the importance of the larger community and the environment may ensure the successful pursuit of social integrity.

SUMMARY

Recognizing that the pursuit of quality in contemporary organizations has significant effects upon the day-to-day experiences of various organizational stakeholders, this chapter inquires into the morality of quality programmes. It also ponders the question of whether organizations can meet customers' expectations in a manner that does not harm the interests of the other stakeholders. The chapter urges organizations to question the purpose and morality of their quality management programmes, in particular how they affect the experiences of all existing stakeholders and to what extent these experiences are viewed in positive or negative terms. organizations must also work hard at raising awareness of the moral and ethical consequences of quality among organizational members, rather than simply stating (in their codes of conducts) that quality is good business. It may well be so, but it is equally important to provide the employees with the appropriate material and symbolic resources to help them make informed choices and act according to those. Without realizing this democratic project, there is no hope that the morality of quality will be simply realized on the market through a spontaneous process in which customers recognize product integrity and confer social and technical legitimacy to the organization.

KEY CONCEPTS

Here are the key concepts covered in this chapter: morality, ethics, technical integrity, social integrity, product liability;

QUESTIONS

At the end of this chapter you should be able to answer the following questions:

- What is morality and what is its relationship with ethics and integrity?
- What are the most important approaches to business ethics and to what extent do they lead to moral behaviour in organizations?
- What is product integrity? Is it a mere technical issue?
- Why is the pursuit of quality a moral issue?
- Can you suggest ways in which quality management can be implemented in a more ethical manner?

12 Making quality critical

Quality management has been construed, among other things, as a social practice that professes to fill the gap left open by the decline of earlier forms of collectivism (Kerfoot and Knights, 1995) and as a totalizing discourse which exploits workers and reinforces the privileged position of management (Steingard and Fitzgibbons, 1993). Such criticisms and others are reviewed by Wilkinson and Willmott (1995) in their edited book from which this chapter borrows its title. In this chapter, rather than simply reviewing these criticisms, I discuss my own concerns about quality programmes but remain optimistic that quality can be pursued in a moral fashion and can contribute effectively to the construction of a more pluralistic and democratic future.

QUALITY: AN OPERATIONAL OR A POLITICAL ISSUE?

For a majority of scholars, quality management is a body of knowledge deeply rooted in operational research having as a prime concern the control and continuous improvement of processes of production and service delivery with the view to increasing the efficiency and effectiveness of the organization. From this operational perspective, quality management is viewed as a rational activity relying on seemingly objective (i.e., statistical) means of gaining hard information about processes of production and service delivery in order to reduce a messy and complex organizational reality to technical problems which are relatively easy to diagnose and solve. TQM is one of the most celebrated and widely used forms of quality management; its promise to deliver a total solution in the form of a unified set of rational principles and procedures entices managers to join in (Huczynski, 1993). The management of quality relies on the application of gurus' prescriptions which are intended

This chapter draws on material published by the author in *Journal of Management Studies* (2000), 37(4): 483–98, 'Too much or too little ambiguity: the language of total quality management'.

primarily to ensure that products and processes conform to set standards. Insofar as the workforce is concerned, quality does not necessarily mean the attainment of 'excellence' in working conditions and terms of employment: rather it refers to the development of 'uniform and dependable' work practices which are congruent with delivering low costs, value for money products and services to the customers.

More recently, however, there has been a shift away from operational concerns towards softer issues which point to the need to change employees' attitudes and behaviours in line with a customer-focused philosophy. This approach suggests that it is not enough to get the system right; if the system is disconnected from the people who are supposed to operate it, quality remains a chimera. Top managers are accorded a central role in motivating and empowering the employees with the view to gaining their active consent and commitment to achieving quality. This perspective, while recognizing the socially constructed nature of quality, embraces a unitarist view assuming that employees and managers have similar interests and are willing to work together towards the agenda set by the customer.

Moreover, quality cannot be entirely set and controlled from the top because it is the result of complex social relationships whose outcomes are difficult to predict (Grint and Case, 1995). Thus, far from being an operational issue, quality is in fact a political one. Various researchers have started to problematize the apparently benign façade of quality management programmes, the ways in which quality is identified and pursued in organizations and the purposes it may in fact serve (Wilkinson and Willmott, 1995). This line of inquiry does not deny the importance of operational issues in pursuing quality management: of course, without safety standards and clear work procedures most organizations would collapse in chaos. However, rather than viewing these procedures as governing neutrally over the province of quality, this approach sees them as transforming and being transformed by the social and power relations within and across organizations.

THE POLITICS OF QUALITY

The operational perspective on quality management has often been criticized for failing to grasp the complex social nature of organizational realities and the processes by which individuals interpret, negotiate, challenge and enact their environments. Rather than being solely the domain of experts (managers and quality professionals), quality is the result of and influences the identity work performed by all employees. Here identity work refers to the processes by which employees attempt to understand their role in the organization with respect to quality practices. In order for procedures, standards, and requirements to be translated into material practice, they must be understood and shared by a majority of organizational actors. Thus, building consensus around the meaning of quality and quality systems becomes a crucial task of top managers. Such consensus is fraught with difficulty for it requires attitudinal and behaviour shifts from the employees and occasionally from management. Consensus building is usually pursued through programmes of culture change which aim to equip the employees with socially acceptable tools they can use to understand themselves and their roles within the broader context of quality goals and objectives. However, what may appear to be simple, rational tools and solutions of management carry with them distinct moral commitments and preferences. What appears commonsensical and rational is in fact socially constructed and may not be the best or the only way to behave in the world. Best managerial practice is not simply about identifying the most suitable technical and rational solutions but should be evaluated in terms of its contribution to realizing the objectives of autonomy, democracy and human betterment (Willmott, 1993).

Most of the knowledge regarding quality, or the so-called science of quality, is subordinated to the production of efficiency, to producing more with less, to predicting and controlling human and non-human behaviour. Here management is represented as a neutral technology of goal achievement that carries with it no implicit moral commitments and consequences (Alvesson and Willmott, 1992). The representation of management as a technical, scientific activity turns a blind eye to the social relations through which management practice is constituted and upon which knowledge ultimately depends (Alvesson and Willmott, 1996). Quality management as a body of knowledge structures reality by reflecting the views and interests of privileged categories of people, by setting evaluation standards for everybody and ultimately by fundamentally affecting individual identities. The language of quality rather than being neutral and non-intrusive is intertwined with existing power arrangements, influencing individual and collective beliefs, attitudes and behaviours in the organization. A critical analysis of TQM language points to the pervasive effects the discourse of quality management has upon managers and employees alike. The analysis below subscribes to the discursive approach to quality discussed in Chapter 1.

THE LANGUAGE OF TQM

The centrality of language in analysing and understanding organizational life has been advocated by many authors. People in organizations use language in order to make meaning, to understand what is going on around them and to express their views on particular issues. It is through and with language that organizational members, be they top managers, middle managers or employees, describe and provide accounts of their activities and decisions (Boden, 1994). It is through language that individuals attempt to justify themselves, legitimize their actions and persuade other people (Davis and Luthans, 1980). Thus, language contributes to the enactment of the world where people not only perceive their environments but also create and interpret them (Gowler and Legge, 1983).

The language of TQM becomes operational as top managers learn about it and start using it in organizations. As a result of the acquired vocabulary, managers are thought of and think of themselves as being better positioned to know what is 'best' for the organization. This allegedly privileged access to 'truth' legitimizes their quest for attempting to build consensus around the institutionalized meaning of quality.

In attempting to construct consensus managers use language both in semantic and poetic fashions (Burke, 1966). The semantic use of language aims at instilling clarity and specificity, while the poetic use of language invites multiple interpretations from the employees. While both managers and employees might have a certain amount of discretion over the use of language, the consequences of using language cannot be predicted or indeed known. For example, managers may think that a clear, straightforward message, devoid of ambiguity leads to employees acting according to the preferred rationality, while a message riddled with ambiguity may give employees room for manoeuvring meaning. However, the picture is not as static and as simplistic as implied here. The use of ambiguous language could potentially facilitate control to be exercised more effectively by managers while at the same time creating spaces for resistance. Employees may choose to respond to ambiguous language with their own ambiguous language so that top managers will find themselves in a position of having to decipher the meanings coming from below. Ambiguity may also act as the social glue that keeps subordinates together. For example, when employees do not understand what is going on at the top level, they usually stick together and attempt to find comforting meanings around ideas of survival.

Some language devices, such as platitudes and labels, attempt to build consensus through a reduction in ambiguity, while other devices such as metaphors aim at consensus making using an increase in ambiguity (Czarniawska-Joerges, 1990, 1993). For heuristical purposes, the chapter treats these language devices as distinct, while recognizing the problematic nature of this taxonomy and the impossibility of maintaining it outside this exercise. Indeed, metaphors are often used in platitudes and labels, and similarly, platitudes and labels could be used in metaphors. Thus, these categories are not exclusive or indeed exhaustive: quality, for example, may well be a metaphor which acquires multiple meanings depending on the interpreter, a label which defines provinces by drawing boundaries around them, as well as a platitude whose meaning is taken for granted by organizational members (as indeed, who is against quality?).

Labels not only tell us what things are; they also classify, they sort through and separate entities from one another. Labels order the reality in a particular way, for the moment we label something, we single it out (Burke, 1966). By labelling activities and practices one defines boundaries: one includes and excludes things from the province of quality, for example. By labelling certain practices 'quality improvement projects', 'quality circles' or 'total customer satisfaction', labels make transparent those behaviours that are valued by the organization and are to be included into the province of quality.

In one British organization I studied there were more than 50 Quality Improvement Projects going on at a time. Such projects aimed to 'identify and prioritize improvement opportunities, to plan and implement solutions and to continuously improve everything we do in the company' (internal document: 3). This label hints at the sorts of activities constitutive of quality in this organization. In another British company, quality circles allowed 'the employees to get together in a structured way to identify, evaluate, recommend and implement improvements in quality, customer service and the way things are done in general' (internal document: 2), once again pointing to those practices which are being valued and encouraged by top managers in this organization. By labelling certain practices in quality terms, managers ensure that these practices take up an 'identity' of their own that can be monitored, manipulated and used for legitimation purposes.

Furthermore, labels are not neutral sorting devices. The effects of naming are more clear when the naming is moved from processes to people. By labelling individuals 'quality champions', 'missionaries' or 'dinosaurs', for example, labels make a clear distinction between those who are in favour and those who oppose quality. Consequently, quality champions and missionaries reflect a type of employee to be emulated by the rest of the organization, while the dinosaurs are irresponsible and, therefore, should be disregarded, ignored or punished until eventually they become extinct.

Platitudes are those words whose repetitive character makes them obvious and easy to understand. The use of platitude gives an illusion of a unitary meaning that is taken for granted by all employees. Platitudes, such as, 'do it right first time', 'customer is king', 'people make the difference', 'towards world class', invite consensus over the meaning of quality which, otherwise, may be controversial. The use of platitudes may be directed to producing a sense of normality that hides the contentious, political nature of most organizational practices.

The role of platitudes is to smooth out potential conflicts and build consensus by inculcating 'the one right way' into the language, thoughts and behaviour of employees. 'My contribution counts', one of the many quality initiatives present in a UK service organization I studied, appears to make a plain but appealing statement that nobody can negate. But 'My contribution counts' is more than a platitude. Compare it with 'everybody's contribution counts' which may be nauseatingly 'true' but is also immediately contestable. But when someone puts their bodies in the way, it is harder to get past. Indeed, 'My contribution counts' suggests that I, myself, am taking personal pride in my work and my contribution to the success of the organization is not only undeniable but paramount (i.e., it counts). The effect of this statement is quite powerful due to the embodiment of ideology in a person as a person rather than merely trying on an idea.

However, the effectiveness of platitudes in achieving consensus depends to a considerable degree on drawing on language that encapsulates assumptions that are taken for granted as mere commonsense (Fairclough, 1996). However, as soon as one becomes aware that a particular aspect of common sense is sustaining power inequalities at one's expense, it ceases to be commonsense. Thus the production of consensus through using commonsensical language is not a linear exercise as there will always be conflict and struggle coming from below to the extent that ideological uniformity can never be completely achieved. This is not to say that all commonsense is necessarily ideological, in other words, that top managers use taken-for-granted assumptions entirely as a resource to be drawn upon in the service of unbalanced relations of power.

Metaphors line the majority of our messages in everyday life. The metaphor is a substitution of one element of language for another. Such substitution is cultural and aims to stimulate the private world of the addressee in order that she can draw from inside herself some deeper response. Metaphors invite multiple and diverse meanings over the same concept. Such meanings are shaped by the distinct agendas and immediate circumstances of the people who interpret them (Lilley and Platt, 1994). Multiple meanings are a prerequisite of the metaphor's ordering function, ensuring at least on a temporary basis the reproduction of existing power relations and the production of consensus (Alvesson, 1990). For example, controversial issues such as quality could be settled by specifying them in a form requiring subsequent interpretation, thus permitting disparate groups and individuals to redefine issues in ways that are relevant to their immediate interests or circumstances (Astley and Zammuto, 1992).

Quality is a central metaphor in most organizations embarked on TQM programmes. Other metaphors can be brought into play to support or explain what is needed to substantiate and embody quality. In a UK company I studied, the metaphor of the market (with its associated paraphernalia) was used by top managers in order to enforce the quality message. Talk about 'internal customers', 'the chain of quality', 'customer is king' and so forth dominated managerial talk, signalling perhaps, a high level of the commodification of internal organizational relationships (McArdle et al., 1995). The use of the market metaphor aimed to strengthen top managers' attempt to create consensus through the constant reminder of the so-called logics of the market.

Metaphorical language is often used to construct organizational goals that could appeal to most employees. In a UK insurance company I studied, for example, the goals of the TQM programme were to ensure a growth in the company's revenue, develop the company's geographical businesses, and empower and develop the employees. These goals are fuzzy enough to allow different groups in the organization to find meaning in them. As a result, employees may find TQM attractive because of the empowerment side, while the shareholders and the managers might be more interested in the other two promises.

The production of consensus through language use is intertwined with the production of employees of a certain sort, employees who are willing to incorporate the quality message into their way of thinking and being. Managers, however, cannot be entirely successful because employees are not 'cultural dopes' and can judge ideological appearances for what they are, by testing the exhortation of managers against what they perceive to be 'reality' (Hill, 1995).

Indeed, employees respond to such discursive attempts in unpredictable ways: they may subvert the official meanings of quality in order to open up new alternatives for themselves or may simply accept the meanings propagated by top managers. Some employees do in fact resist the official quality language and its associated practices. Individual resistance to quality is quintessential to the reproduction of quality practices. Cases of individual resistance are crucial to the functioning of quality management, as they make visible what cannot be articulated, namely the sanctions attached to the refusal to enrol in quality management initiatives and to comport oneself like a committed employee (Fournier, 1998).

Rather than resisting the discourse of quality management, some employees comply with it selectively or for calculative reasons, in order to protect themselves from the others, ensure that they have a future with the organization and to create a personal space in which personal justifications can be readily manufactured.

Finally, there are other individuals whose responses are in line with managers' expectations. These are the people who make managers think that management indeed holds a privileged position from where it can construct and control what goes on in the organization. These employees appear to have absorbed the language of quality and to be engaged in its associated practices out of their own will. Their autonomy as individuals is established through submission, in that they aspire to become individuals through belonging to the organization and through making statements about their personality via impersonal means. The internalization of quality values may be the ultimate aim of top managers; however, it is difficult to assess to what extent consensus is real and to what extent employees act in the way preferred by top managers out of fear or comfort.

QUALITY AND LEARNING

It is a fact of life that most organizations are riddled with conflicts and attempts to create consensus over the meaning of quality usually result in significant differences of opinion. Changing the culture of an organization is a political process, one which attempts to unsettle taken-for-granted ways of being and doing. This process usually meets resistance and inertia from employees and/or managers. Typically, resistance and inertia are viewed as irrational responses, the consequence of lack of understanding and training. The usual remedy comes in the shape of training programmes which aim to enhance understanding and persuade the employees of the legitimacy and rationality of official courses of action. Thus, training is not as a neutral, apolitical technology of management, but as one which attempts to transform individuals into disciplined subjects, namely, individuals who want on their own what the corporation wants (Townley, 1994; Kelemen, 2001).

Training can be viewed as a technology that attempts to transform the individual into a useful 'subject'. First, one could *be* subject to the control and domination by the other and secondly, one could be *a* subject whose identity is constituted by self-knowledge. Training works through the internalization of a complex set of norms and standard practices which provide common sense and self-evident experience to individuals or in other words, a sense of self, a sense of personal identity. According to Clegg (1989), subjectification (the transformation of the individual into a self) operates primarily through enhancing the calculability of individuals. Calculability is pursued using two types of technologies: technologies of domination and technologies of the self (Foucault, 1977). The former regard the individual as a distinct and coherent entity which can be optimized and integrated into systems of efficient and economic controls; the latter technologies are those practices which allow individuals to have knowledge about themselves in order to transform their conduct and reach a desired state (Kelemen, 2001).

As a technology of domination, training aims to make the individual knowable/visible and controllable in order to reduce the gap between the current and an expected or desired state, derived, for example, from existing organizational or group norms. Top managers are charged with knowing what is best for each employee and providing training that will ensure the transformation. Training acts also as a technology of the self in that it allows individuals to know themselves in order to transform their conduct to reach a desired state. To know oneself presupposes to turn inward and search for the truth from inside. According to McGregor, 'the individual knows more than anyone else about his own capabilities, needs, strengths, and weaknesses' (1975: 136), and it is important that this knowledge be rendered available to the individual and eventually to the organization. However, the knowledge of the self acquired through training is by no means private to the individual, but socially and culturally bound. The individual is expected to use such self-knowledge in order to improve him/herself as well as his/her relationships with significant others. Failure to act upon self-knowledge becomes no more than a story of personal failure, while alignment of the individual to the dominant discourse is heralded as a story of organizational success. The process of knowing oneself is based on given ideas as to how one should be. As Rose (1990) notes, though self-inspection, self-problematization, self-monitoring and confession we evaluate ourselves according to the criteria provided to us by others. In so doing, the private self becomes reconstituted based on external norms (in this case, quality norms) constructed by those in a power position in the organization.

SUMMARY

For most academics and practitioners, quality management is a discipline and a practice of management deeply rooted in system and engineering theory. Indeed, most quality management textbooks (and to a certain extent, the present one, too) privilege the claims of technical reason and subsume other (social and moral) concerns to ideas of rationality and efficiency. However, technical solutions must be negotiated, shared and enacted by a majority of organizational members if they are to work successfully in the organization. Yet, consensus is often difficult to achieve as different groups and individuals have different agendas and understandings of what counts as quality. For the managers, quality may mean product integrity at a reasonable cost for the employees, quality may mean improved working conditions, while for the shareholders quality must translate into financial results. While these definitions may not necessarily be incompatible, they may require different resources and power alignments.

Thus, quality management cannot simply be seen as consisting of a set of neutral technologies which if applied correctly delivers benefits. The managerial approaches to defining quality may be a useful starting point but they are also limiting for they regard quality as an objective phenomenon that can be measured, managed and controlled with the help of various tools and techniques available to the manager. Critical approaches to defining quality, on the other hand, view quality as constituted through social and political processes which support certain interests and marginalize others. As such, quality unfolds itself in organizations in a complex, ambiguous and unpredictable fashion, leading to both positive and negative outcomes for the various parties involved directly or indirectly in the process. When they do not account for the interests of all stakeholders, quality management initiatives may end up imposing a managerialist 'best way' by suppressing discussions of ends and objectives in favour of a technical choice of means as inscribed in the dominant ideology. To make quality critical it is not enough to recognize its importance to the survival and well-being of the organization and allocate resources for its pursuit. Making quality critical presupposes an awareness of its political and contextual character and an interrogation of the consequences it has upon the identity work performed by multiple stakeholders.

KEY CONCEPTS

Here are the key concepts covered in this chapter: metaphor, platitude, label, ambiguity, discourse, identity, resistance.

QUESTIONS

At the end of this chapter you should be able to answer the following questions:

- Is quality an operational or a political issue? Why?
- How do managers use the language of quality and what are some of the consequences of such language use?
- How do the employees respond to managerial attempts to discursively constitute quality as primary organizational goal?
- To what extent can training on quality matters be viewed as a control mechanism?

PART FOUR

Case studies on quality management

Part Introduction

In Part 4, I present six case studies based on empirical data collected in various organizations by myself and three other researchers. Each case illustrates a number of issues which have been discussed theoretically in previous chapters. The first case study by Joan Durose, entitled: 'Quality Management in the British National Health Service', explores the dilemmas faced by the British Health Service with regards to meeting patients' expectations of 'good health care'. In so doing, it revisits some of the themes presented in Chapter 3 regarding the management of quality in the public sector. The second case study, written by Duthika Perera sheds light on the use of Statistical Process Control in a British NHS trust. The case suggests that SPC (reviewed in Chapter 7) may be a useful technique but warns of the dangers of being perceived by some employees as a control mechanism. The third case, written by myself, is about the role of team leaders within a UK logistics company embarked on a quality management programme. In so doing, it makes references to the discussion on leadership and teamwork from Chapter 10. The fourth case written by Duthika Perera discusses, in a rather cynical manner the impact of new technology on customer service and customer satisfaction in the so-called new economy. The next case written by Ioanna Papasolomou-Doukakis looks at the concept of internal marketing, its ambiguous meanings and application within the UK retail-banking sector, unpacking some theoretical claims made by Chapter 3. My last case study looks at the extent to which the rhetoric of quality standards is matched up by a rhetoric of empowerment in a UK insurance company (for a discussion of quality standards see Chapter 5).

Quality management in the British National Health Service

Joan Durose

> The NHS will work continuously to improve quality services and to minimize errors. The NHS will ensure that services are driven by a cycle of continuous quality improvement. Quality will not just be restricted to the clinical aspects of care, but include quality of life and the entire patient experience. (NHS Plan, July 2000)

What do we mean by quality in the NHS? There are potentially as many definitions as there are groups of individuals who work in and use the health service. For most patients, users and their families the definition of quality is about getting the right service at the right time delivered by an appropriate person to a better than acceptable standard. For most staff groups it means all of that, and additionally meeting the expectations and regulations of the particular professional body that holds their accreditation. For health service managers and senior clinicians it also means ensuring that their organizations can complete mounds of paperwork to demonstrate the ability to meet a host of nationally prescribed standards. These potentially different viewpoints frequently come together under an increasingly emotive and public spotlight as the debates about the way in which the NHS fulfils its roles continue to make political headlines in the UK.

Since coming to power in 1997 the British labour government has made clear its intention to 'modernize' the NHS and has stated that improving quality is one of the core principles of the modernization agenda. Actions taken by the government to demonstrate their commitment have increased the quality dilemmas posed to the people who deliver the service, and ultimately, although it may not yet be recognized, to the service user. These dilemmas can be explored under a number of key themes, as set out below.

CONSISTENCY AND ACCESSIBILITY

The UK government perceives any variation in performance across the NHS as a demonstration of poor quality. Several measures have been introduced to ensure that all services are delivered 'at the level of performance of the exemplar services in the NHS' (Clinical Governance White Paper, 1998). One such is the creation of the National Institute of Clinical Excellence (NICE), a national body whose role is to produce and disseminate high quality, evidence-based guidance on the management of diseases (pharmaceutical usage, use of prosthesis, etc) that must be used to inform clinical and financial decisions made locally. Although only in full operation for one year there is already much public debate about how free NICE can be from government intervention, particularly around guidance on high cost drugs.

In addition a series of National Service Frameworks (NSF) are being developed. Each framework refers to a particular disease or population group and makes clear statements about the standards of service that are expected. The first three NSFs are targeted at mental health, coronary heart disease and older people. Unfortunately there is little additional funding to ensure that the targets can be met.

Whilst most people would acknowledge that measures to standardize performance are helpful, the impact of these interventions may well be to move health services from locally accessible venues. For instance if a hospital cannot deliver certain services to the standard required – because of lack of highly trained specialists in a certain area of work, or lack of money – the service will be moved to another hospital perhaps 50 miles away. It is questionable whether members of the public realize the relationship between the desire for consistent standards and local access to health care. A similar tension arises for individual clinicians. The government emphasis is on ensuring everyone is trained to meet the standards of the best, but clinical expertise can be seen as being dependent on interest as well as technical skills, and there is always an alternative career within the private sector.

EMPOWERMENT AND STANDARD SETTING

'The time has now come to free the NHS frontline,' said Alan Milburn, UK Secretary of State for Health in a speech in June 2001. He went on to describe how this would be realized. During 1999 the Commission for Health Improvement (CHI) had been set up to monitor the standards achieved by health service providers, much along the lines of the process of monitoring in schools. Its role is both developmental, visiting each health provider on a rolling programme and advising on improvements, and punitive, publishing the results of performance studies and providing rapid response teams to 'sort out' poor performers. One of the freedoms referred to by Milburn was that the best performers would have less frequent monitoring from the centre, and fewer inspections by CHI. In addition they would have extra resources for certain central programmes and for taking over and turning round the performance of 'failing' hospital Trusts.

Failing Trusts are identified by their inability to meet the targets set nationally on a range of aspects including waiting times (for admission, for appointments, etc.), environment (mortuary standards) and catering. Regular measurements result in a traffic light labelling; too many red lights can potentially lead to the termination of the contract of the chief executive and the intervention of a 'hit squad'. The incentives are pushing managers to aim for the upper end of orange – not to draw attention to the organization in any way, good or bad. Working in the high-pressure environment of health service delivery, and being constantly pushed to deliver targets can result in a culture in which empowerment is difficult to achieve and where staff often have to make uncomfortable decisions. Should Mrs X be discharged when it is known that she is not quite as fully recovered as was expected, but also knowing that to keep her in the bed will result in yet another person on the waiting list for a hip replacement operation? The number of revolving door patients (discharged on day one and returned unwell on day three) is testimony to the pressure on staff to make those decisions. Which one is the 'quality' decision?

Each health organization is expected to set up a process of Clinical Governance: 'a framework through which the organization is accountable for continually improving the quality of their services and safeguarding high standards of care by creating an environment in which excellent clinical care will flourish.' (Clinical Governance, 1998). The philosophy of Clinical Governance is founded on openness and a supportive environment. Many health service organizations struggle to develop such characteristics while operating in a national system that can be more focused on failure and punishment.

HIDDEN AGENDAS

Quality management in the NHS is wrapped around with very strong organizational issues of personality, professionalism and power, and overlaid with the political dimension. The national tussles about how powerful trade unions and professional bodies such as the Royal College of Surgeons impact on the service have always been apparent, but are becoming more confusing. There is a view that the increasing imposition of national standards and the rigour of performance management have a hidden agenda, to enable greater control of some of the most powerful players, the doctors. High profile cases of poor clinical performance have rightly pushed the need to make public the information on the results of hospital departments (perhaps even league tables on individual doctors' success rates), and have also challenged the 'old boy' behaviour of many doctors. Managers have become more confident in their responsibility to ask questions about quality decisions in areas where they may have no technical knowledge. On the flip side the increasing lack of public trust in the NHS is resulting in severe recruitment difficulties.

The most recent structural changes to the management of the service will also affect the current power balance. The commissioning of services in hospitals is becoming the responsibility of Primary Care Trusts, community-based health organizations led by general practitioners. The 'family' doctor will lay down their expectations of the quality of the service given by the powerful hospital consultant.

THE USER/CITIZEN DIMENSION

Throughout all of the modernization changes there is a constant emphasis on the role of patients/service users and carers within systems designed to enable improved quality management. Some examples are:

- Patient representatives on Clinical Governance groups.
- Patient-friendly versions of clinical guidelines from NICE.
- Plans for patient choice regarding appointment dates.
- A patient advocacy service in all NHS Trusts.
- Increased rights of redress.
- An annual National Patients Survey that links to financial rewards for NHS institutions.

However, although the requirements are clear there are two issues that indicate that it may prove difficult to realize them. First the record of past attempts, as for over ten years specific requirements to take action to increase public involvement have been generally overlooked or fudged, and the main impact that the public have had on the NHS is visible only when serious mistakes are made. Much of that difficulty stems from a lack of understanding of the complexities within public service delivery; and second, the level of understanding reached about the differing responses of members of the public to the health quality dimension. Do they behave as a citizen, paying for the service through taxation, or as a user who wants immediate effective and efficient treatment even if it can be detrimental to the next person on the waiting list? The person stake in health service quality management creates additional dilemmas for all.

This brief picture of some of the forces interacting in the quality agenda of the British NHS has demonstrated the complexity of the challenge. There is no doubt that the health service needs rigorous, understandable and open systems to manage managerial and clinical performance, but also no doubt that such systems will only work well in a learning and supportive culture. Private sector organizations face a similar balancing act, but can do so without the added impact of public scrutiny and political manipulation.

CASE STUDY QUESTIONS

- Quality in the NHS is founded on the relationship between the user, the health professional and the manager. How does the political focus change that relationship and the resultant quality outcome?

- Power and quality – how uncomfortable are they as bedfellows in the NHS?

- How do the quality dilemmas faced by NHS managers differ from those faced by managers in the private sector?

Statistical process control in the National Health Service

Duthika Perera

In recent years, the boundaries between the private and the public sectors have become more blurred. The public sector has embraced many of the quality management practices from the private sector. The aim of this case study is to illustrate the application of Statistical Process Control in a UK NHS Trust.

The British NHS, which was once considered to be a highly structured and bureaucratic structure, is now transitioning to a more flexible, more participative, patient-centred structure. The UK healthcare sector was initially sceptical about the usefulness of quality tools and techniques: there seemed to be a feeling that such managerial tools were more applicable to the private sector than the public sector, and to the manufacturing rather than service industries (Feeney and Zairi, 1996). Moreover, the appropriateness of the concept of the 'customer' to health care provision was also questioned on the basis that patients do not necessarily enjoy going to hospitals and their requirements – treatments – are not necessarily dictated by choice but rather by need. The 1980s and 1990s, however, saw radical changes within the UK health service with increasing customer choice – for both doctors and patients – and an increasing emphasis on patient satisfaction (Feeney and Zairi, 1996).

Despite such changes, a study conducted by Wright (1997) among quality managers in the UK, found both a lack of understanding of the theory behind quality tools and techniques, and a relatively low frequency of managerial use of such techniques. Interestingly enough, a majority of quality managers surveyed argued that an understanding of theory lies at the basis of the successful implementation and integration of quality in everyday work practices. The NHS Trust in which this study was conducted had implemented several quality initiatives such as the ones described below.

HOOP (Head Office Organizational Project) was a continuous improvement initiative where head office administrative and clerical staff worked in teams to improve the ways in which services were provided. It was aimed at encouraging staff to discover innovative ways of reducing costs.

Team Talk was an initiative implemented with the view to bypassing bureaucracy and creating a more open and communicative organization.

Team Talk was led by the chief executive and each senior manager was expected to take the process forward within his/her managerial sphere of activity. The purpose was to create a two-way communication process by which staff could be kept aware of and have an input to developments and changes occurring within the Trust.

Delivering Health was another initiative which encouraged organizational-wide participation to the development of business plans. Staff were encouraged to view the plan, assess what every manager did and also provide suggestions themselves.

Statistical Process Control (SPC) was also in operation in a learning disabilities directorate of the NHS Trust under the study. In this directorate, learning-disabled patients were domiciled in special purpose-built bungalows and referred to as residents. They were supervised by nursing staff assigned to the particular bungalows. The process aimed to facilitate 'normal living', as opposed to the previous practice of keeping them warded in hospital wards. The staff was organized into teams and each team had a home leader responsible for the running of his/her bungalow ranging from around six to eight residents. Such teams were self-managed and were based on flexible tasks or function performance arrangements (Siegel and Seidler, 1996). This concept, usually referred to as 'systemic process thinking', was widely used in many parts of the NHS as part of the quality management process.

The team leader, who was responsible for all the bungalows explained how they utilized the practice of SPC to look after the residents living in these purpose-built bungalows.

> There are enough registered nurses so that each resident has one named nurse (a point of communication for each patient). When the named nurse makes detailed assessments and histories, we can look at strengths and weaknesses of the residents, assess their needs . . . all in order to do good care planning. Care planning as the name suggests, outlines the procedures of care the resident should receive.

The idea is that the named nurse monitors the care plan of each resident using daily recordings and charting the results on a so-called process chart. These results are discussed informally at weekly staff meetings with the home leader and formally reviewed on a monthly basis with the team leader. Despite working as a team, named nurses are empowered to take a great deal of individual responsibilities on:

> They do all the careplans and all the assessments. In this way we make sure that everything is done properly. . . . The team leader meets with the named nurse monthly to discuss and review the care plans and assessments, almost like an action plan. In a way it's like a monitoring system or an audit.

Statistical process control was adopted to provide both a way of identifying problems quickly and as a means of understanding and making more visible existing processes. This facilitated the discussion and the review of care plans on a periodic basis, thus encouraging both teamwork and individual responsibility. SPC operated as a double-loop learning mechanism. Unlike single-loop learning, where the aim is to merely solve the problem, double-loop learning concentrates on identifying the reasons as to why the problem has occurred in the first place.

From talking to many members of staff, it became apparent that the use of SPC made the staff appreciate the importance of understanding processes and the positive effects this had on both patient care and staff moral. They recognized that a process that is stable, in a statistical sense, helped management predict with a reasonable degree of confidence its future performance and contain it within the boundaries of the upper and lower control limits, thus reducing costs and improving patient satisfaction. Despite the flexibility offered by the SPC practices described, some nurses argued that there still remained tight control. In their view, staff was given freedom to operate but only within clearly set parameters; meetings were held periodically to ascertain whether standard practices were being adhered to rather than to monitor patient satisfaction. As such, SPC was perceived by some as a silent monitoring system, more powerful than overt management control.

CASE STUDY QUESTION

- To what extent can the standardization of health care provision and empowerment programmes can go hand in hand in the NHS?

Team leadership in a UK logistics factory

Mihaela Kelemen

The company presented below is a major UK wholesaler and retailer of automotive and industrial components and accessories (named here Discom). The services offered by the company include procurement, warehousing, distribution and marketing.

At the beginning of the 1990s the company implemented a radical package of measures among which the cessation of union recognition and the creation of a teamworking environment to replace the previous operator/ supervisor relationship. A new team leader role was introduced to act as a catalyst 'to harness the creativity of all staff in the organization in the drive for significantly improved business performance' (Team Leader internal document: 1). In 1995 a Working Group chaired by two senior managers was established to assess the role, selection and training of team leaders.

Initially the working party reviewed known role models within Japanese organizations: these reviews showed, however, highly layered, hierarchical organizational structures. The typical Japanese organization reviewed had six levels of staff from operator to general manager, with the team leader having a narrow line of responsibility, normally focusing his/her attention on production planning and ensuring that *kaizen* activities were implemented. Both Nissan and Honda employed team leaders whose main role was to overlook *kaizen* activities but held no departmental budgetary control.

It was then decided to review best practices on team leaders in a number of American organizations. In the US organizations under study:

- The team leader role was narrowly focused and clearly defined.
- The team leader was focused on teamwork and the team, rather than other managerial issues.
- The team leader was supported by a co-ordinator to whom the team leader reported.
- As the team matured the role of the team leader became less important.
- Training and development of team leaders had high priority.
- There were mechanisms in place for rewarding idea generation.

The working party recommended the US model on team leadership as a framework for developing practices in Discom with regards to: the role of the team leader; the selection of the team leaders; and training and development of the team leaders. Recommendations were put forward in each of the area as follows.

THE ROLE OF THE TEAM LEADER

A statement of the purpose of the team leader job was developed by the working party as follows:

> A team leader must enable his or her team to contribute fully to the team goals, through maximizing their own contribution, by resolving issues which create barriers and through the development of the team. (Internal Document: 6).

A number of behavioural competences for the team leader job were put forward in three significant areas: managing yourself, people management and attitude to the customer. The Working Party also developed job descriptions for team leaders and stipulated that his/her qualifications must include some operational experience, competence in functional processes and people skills. The principal accountabilities of the role were described as follows:

- Prioritize and organize the workload to best match the business needs, in the most effective and cost-efficient manner possible.
- Monitor performance, looking for practical ways to make improvements and encouraging the team to produce best results.
- Talk to customers to understand their needs and ensure that the team shares this information, and find ways to satisfy customer expectations.
- Operate company procedures to assist in achieving best performance of staff (target setting, monthly review, quarterly review, appraisal and disciplinary).
- Ensure staff is motivated to achieve targets through communication, involvement, support and encouragement in the workplace.

SELECTION OF TEAM LEADERS

Following the identification of the behavioural competences required to fulfil the team leader role, a selection process was developed during which individual's ability to demonstrate these competences was assessed prior to appointment. US best practice companies placed a great emphasis on pre-appointment training for team leaders and the process proposed by the working party adopted a similar approach.

Thus, identification of potential was to take place initially through appraisal and career development discussions and would include the development of a personal competency profile. A personal development plan would then be developed such that the individual could commence the appropriate training prior to appointment. This would generate a 'pool' of potential team leaders who had, or were developing the necessary skills before rather than after appointment.

TRAINING AND DEVELOPMENT

The working party recommended that team leader training should consist of core modules and local modules. The core modules should be specifically designed to address the behavioural competences previously identified while the local modules should cover technical skills specifically required to support each department's business plan. Core modules would include: time management, problem solving, customer service, health and safety, world class production systems, team leadership, teamworking, managing change, stress management, effective written communication, presentation skills, project management and so on. Team leaders were to also receive on the job coaching and be appraised regularly by the section leader.

CONCLUSIONS

The company under study is one of the very few British organizations to be regarded as 'world class'. It has been awarded numerous quality prizes domestically and abroad. Teamworking is considered to be an essential ingredient of the company's success in achieving high levels of customer satisfaction and improved financial performance. As such, the role of team leader has gained special attention from top management in an attempt to redesign it along the lines of lean and customer-focused production processes. A great deal of pressure and high expectations are placed on team leaders. Some may argue that this is not empowerment but work intensification and the removal of personal rights in the name and for the sake of team performance.

CASE STUDY QUESTIONS

- To what extent will the new team leader role be successful in Discom?
- Are you surprised that this UK company chose a US model of team leadership rather than a Japanese one? Discuss.
- What sorts of rewards should be attached to the Team Leader role? Should they be dependent on individual performance or team performance?

New technology and customer satisfaction

Duthika Perera

It would be hard to overstate the influence that information and communication technologies have had on reshaping the global economy. In developed nations, new technology has become an increasing part of everyday life, accounting for an increasing share of overall economic activity. Rather than necessarily surpassing traditional industries, new technology is smoothly assimilated into them, creating opportunities for improvements and competitive advantage (Regalia, 2000).

The Internet is perceived to provide enhanced tools to better serve consumers, offering the greatest opportunity to maximize customer relationship management (CRM). CRM refers to the segmentation of customers and tailored offerings to create value (Kalakota and Robinson, 1999; Ptacek, 2000). As new technologies facilitate a more efficient approach to dealing with customer requests and problems via Internet-enabled channels, both private and public organizations are developing or simply transforming themselves into fully-fledged contact centres. Call centres, as they are also known, are a prime example of the ways in which new technology is penetrating relatively 'old' industries such as banking and insurance but also some public organizations such as the British NHS. Most of them operate a round the clock schedule, offering customers what they perceive to be tailored service. Using amassed customer information these call centres are allegedly better positioned to segregate – tier – customers into groups to better serve their needs. In so doing, call centres are apparently aiming to improve customer satisfaction.

New technology promises, and most often than not, delivers the tiering of customer information with the view to facilitate better targeted customer service. But why should one expect superior quality service as a result of this practice? Studies by groups ranging from the council of Better Business Bureaus Inc. to the University of Michigan suggest that call centres have lead in fact to a decrease in customer satisfaction and have made customers rather cynical: most customers of such call centres believe that 'Good service is increasingly rare' and as time goes on, the service gap will grow wider (Brady,

2000). These days, passengers languish in airport queues, consumers are caught in voice-mail hell and corporations push for profits and productivity (Brady, 2000).

The ability to provide preferred customer service is being exploited and, increasingly, organizations have made a deliberate decision to give some people skimpy service based on how much their business is worth. This is the dark side of technology where marketers can amass a mountain of data that gives them an almost Orwellian view of each consumer (Brady, 2000). Unlike traditional loyalty programmes, the new 'tiers', that is, segregating consumers according to their potential value, are on many occasions working against the customer, being enacted as a strategy whereby the consumer is invisibly deceived into sealing his/her own doom.

The following is an example of how increased access to customer information can be used to the detriment of some customers rather than leading to universal customer satisfaction. A premier bank in the US codes its credit card customers with tiny coloured squares that flash when service representatives call up an account. Green indicates a profitable customer who should be granted waivers or, differently put, given white-glove treat-ment. Red indicates money losers who have no negotiating power while yellow is the in-between discretionary category. This tiering system was defended by a company's spokesperson as facilitating better decision-making in the following way: 'The information helps our people make decisions on fees and rates.'

In November 1999 a group of technology companies led by IBM (Inter-national Business Machines) began building an Internet standard that gives companies a common platform for exchanging information. The aptly named Customer Profile Exchange (CPExchange) network proposes swapping cus-tomer names, addresses, phone numbers and ages plus hard-to-track data like transaction information and purchases. Unlike in Europe where strict privacy laws would not permit such a venture in the first instance, there are few US laws that limit customer information-sharing among companies (*American Banker*, 2001). The rationale for this standard is presented in terms of 'better information, better service to the customer', as the more easily customer information is exchanged, the more easily organizations can provide tailored service. Quoting an executive from a premier US bank, 'Our top priority is clearly serving our customers, and we would not use technology that would violate the privacy or security of our customer information', it becomes clear that such endeavours are justified by a consumerist discourse rather than by one rooted in profit and business results.

But there are many cynical views regarding the use of new technology to tier consumers and facilitate the exchange of customer information. First, measuring current customer potential with the view to offer so-called tailored service may not be the most appropriate approach. Life situations and spending habits can change and current spending potential may be very different from the future one. If such technologies are let free, in the future the service divide may become more transparent and more acceptable from an ethical standpoint, while customer service will become just another product for sale: 'Consumers have become commodities to pamper, squeeze or toss away . . . [we have seen] a decline in the level of respect given to the customers and their experiences' (Berry in Brady, 2000).

What is disconcerting is not only the ability of new technology to make visible and record the spending preferences of the consumer: such data is consequently acted upon in a manner that may have little to do with customer satisfaction and more to do with profit concerns. If consumerist discourses insist that consumers are equal and have power over their spending choices, this envisaged scenario makes improbable both the fairness with which different tiers of consumers are to be treated and the image of the consumer as a winner.

CASE STUDY QUESTION

- What do you think will happen to customer privacy if CPExchange gets built?

Managing quality through internal marketing: the case of the UK retail banking sector

Ioanna Papasolomou-Doukakis

This case study presents some of the findings that emerged from research carried out within the UK retail banking sector on the relationship between internal marketing (IM), quality management (QM) and human resource management practices (HRM). The study was primarily qualitative in nature since its main aim was to unearth people's views and experiences rather than reflect objectively an a priori reality. Thirty-five business units from seven different UK banking organizations participated in the study. Data was generated mainly from in-depth qualitative interviews with 35 branch managers and 21 employees. A structured questionnaire was also administered to all the interviewees and documents related to internal marketing were examined. A systematic review of the current literature on IM, QM and HRM was an integral part of the study in order to allow for a comparison between the study's own conclusions and the findings from the literature.

The empirical evidence suggests that there is an increased pressure on UK retail banks to improve their service in order to differentiate themselves from the competition. In their quest to become more market-led, UK retail banks have attempted, with a higher or lower degree of success, to adopt the practice of internal marketing. In the words of a bank manager: 'The internal marketing initiative emphasizes the importance of being customer-focused all the time.'

Internal marketing views internal relationships and structures within the organization as governed by the same (exchange) logic that governs external markets. Thus, if the organization implements effective exchanges between its members/departments and between the organization and various groups of employees, this will eventually lead to successful exchanges on the external market.

The overall conclusion of the study is that internal marketing programmes have a strong human resource flavour and are an integral part of service quality initiatives. Internal marketing seems to be a 'soft' quality management initiative that aims to inculcate a service mentality by means of:

1   an emphasis on the notion of internal customers;
2   the importance placed on training;
3   the weight accorded to meeting internal service standards, and
4   the alignment of reward strategies with service performance targets.

Internal marketing aims to please both internal and external customers, but the evidence suggests that in many cases, it is no more than a rhetorical ploy which, in the name of customer care, is directed to achieving higher profits for the corporation.

INTERNAL CUSTOMERS

By viewing employees as internal customers, UK retail banks aim to achieve internal customer satisfaction, which is seen to be a prerequisite for external customer satisfaction. If staff is motivated, the exchanges between them are more effective, and this will ultimately lead to improved customer satisfaction on the external market.

The banks studied recognize that they will be in a better position to satisfy their external customers by designing internal products that satisfy the needs of the internal customers. By satisfying such internal needs, UK retail banks hope to enhance employees' ability to, among others but primarily so, deliver external customer satisfaction. At the heart of the internal marketing practice within these banks is the view that the needs of internal customers must be fulfilled first, before the needs of external customers can be satisfied. To do so, most of the banks under the study have embarked on internal market research in an attempt to identify, assess and measure internal customer expectations in terms of, for example, needs and concerns, internal service quality levels and internal service quality gaps. One of the branch managers said: 'As part of the "investment in people" initiative we have done internal surveys to investigate subordinates' views regarding their superiors on issues such as motivation, training opportunities, expressing ideas.'

Selling the bank's products to employees is another way in which employees are transformed into internal customers. This is an activity typically implemented by head offices. Its purpose is the enhancement of the employees' knowledge and competence in relation to the bank's products. Banks attempt to motivate their personnel to purchase the bank's products by offering them at a reduced price. Examples include loans sold to personnel at a lower interest rate (however, certain loans can only be used for specific purposes such as for the pursuit of academic qualifications).

By using such marketing techniques, internal marketing attempts to ensure that the relationship between the organization and individual employees is optimized. In exchange, individuals are expected to treat their colleagues as customers and deliver a high standard of service, as they themselves would expect in the external marketplace. According to a branch manager:

> If you treat people the way you want to be treated, the quality of internal service will improve. Everybody needs to be given the same standard of service. The notion of internal customers highlights that. Internal Marketing encourages everybody to provide each customer, internal and external, with the best possible service.

TRAINING

In the banks studied, training does not merely emphasize employees' technical skills but, more importantly, softer skills related to service and customer consciousness. From an interview with a branch manager:

> Training courses make everybody aware that they have internal customers to serve. A lot of the training programmes are aimed at highlighting the importance of achieving service quality in internal encounters and of treating fellow workers as internal customers. As a result, customer and service orientation are strengthened.

Most training programmes aim to inculcate a service mentality throughout the organization by emphasizing the importance of treating employees as internal customers. Training is mainly directed at 'shaping' employees' attitudes and behaviour towards recognizing the importance of both internal and external customers and acting to please them. One could argue that internal marketing is the process of 'selling' to the employees a certain set of values which puts on a pedestal the demands of the market and the importance of service quality in meeting and exceeding customer expectations.

The evidence suggests that despite the rhetoric surrounding such training programmes, they are used in a manipulative way. Banks may use these programmes to demonstrate that the organization cares about the needs and wants of staff but the genuine nature of this concern is debatable. Very often, these programmes are 'revamped', within the context of internal marketing, in order to signal a more people-oriented culture that benefits the bottom line of the organization through improved staff performance and productivity rather than through improved morale and employee satisfaction.

INTERNAL SERVICE STANDARDS

Internal standards are another important element of the Internal Marketing programmes implemented by the banks under the study. These banks set desired levels of quality for all internal service encounters. Most branch managers and employees see these standards as vital in ensuring internal service quality. In the words of an employee:

> Each branch has its own internal service standards. We also have standards on a group-wide basis . . . so we know what level of service to expect from the support departments. Internal marketing has highlighted the importance of meeting these standards in order to satisfy our internal customers as a way of achieving external customer satisfaction.

This message is reinforced by a bank manager:

> Everybody is aware of the quality standards and everybody has service quality targets. Internal marketing emphasizes the importance of meeting service standards in every internal service encounter. IM is motivating individuals to be customer-focused and service-oriented, and everything is geared towards that . . . our personal targets, our team objectives, the organizational objectives.

REWARD SYSTEMS

The UK retail banks studied tie individual objectives to the organizational aim of customer satisfaction and reward the achievement of those objectives. They use both extrinsic and intrinsic rewards. In particular, monetary rewards are used to reward individual performance related to the opening of new accounts and sales achieved against set targets. Such monetary rewards take the form of bonuses and commissions. Thus, the front-line staff have more opportunities to obtain monetary rewards than the back-room staff. The key reason for this tendency is that banks link monetary rewards to quantitative targets such as sales figures. Since only customer-contact personnel have sales targets, only they have an opportunity to obtain these rewards.

The achievement of qualitative targets, such as service quality, is rewarded mainly by intrinsic non-monetary rewards such as gifts, medals and plaques. In certain cases, these may be instigated by head office, but more usually, they are left at the branch managers' discretion. What is puzzling is the fact that only quantifiable matters seem to be recognized as crucial and therefore rewarded financially (sales/account openings). Service quality, being intangible, takes a back stage position: a few words of praise, an insignia or a badge with the 'employee of the month' are supposed to be of sufficient standing to motivate the back office employees to deliver service quality.

CONCLUSIONS

The four practices reviewed above are constitutive of internal marketing and according to the senior management of the banks, are the prerequisite for achieving customer satisfaction. Through these levers, individuals are encouraged to provide outstanding service that meets and exceeds the expectations of both internal and external customers. Hence, the internal marketing practice within UK retail banks aims at achieving an attitudinal change among staff towards market responsiveness and service quality A branch manager said:

> You are bound to have an increase in customer service because you are influencing the behaviour of the individuals in a planned process. IM is aimed at achieving a shift in the attitude of employees towards being more customer and service oriented. You can easily improve customer service by highlighting it, rewarding it and making people understand how the level of service they provide to their internal and external customers affects the success of the organization.

The findings of this study suggest that the banks studied have attempted to combine the principles of marketing, quality management and human resource management under the umbrella of internal marketing, in an attempt to improve organizational effectiveness and efficiency. Internal marketing is used as a means for enabling individuals to understand their role within the internal customer–supplier chain, with the ultimate view of achieving outstanding external customer service. By and large the UK banking industry seemed to have successfully adopted the practice of internal marketing in that it has recently become more responsive to customer needs and expectations. To what extent this is the result of more empowered and happier internal customers, remains to be seen.

CASE STUDY QUESTIONS

- Can the objective of profit making be reconciled with the objective of employee satisfaction? Discuss.
- Is internal marketing the most appropriate technique for improving customer service in the UK retail-banking sector?

Quality standards and the journey to total quality: the case of Inscom UK

Mihaela Kelemen

This case traces the quality journey of a major insurance company. The company (which will be called Inscom UK for the purpose of this case study) is part of an international financial group which offers international risk consultancy, insurance broking, employee benefits and financial services having a network of more than 260 offices in 60 countries around the world. Inscom UK has a number of operations, among which are retailing, special risks, and international broking. Inscom UK embarked on a total quality programme in 1996 which was labelled 'Win with Quality'.

The 1997 annual report states in the opening page: 'Our aim is to "Win with Quality". Inscom is committed to quality and client service. It is also committed to staff training and development, to improving shareholder value and to being a good citizen of the communities in which it operates.' Prior to the adoption of the 'Win with Quality' programme, the company was preoccupied mainly with the standard aspect of quality. Inscom UK was the first broker 'to achieve accreditation to the international quality standard, ISO 9000, across a network of offices' (1995 annual report). But the preoccupation with standards started earlier than that.

In 1993 Inscom launched an in-house set of standards entitled Professional Accounting Management (PAM) standards, with the objective of creating a consistent quality of service throughout its international network. In the words of the marketing director, 'PAM is about agreeing what you give to the client and how you go about it'. The originators and main drivers of these standards were the company's quality professionals. The company's statistics regarding the implementation of PAM in the UK shows that in many offices PAM had not been introduced as yet.

This may have a great deal to do with the way in which PAM standards were launched. In the words of a senior manager: 'we did not launch PAM. We threw it at people. Launching is about winning people's minds and hearts and making sure they understand what PAM is all about.' His view is supported by a number of quality managers from various UK offices. There seems to be a general view that the launch of PAM 'emphasized the administrative parts, but not the benefits PAM could deliver for the clients and the organization, itself'.

In this context, people's understanding of PAM standards seems to be parochial and limiting. A London-based quality manager said, for example: 'Many people think that PAM is just an extra task or a set of rules and are very cynical about it. People keep files on things just in case someone from above comes to check on them.' Another quality manager said: 'It is annoying when people say we have PAM. We have the PAM brochure in the cupboard, but that does not mean we apply it.'

Rather than taking the blame, quality professionals see senior management as the main culprits. It is the latter who do not seem to understand what PAM standards are trying to achieve and who, consequently, make no effort to enthuse their subordinates with respect to the potentialities offered by these standards. PAM is not on the board of directors' agenda and as such it lacks a strategic focus and the necessary resources to make it happen.

Despite such negative feelings displayed by quality professionals towards the board of directors, some progress has been made on achieving accreditation to the ISO 9000 series by many offices across the UK in 1995. The 1997 annual report regards this accreditation as providing 'evidence that the company's success in the field of quality is recognized externally as well as internally'.

The drivers behind this process, two senior managers based in the London office, gave their accounts on the difficulties of achieving the ISO accreditation. One of them said: 'When we started ISO, a small part of the people were enthusiastic about it, a small part was against it but the majority was open minded enough to accept that this is a serious initiative. We learnt as we went along and the whole process lasted 12 months.' The other one said that she 'had to go out and sell the project to all UK branches. I had to run training courses for auditing. It was stressful. Initially we struggled to understand what it meant. Not all branches were so positive at the beginning and in fact not all have been accredited.'

The benefits of ISO are, however, debatable and there are voices who claim that internally ISO achieves very little. The chairman himself argues: 'ISO is just a marketing tool but does not put too much internal discipline into the company. It is just a gloss, something that the market requires.' Another board member has a similar opinion: 'ISO is much more to do with marketing, it is a means by which you can explain the world how clever you are.' Indeed, having standards and procedures in place does not automatically mean more discipline because 'as soon as these procedures were implemented they got forgotten'. The external consultant who helped with the process warns against complacency:

> Having ISO 9000 in place is only the infrastructure of a quality organization and you should not be complacent and content with yourselves and stop

here. Your competitors will achieve accreditation sooner or later and you will have to find something else that differentiates you.

Despite scepticism regarding the benefits of the ISO series, the board of directors has heavily backed up the initiative (much more so than in the case of PAM standards):

> There are three reasons we have decided to do it: firstly, the marketing value of having ISO at present, secondly, the potential for driving costs out of our business by doing it right first time, and thirdly, the future institutionalization of ISO which will make our clients ask for it. (Marketing Director)

The launch of the 'Win with Quality' programme in 1996 took place in response to two needs: the need to supplement existing standards packages with a more human driven approach (i.e., empowerment, culture change) and the need to unite the existing initiatives under a big umbrella. Indeed, there seemed to be a constant tension between 'quality' as a continuous process and 'quality' as a sum of discrete initiatives. One of the quality managers argued that 'on the one hand, you fight for attention to keep the interest going by promoting discrete events such as empowerment, PAM, ISO etc., on the other hand, you want to have it as a continuous process that permeates everybody's job'. The chairman of the company appears to be confident that the consultants will sort things out since 'the company put a lot of thought and money into the process'. Other organizational members are more pessimistic because 'nobody has the total answer as to how to continuously make it meaningful to people' and 'top management bullshits a lot about quality these days but it is just for public relations'.

A year after its launch, the evidence on the state of the 'Win with Quality' programme remained rather controversial. The objectives of the 'Win with Quality' programme were not reflected in specific action plans and, as such, did not appear to be understood in a consistent manner across the organization. Due to the broker/hard selling mentality, a great deal of emphasis was still put on the external customers at the expense of the internal ones, the employees. And despite empowerment promises the emphasis remained on standardization, quality control and employee monitoring.

CASE STUDY QUESTIONS

- To what extent has Inscom UK taken on board the philosophy of total quality management?
- What should the board of directors do to ensure that employees are less cynical about and more committed to quality?

Final remarks

The cases presented above explore the processes by which quality is constructed, understood, expressed, managed, controlled and portrayed in various organizations by various organizational stakeholders. As such, the result is more messy and complex than the previous chapters might have suggested. Quality is not an objective phenomenon that can be instantly and remotely controlled: although the most powerful organizational members may attempt to do just that. It is a process influenced by and influencing existing power discourses and regimes of truth. As such, although the author is pro-quality, a stance that hopefully comes through clearly in the book, she cannot take quality at its face value and simply regurgitate what quality gurus have said for decades, namely, 'that quality is good'. The questions that need asking are: 'What is good?', 'Who decides what is good?', 'Good for whom?', 'Does good come at an easy cost?', and so on.

There are no easy answers, yet it is important that one asks these questions rather than simply embrace the missionary message of quality gurus. We live in a consumerist society but this does not automatically lead to better, more fulfilled lives for all of us: work intensification, the exploitation of third world countries, natural resource depletion and other environmental concerns are the price we pay for our daily conveniences. But this is all relative: if we compare standards of living now with standards of living 300 years ago, it is a fact that a much higher proportion of people have access to quality, convenience and value for money. The consumerist discourse could be seen to democratize rather than exploit the 'masses', for the 'masses' now could have a say in what is going on in the world. People can choose not to buy from companies that are perceived as socially irresponsible. Their voice could be given weight by legislation that protects their rights. Quality and consumerism could be positive forces shaping the society: yet, they could also be manipulated by multinational corporations, governments and powerful individuals. The challenge lies in being aware of and constantly assessing the dangers hidden behind the seductive face of quality.

Bibliography

Abbott, L. (1955) *Quality and Competition: An Essay in Economic Theory.* Westpoint, CT: Greenwood Press.

Abrahamson, E. (1996) Management fashions, *Academy of Management Review*, 21: 254–85.

Abrahamson, E. and Fairchild, G. (1999) Management fashions: lifestyles, triggers and collective learning processes, *Administrative Science Quarterly*, 44: 708–40.

Ahire, S.L. and Dreyfus, P. (2000) The impact of design management and process management on quality: an empirical investigation, *Journal of Operations Management*, 18(5), 549–75.

Albert, S. and Wetten, D. (1985) Organizational identity, in L.L. Cummings and B.M. Staw (eds) *Research in Organizational Behaviour*, vol. 7. Greenwich, CT: JAI Press. pp. 263–295.

Alvesson, M. (1990) Organization: from substance to image?, *Organization Studies*, 11(3): 373–94.

Alvesson, M. and Willmott, H. (eds) (1992) *Critical Management Studies.* London: Sage.

Alvesson, M. and Willmott, H. (1996) *Making Sense of Management: A Critical Introduction.* London: Sage.

American Banker (2001) The tech scene: a new privacy flash point, 3 January.

Ammons, R.E. and Vujasinovic, V.S. (2000) Times that kill, *Trial*, 36(12): 52–60.

Ascari, A., Rock, M. and Dutta, S. (1995) Re-engineering and organizational change: lessons from a comparative analysis of company experiences, *European Management Journal* 13(1): 1–30.

Astley, W.G. and Zammuto, R.F. (1992) Organization science, managers, and language games, *Organization Science*, 3(4): 443–61.

Babicz, G. (2000) ISO changes its quality approach, *Quality*, 39(6): 56–58.

Bank, J. (1992) *The Essence of Total Quality Management.* Hemel Hempstead: Prentice Hall.

Barnard, C. (1938 [1968]) *The Functions of the Executive.* Cambridge, MA and London: Harvard University Press.

Barney, J. (1991) Firm resources and sustained competitive advantage, *Journal of Management*, 17: 99–120.

Bass, B.M. (1990) *Handbook of Leadership: Theory Research and Managerial Applications*, 3rd edn. New York: Free Press.

Baston, R.G. (1988) Disovered: quality's missing link, *Quality Progress*, October: 61–4.

Bauman, Z. (1995) *Life in Fragments*. Oxford: Blackwell.

Bayton, J.A. (1958) Motivation, cognition, learning-basic factors in consumer behaviour, *Journal of Marketing*, 22(3): 282–9.

Beckford, J. (1998) *Quality: A Critical Introduction*. London: Sage.

Bendell, T. (1991) *The Quality Gurus: What Can they do for your Company?* London: DTI.

Bennis, W. (1993) *An Invented Life: Reflections on Leadership and Change*. Reading, MA: Addison-Wesley Publishing Co.

Berggren, E. and Nacher, T. (2000) Why good ideas go bust?, *Management Review*, 82(2): 32–6.

Berry, L.L. (1986) Big ideas in services marketing, *Journal of Consumer Marketing*, Spring: 47–51.

Bigliazzi, M. (1995) A history of managing for quality, *Quality Progress*, 28(8): 125–9.

Blackburn, R. and Rosen, B. (1993) Total quality and human resource management: lessons learnt from Baldrige Award-winning companies, *Academy of Management Executive*, 7(3): 49–79.

Blair, H., Grey Taylor, S. and Randle, K. (1998) A pernicious panacea: a critical evaluation of business re-engineering, *New Technology, Work and Employment*, 13(2): 116–28.

Boden, D. (1994) *The Business of Talk: Organizations in Action*. Cambridge: Polity Press.

Bond, S. (2001) When they built the ship *Titanic*, *National Forum*, 18(1): 33–8.

Bowie, N.E. (1999) *Business Ethics: A Kantian Perspective*. Oxford: Blackwell.

Brady, D. (2000) Why service stinks, *Business Week*, 23 October.

Brown, W. (2000) The great foreign car myth: are Japanese and European cars truly better than American ones, or just better at hiding their defects?, *The Washington Post*, 29 October.

Bryman, A. (1992) *Charisma and Leadership in Organizations*. London: Sage.

Bucklin, L.P (1963) Retail strategy and the class of consumer goods, *Journal of Marketing*, 27: 51–6.

Burke, K. (1966) *Language as Symbolic Action: Essays on Life, Literature and Method*. Los Angeles: University of California Press.

Burns, J.M. (1978) *Leadership*. New York: Harper & Row.

Burrell, G. (1996) Normal science, paradigms, metaphors, discourses and genealogies of analysis. In S.R. Clegg, C. Hardy and W.R. Nord (eds) *Handbook of Organization Studies.*, London: Sage. pp. 31–56.

Caulkin, S. (2002) Running a business is studied to death in UK, *The Observer*, 13 January: 9.

Chase, R.B. (1981) The customer contact approach to services: theoretical basis and practical extensions, *Operational Research*, 29: 698–706.

Chatterjee, S. and Yilman, M. (1993) Quality confusion: too many gurus, not enough disciples, *Business Horizons*, 36(3): 15–18.

Chia, R. (1996) The problem of reflexivity in organizational research: towards a postmodern science of organization, *Organization*, 1: 149–78.

Choi, T.Y. and Behling, O.C. (1997) Top managers and TQM success: one more look after all these years, *The Academy of Management Executive* 11(1): 37–47.

Chorn, N.H. (1991) Total quality management: panacea or pitfall?, *International Journal of Physical Distribution and Logistics Management*, 21(8): 31–5.

Clegg, S. (1989) *Frameworks of Power*. London: Sage.

Conti, R.F. and Warner, M. (1994) Taylorism, teams and technology in re-engineering work-organization, *New Technology, Work and Employment* 9(2): 93–102.

Coulson, H. (1993) Putting theory into practice: tailoring current cost of quality models to suit your company, *IIR Limited Industrial Conference*, London, February.

Coulson-Thomas, C. (1991) Competent directors: boardroom myths and realities, *Journal of General Management*, 17(1): 1–26.

Crosby, P.B. (1979) *Quality Is Free: The Art of Making Quality Certain*. New York: Mentor Books, New American Library.

Crosby, P.B. (1983) Don't be defensive about the cost of quality, *Quality Progress*, April: 38–9.

Crosby, P. (1984) *Quality Without Tears: The Art of Hassle-free Management*. New York: McGraw-Hill.

Curtis, N., Kelemen, M. and Oren, J. (1992) Process modelling, *Communications of the ACM*, 35(9): 75–90.

Czarniawska-Joerges, B. (1990) Merchants of meaning: management consulting in the Swedish public sector. In B.A. Turner (ed.) *Organizational Symbolism*. Berlin: de Gruyter. pp. 139–150.

Czarniawska-Joerges, B. (1993) *The Three-dimensional Organization: A Constructivist View*. Sweden: Studentlitteratur.

Dahlgaard, S.M.P. (1999) The evolution patterns of quality management: some reflections on the quality, *Total Quality Management*, 10(4): 473–80.

Dahlgaard, S.M.P., Krustensen, K. and Kanji, G.R. (1994) Strategic quality management and quality costs, *Advances in Total Quality Management*, 5: 111–7.

Dale, B.G. (ed.) (1994) *Managing Quality* (2nd edn). Hemel Hempstead: Prentice Hall.

Dale, B.G. and Boaden, R.J. (1994) The use of teams in quality improvement. In B.G. Dale (ed.) *Managing Quality* (2nd edn). Hemel Hempstead: Prentice Hall. pp. 514–32.

Dale, B.G. and Shaw, P. (1994) Statistical process control. In B. Dale (ed.) *Managing Quality*. Hemel Hempstead: Prentice Hall. pp. 469–97.

Davenport, T.H. (1993) *Process Innovation: Re-engineering Work Through Information Technology*. Boston, MA: Harvard Business School Press.

Davenport, T.H. and Short, J.E. (1990) The new industrial engineering: information technology and business process redesign, *Sloan Management Review*, 31(4) (Summer): 11–27.

Davis, T.R.V. and Luthans, F. (1980) Managers in action: a new look at their behaviour and operating modes, *Organizational Dynamics*, 9(1): 64–80.

Dawson, P. and Webb, J. (1989) New production arrangements: the totally flexible cage, *Work, Employment and Society*, 3(2): 221–38.

de Cock, C. (1998) 'It seems to fill my head with ideas': a few thoughts on postmodernism, TQM and BPR, *Journal of Management Inquiry*, 7(2): 144–53.

Deal, T. and Kennedy, A. (1982) *Corporate Cultures: The Rite and Rituals of Corporate Life*. Harmondsworth, Mx: Penguin.

Dean, J.W. and Snell, S.A. (1991) Integrated manufacturing and job design: industry effects of organizational inertia, *Academy of Management Journal*, 34: 776–804.

Delbridge, R. and Turnbull P. (1992) Human resource maximisation: the management of labour under just-in-time manufacturing systems. In P. Blyton and P. Turnbull (eds) *Reassessing Human Resource Management*. London: Sage. pp. 56–73.

Deming, W.E. (1986) *Out of Crisis*. Cambridge, MA: MIT Press.

Dixon, J.R., Arnold, P., Heineke, J., Kim J.S. and Mulligan, P. (1994) Business process re-engineering, *California Management Review*, Summer: 93–108.

Doyle, K. (1992) Who's killing total quality management, *Incentive (IMK)*, August: 59.

Earl, M. (1994) The new and the old business process undersign, *Journal of Strategic Information Systems*, 3(1): 5–22.

Eco, U. (1979) *The Role of the Reader*. Indianapolis: Indiana University Press.

Fairclough, N. (1996) *Language and Power*. Harlow: Addison Wesley Longman.

Farnworth, N.R. (1994) Strict product liability and its impact on the management of quality. In B.G. Dale (ed.) *Managing quality*, (2nd edn). Hemel Hempstead: Prentice-Hall. pp. 149–62.

Feeney, A. and Zairi, M. (1996) TQM in healthcare, *Journal of General Management*, 22(1): 35–47.

Feigenbaum, A.V. (1951) *Quality Control: Principles, Practice and Administration*. New York: McGraw-Hill

Feigenbaum, A.V. (1961) *Total Quality Control: Engineering and Management*. New York: McGraw-Hill.

Feigenbaum, A.V. (1983) *Total Quality Control*. New York: McGraw-Hill.

Flood, R.L. (1993) *Beyond TQM*. Chichester: Wiley.

Foucault, M. (1977) *Discipline and Punish: The Birth of the Prison*. London: Penguin.

Foucault, M. (1980) *Power/Knowledge: Selected Interviews and Other Writings, 1972–1977*. New York: Pantheon.

Fournier, V. (1998). Stories of development and exploitation: militant voices in an enterprise culture, *Organization*, 5(1): 55–80.

Fritsche, D.J. and Becker, H. (1984) Linking management behavior to ethical philosophy: an empirical investigation, *Academy of Management Journal*, 27: 166–75.

Gabriel, Y. and Lang, T. (1995) *The Unmanageable Consumer*. London: Sage.

Garvin, D. (1987) Competing on the eight dimensions of quality, *Harvard Business Review*, 65(6): 101–9.

Garvin, D.A. (1984) What does product quality really mean?, *Sloan Management Review*, Fall: 25–43.

Garvin, D. (1988) *Managing Quality: The Strategic and Competitive Edge*. New York: Free Press.

Gaster, L. (1995) *Quality in the Public Sector: Managers' Choice*. Buckingham and Philadelphia: Open University Press.

George, C.S. (1972) *The History Of Management Thought*. Englewood Cliffs, NJ: Prentice Hall.

Giakatis, G. and Rooney, E.M. (2000) The use of quality costing to trigger process improvement in an automotive company, *Total Quality Management*, 11(2): 155–70.

Giakatis, G., Enkawa, T. and Washitani, K. (2001) Hidden quality costs and the distinction between quality cost and quality loss, *Total Quality Management*, 12(2): 179–90.

Gill, J. and Whittle, S. (1993) Management by panacea: accounting for transition, Journal of Management Studies, 30(2): 281–393.

Gilmore, H.L. (1974) Product conformance cost, *Quality Progress*, June: 16–19.

Gioia, D. (1992): at Keele

Gioia, D. (1999) Personal reflections on the Pinto fires case. In L.K. Trevino and K.A. Nlson (eds) *Managing Business Ethics: Straight Talk About How to Do It Right* (2nd edn). New York: Wiley.

Gowler, D. and Legge, K. (1983) The meaning of management and the management of meaning: a view from social anthropology. In M. Earl (ed.) *Perspectives on Management: A Multidisciplinary Analysis*. Oxford: Oxford University Press. pp. 197–234.

Grey, C. and Mitev, N. (1995) Re-engineering organizations: a critical appraisal, *Personnel Review*, 24(1): 6–18.

Grint, K. (1994) Re-engineering history: social resonances and business process re-engineering, *Organization*, 1(1): 179–201.

Grint, K. (1997) *Leadership: Classical, Contemporary And Critical Approaches*. Oxford: Oxford University Press.

Grint, K. and Case, P. (1995) Now where were we? BPR lotus-eaters and corporate amnesia, Paper for the workshop on *Critical Studies of Organizational and Management Innovations*, European Institute for Advanced Studies in Management, Brussels, 8–9 May.

Grint, K. and Case, P. (1998) The violent rhetoric of re-engineering: management consultancy on the offensive, *Journal of Management Studies*, 35(5): 557–77.

Grint, K. and Willcocks, L. (1995) Business process re-engineering in theory and practice: business paradise regained?, *New Technology, Work and Employment*, 10(2): 99–109.

Gronroos, C. (1983) *Strategic Management And Marketing In The Service Sector*. Cambridge, MA: Marketing Science Institute.

Guillen, M.F. (1997) Scientific management lost aesthetic: architecture, organization and the Taylorized beauty of the mechanical, *ASQ*, 42: 682–715.

Guimares, T. and Bond, W. (1996) Empirically assessing the impact of BPR on manufacturing firms, *International Journal of Operations and Production Management*, 16(8): 5–29.

Gummesson, E. (1991) Truths and myths in service quality, *International Journal of Service Industry Management*, 2(3): 7–16.

Hall, G., Rosenthal, J. and Wade, J. (1993) How to make re-engineering really work, *Harvard Business Review*, November–December: 119–30.

Hall, R.H. (1991) *Organizations: Structures, Processes and Outcomes*, 3rd edn. Englewood Cliffs, NJ: Prentice Hall.

Hamm, S. and Stepanek, M. (1999) From re-engineering to e-engineering, *Business Week*, 22 March.

Hammer, M. (1990) Re-engineering work: don't automate, obliterate, *Harvard Business Review*, July–August: 104–12.

Hammer, M. and Champy, J. (1993) *Re-engineering the Corporation: A Manifesto for Business Revolution*. New York: Harper Business.

Hammer, M. and Stanton, S. (1999) How process enterprises really work, *Harvard Business Review*, 77(6): 108–18.

Hassard, J. and Parker, M. (1993) *Postmodernism and Organizations*. London: Sage.

Haywood-Farmer, J. (1987) A conceptual model of service quality, *International Journal of Operations and Production Management*, 8(6): 19–29.

Hegarty, S. (1993) On the quest for quality, *Personnel Today*, July: 19–22.

Heller, R. (1993) *TQM: the quality makers*, Switzerland: Norden Publishing House.

Hendricks, K.B. and Singhal, V.R. (1997) Does implementing an effective TQM program actually improve operating performance? Empirical evidence from firms that have won quality awards, *Management Science*, 43(9): 1258–74.

Hendricks and Singhal (1999) Don't count TQM out: evidence shows implementation pays off in a big way, *Quality Progress*, April: 35–42.

Hill, S. (1991) Why quality circles failed but total quality management might succeed, *British Journal of Industrial Relations*, 29(4): 541–68.

Hill, S. (1995) From quality circles to total quality management. In A. Wilkinson and H. Willmott (eds) *Making Quality Critical: New Perspectives on Organizational Change*. London: Routledge. pp. 33–53.

Hogarth, S. (1999) On the horizon, ISO 14000, *Manufacturing Engineering*, 122(3): 118–28.

Hopfl, H. (1995) Organizational rhetoric and the threat of ambivalence, *Studies in Cultures, Organizations and Societies*, 1: 175–87.

Hopper Wruck, K. and Jensen M. (1994) Science, scientific knowledge and total quality management, *Journal of Accounting and Economics*, 18: 274–87.

Horsted, J. and Doherty, N. (1994) Poles apart?: integrating business process redesign and human resource management, *Business Change and Re-engineering*, 1(4): 49–56.

Huczynski, A. (1993) *Management Gurus*. London: Routledge.

Hunt, V.D. (1993) *Managing Quality: Integrating Quality and Business Strategy*. Homewood, IL: Irwin.

Ishikawa, K. (1985) *What is Total Quality Control? The Japanese Way*. Englewood Cliffs, NJ: Prentice Hall.

Jacobs, F.A. and Kamm, C. (1998) The relationship of customer satisfaction to strategic decisions, *Journal of Managerial Issues*, 10(2): 165–82.

Janis, I.L. (1972) *Victims of Groupthink*. New York: Houghton Mifflin.

Johansson, H.J., McHugh, P., Pendlebury, A.J. and Wheeler, W.A. (1993) *Business Process Re-engineering*. London: John Wiley.

Juran, J.M. (ed.) (1979) *Juran's Quality Control Handbook* (3rd edn). New York: McGraw-Hill.

Juran, J.M. (1988) *Juran on Planning for Quality*. New York: Free Press.

Juran, J.M., Goyna, F.M. and Bingham, R.S. (eds) (1974) *Quality Control Handbook* (3rd edn). New York: McGraw-Hill.

Kahn, R. (1964) *Organizational Stress: Studies in Role Conflict and Ambiguity*. New York: John Wiley.

Kalakota, R. and Robinson, M. (1999) *E-Business: Roadmap for Success*. Reading, MA: Addison Wesley.

Kanji, G.K. and Asher, M. (1996) *Methods for Total Quality Management*. London: Sage.

Keat, R. and Abercrombie, N. (eds) (1991) *Enterprise Culture*. London: Routledge.

Kelemen, M. (1998) Total quality management in the UK service sector: a social constructivist study. In S. Clegg, E. Ibarra and L. Bueno (eds) *Global Management: Universal Theories and Local Realities*. London: Sage.

Kelemen, M. (2000) Too much or too little ambiguity: the language of total quality management, *Journal of Management Studies*, 37(4): 483–98.

Kelemen, M. (2001) Discipline at work: distal and proximal views, *Studies in Cultures, Organizations and Societies*, 7: 1–23.

Kelemen, M., Forrester, P. and Hassard, J. (2000) BPR and TQM: divergence or convergence. In D. Knights and H. Willmott (eds) *The Re-engineering Revolution*. London: Sage. pp. 154–173.

Kerfoot, D. and Knights, D. (1995) Empowering the quality worker? In A. Wilkinson and H. Willmott (eds) *Making Quality Critical: New Perspectives on Organizational Change*. London: Routledge. pp. 219–39.

Kirkpatrick, I. and Lucio, M. (1995) The uses of 'quality' in the British government's reform of the public sector. In I. Kirkpatrick and M. Lucio (eds) *The Politics of Quality in the Public Sector*. London: Routledge. pp. 16–43.

Knight, F. (1921) *Risk, Uncertainty and Profit*. Boston, MA: Houghton Mifflin.

Knights, D. (2000) Bewitched, bothered and bewildered: the meaning and experience of teamworking for employees in an automobile company, *Human Relations*, 53(11): 1481–517.

Knights, D. and McCabe, D. (1998a) 'What happens when the phone goes wild?': staff, stress and spaces for escape in a BPR telephone banking work regime, *Journal of Management Studies*, 35(2): 163–94.

Knights, D. and McCabe, D. (1998b) When 'life is but a dream': obliterating politics through business process re-engineering, *Human Relations*, 51(6): 761–98.

Knights, D. and Willmott, H. (2000) (eds) *The Re-engineering Revolution: Critical Studies of Corporate Change*. London: Sage.

Kunda, G. (1992) *Engineering Culture: Control and Commitment in a High Tech Corporation*. Philadelphia, PA: Temple University Press.

Lawler III, E.E. (1986) *High Involvement Management*. San Francisco, CA: Jossey-Bass.

Lawrence, T.B. and Phillips, N. (1998) Commentary: separating play and critique – postmodern and critical perspectives on TQM/BPR, *Journal of Management Inquiry*, 7(2): 154–60.

Lehtinen, U. and Lehtinen, J.R. (1982) Service quality: a study of quality dimensions. Working paper in *Service Management Institute*, Helsinki, Iceland.

Levhari, D. and Srinivasan, T.N. (1969) Durability of consumption goods: competition versus monopoly, *American Economic Review*, March: 102–7.

Lilley, S.J. and Platt, G.M. (1994) Correspondents' images of Martin Luther King Jr: an interpretive theory of movement leadership. In T.R. Sarbin and J.I. Kitsuse (eds) *Reconstructing the Social*. London: Sage. pp. 65–83.

Ligus, R.G. (1993) Methods to help reengineer your company for improved agility, *Industrial Engineering*, January.

Lovelock, C.H. (1992) *Managing Services: Marketing, Operations and Human Resources*, 2nd edn. Englewood Cliffs, NJ: Prentice Hall.

McArdle, L., Rowlinson, M., Procter, S., Hassard, J. and Forrester, P. (1995) Total quality management and participation: employee empowerment, or the enhancement of exploitation. In A. Wilkinson and H. Willmott (eds) *Making Quality Critical: New Perspectives on Organizational Change*. London: Routledge. pp. 156–73.

McCabe, D. and Wilkinson, A. (1998) The rise and fall of TQM: the vision, meaning and operation of change, *Industrial Relations Journal*, 29(1): 18–29.

McGregor, D. (1975) An uneasy look at performance appraisal, *Harvard Business Review*, 43: 89–94.

Maister, D.H. and Lovelock, C.H. (1982) Managing facilitator services, *Sloan Management Review*, 23(4): 19–31.

Merino, D.N. (1988) Economics of quality: chosing among prevention alternatives, *International Journal of Quality and Reliability Management*, 7: 13–23.

Merton, R. (1957) *Social Theory and Social Structure*. New York: The Free Press.

Meyerson, M. and Martin, J. (1987) Cultural change: an integration of three different views, *Journal of Management Studies*, 24(6): 623–47.

Millar, C. (1998) The town hall factory: the applicability of manufacturing operations management to public services, *Total Quality Management*, 9(2–3): 298–301.

Morgan, G. (1986) *Images of Organization*. London: Sage.

Morishima, M. (1982) *Why has Japan Succeeded? Western Technology and the Japanese Ethos*. Cambridge: Cambridge University Press.

Morrison, S.J. (1994) Managing quality: a historical review. In B.G. Dale (ed.) *Managing Quality* (2nd edn). Hemel-Hempstead: Prentice Hall. pp. 41–79.

Muschamp, H. (2000) Fusing beauty and terror: reverence and desecration, *New York Times*, 31 July.

Nwabueze, U. (1998) Managing innovation in public services, *Total Quality Management*, 2(3): 155.

Oakland, J. (1989) *Total Quality Management*. Oxford: Butterworth-Heinemann.

Olaru, M. (1999) *Managementul Calitatii*. Bucharest: Editura Economica.

Olian, J.D. and Rynes, S.L. (1991) Making total quality work: aligning organizations, performance measures and stakeholders, *Human Resource Management*, 30: 303–33.

Oliver, R.L. (1981) What is customer satisfaction?, *Wharton Magazine*, 5(3): 36–41.

Parasuraman, A., Zeithaml, V.A. and Berry, L.L. (1985) A conceptual model of service quality and its implications for future research, *Journal of Marketing*, 4(4): 41–50.

Parasuraman, A., Zeithaml, V.A. and Berry, L.L. (1988) SERVQUAL: a multiple-item scale for measuring customer perceptions of service quality, *Journal of Retailing*, 64(1): 12–40.

Parker, M. (1997) Organization, community, utopia, *Studies in Cultures, Organizations and Societies*, 4(1): 1–25.

Paul, R.J., Giaglis, G.M. and Hlupic, V. (1999) Simulation of business processes, *The American Behavioural Scientist*, 42(10): 1551–70.

Pearch, C. and Kitka, J. (2000) ISO 9000: 2000: the new kid on the block, *Machine Design*, 72(14): 30–5.

Pearson, G. (1995) *Integrity in Organizations: An Alternative Business Ethic.* Maidenhead: McGraw-Hill.

Pearson, G. and Parker, M. (2001) The Relevance of Ancient Greeks to Modern Business?: a dialogue on business and ethics, *Journal of Business Ethics*, 31: 341–53.

Personnel Today (1994) Cut out the middle men, 22 March.

Peters, T. (1987) *Thriving on Chaos: Handbook for a Management Revolution.* London: Macmillan.

Peters, T.J. and Austin, N. (1985) *A Passion for Excellence: The Leadership Difference.* London: Collins

Peters, T. and Waterman, R.H. (1982) *In Search of Excellence: Lessons from America's Best-Run Companies.* New York: Harper & Row.

Pettigrew, A. (1979) On studying organizational cultures, *Administrative Science Quarterly*, 24: 570–81.

Pettigrew, A. (1985) *The Awakening Giant: Continuity and Change at ICI.* Oxford: Blackwell.

Pfeffer, J. and Koote, A. (1991) Is quality good for you? A critical review of quality assurance in welfare services, *Social Policy Paper 5*, London: Institute for Public Policy Research.

Piore, M.J. and Sabel, C.F. (1984) *The Second Industrial Divide: Possibilities for Prosperity.* New York: Basic Books.

Pirsig, R.M. (1974) *Zen and the Art of Motorcycle Maintenance.* New York: Bantam Books

Price, F. (1989) Out of Bedlam: management by quality leadership, *Management Decision*, 27: 15–21.

Ptacek, M. (2000) Bank of America to set up an online B-to-B Market, *American Banker*, April 5.

Quinn, J.B. (1978) Strategic Change: logical incrementalism, *Sloan Management Review*, Fall.

Rae, S.B., and Wong, K.L. (1996) *Beyond Integrity: A Judo-Christian Approach to Business Ethics.* Grand Rapids, MI: Zondervan Publishing House.

Rao, C.R. (1989) *Statistics and Truth: Putting Chance to Work.* Fairland, MD: International Co-operative Publishing House,

Redman, T. and Grieves, J. (1999) Managing strategic change through TQM: learning from failure, *New Technology, Work and Employment*, 14(1): 45–61.

Redman, T., Snape, E. and Wilkinson, A. (1995) Is quality management working in the UK?, *Journal of General Management*, 20(3): 45–59.

Reed, M. (1995) Managing quality and organizational politics: TQM as a governmental technology. In I. Kirkpatrick and M. Lucio (eds) *The Politics of Quality in the Public Sector*. London: Routledge. pp. 45–63.

Rees, C. (1995) Quality management and HRM in the service industry: some case study evidence, *Employees Relations*, 17(3): 99–109.

Reeves, C.A. and Bednar, D.A. (1994) Defining quality: alternatives and implications, *The Academy of Management Review*, 19(3): 419–45.

Regalia, M. (2000) Gridlock (and Greenspan): a vigilant Fed and a mandate-free presidency mean mostly fair skies in 2001, *Time Magazine*, 18th December.

Reger, R.K., Gustafson, L.T., DeMarie, S.M. and Mullane, J.V. (1994) Reframing the organization: why implementing total quality management is easier said than done, *Academy of Management Review*, 19(3): 565–84.

Reitsperger, W.D. and Daniel, S.J. (1991) A comparison of quality attitudes in the USA and Japan: empirical evidence, *Journal of Management Studies*, 28: 85–96.

Remeny, D. and Whittaker, L. (1994) The cost and benefits of BPR, *Business Change and Re-engineering*, 2(2): 51–65.

Rice, J. (1992/1993) Cascaded training at Hughes Aircraft help ensure continuous measurable improvement, *National Productivity Review*, 12(1): 111–16.

Robinson, T.L. and Kimod, J.R. (2000) SPC: it's a tool not a cult, *Manufacturing Engineering*, 124(3): 104–77.

Rose, N. (1990) *Governing the Soul: The Shaping of the Private Self*. London: Routledge.

Rothschild, M. (1992) How to be a high IQ company, *Forbes*, 7 December.

Russell, S. (2000) ISO 9000: 2000 and the EFQM Excellence Model: competition or co-operation?, *Total Quality Management*, 11: 4–6.

Samuelson, B.A., Galbraith, C.S. and Maguire, J.W. (1985) Organizational performance and top-management turnover, *Organization Studies*, 6(3): 275–91.

Schein, E.H. (1980) *Organizational Psychology* (3rd edn). Englewood Cliffs, NJ: Prentice Hall.

Schein, E. (1983) The role of the founder in creating organizational culture, *Organizational Dynamics*, Summer: 13–28.

Schmenner, R.W. (1986) How can service business survive and prosper, *Sloan Management Review*, 27(3): 21–32.

Schmidt, S.R., Kiemele, M.J, and Cheek Jr. T.F. (1992) Don't let TQM drain you dry without any ROI, *Business Week*.

Schonberger, D. (1990) *Building a Chain of Customers*. New York: Free Press.

Schonberger, J.R. (1988) *Operations Management: Serving the Customer*. Homewood, IL: Irwin.

Seddon, J. (1994) History shooting quality in the foot, *Managing Service Quality*, 4(4): 9–12.

Selznick, P. (1957) *Leadership in Administration*. New York: Harper & Row.

Selznick, P. (1965) *TVA and the Grass Roots*. New York: Harper & Row.

Sewell, G. (1998) The discipline of team: the control of team-based industrial work through electronic and peer surveillance, *Administrative Science Quarterly*, 43: 397–428.

Sewell, G. and Wilkinson, A. (1992) Environment or Emasculation: A Tale of Workplace Survailance in the Total Quality Organization. In P. Blyton and P. Turnball (eds), *HRM: Conflicts and Contradictions*. London: Sage. pp. 97–115.

Shah, K.K.R. and Fitaroy, P.T. (1998) A review of quality cost surveys, *Total Quality Management*, 9(6): 479–86.

Siegel, G.B. and Seidler, E. (1996) Towards a public service blend of human resource management and TQM, *International Journal of Public Administration*, 19(10): 1781–1810.

Shingo, S. (1986) *Zero Quality Control: Source Inspection and the Poka-yoke System*, Cambridge, MA: Productivity Press.

Sitkin, S.B. (1995) Learning through failure: the strategy of small losses. In B.M. Staw and L.L. Cummings (eds) *Research in Organizational behaviour*, Vol. 14. Greenwich, CT: JAI Press. pp. 231–66.

Slack, N., Chambers, S., Harland, C., Harrison, A. and Johnston, R. (1995) *Operations Management*. London: Pitman Publishing.

Smedes, L.B. (1991) *Choices: Making Right Decisions in a Complex World*. San Francisco, CA: Harper.

Smircich, L. (1983) Concepts of culture and organizational analysis, *Administrative Science Quarterly*, 28(3): 203–20.

Smircich, L. and Morgan, G. (1982) Leadership: the management of meaning, *Journal of Applied Behavioural Science*, 18(3): 257–75.

Southern, G. (1994) Introducing business process re-engineering: a brainstorming approach, *Business Change and Re-engineering*, 2(1): 39–47.

Spencer, B.A. (1994) Models of organization and total quality management: a comparison and critical evaluation, *The Academy of Management Review*, 19(3): 446–71.

Steingard, D. and Fitzgibbons, D. (1993) A postmodern deconstruction of total quality management (TQM), *Journal of Organizational Change*, 6(5): 27–42.

Stogdill, R.M. (1974) *Handbook of Leadership: A Survey of the Literature*. New York: Free Press.

Stoumbos Z.G., Reynold, M.R., Ryan, T.R. and Woodall, W.H. (2000) The state of statistical process control as we proceed in the 21st century, *Journal of American Statistical Association*, 95(451): 992–8.

Swan, P.L. (1970) Durability of consumption goods, *American Economic Review*, December: 884–94.

Taguchi, G. (1986) *Introduction to Quality Engineering*. Tokyo: Asian Productivity Organization.

Tai, L.S. and Przasnyski, Z.H. (1999) The Baldrige Award winners beat the S&P 5000, *Quality Progress*, April: 45–51

Tenner, A.R. and DeToro, I.J. (1992) *Total Quality Management: Three Steps to Continuous Improvement*. Reading: Addison-Wesley.

Townley, B. (1994) *Reframing HRM: Power, Ethics and the Subject at Work*. London: Sage.

The Economist (1992) The cracks in quality, 18 April: 67–8.

The Economist (1997) A Wapping mess, 7 December: 54–6.

The Guardian (1999) Ford recalls faulty tires, 17 July.

The Guardian (1999) BMW recalls 3 million faulty cars, 8 October.

Tolstoy, L.N. (1957) *War and Peace*, trans. R. Edmonds. Harmondsworth, Mx: Penguin.

Tönnies, F. (1963) *Community and Society*, trans. C.P. Loomis. New York: Harper & Row.

Trevino, L.K. (1986) Ethical decision making in organizations: a person-situation interactionist model, *Academy of Management Review*, 11: 601–17.

Tuckman, A. (1995) Ideology, quality and TQM. In A. Wilkinson and H. Willmott (eds) *Making Quality Critical: New Perspectives on Organizational Change*. London: Routledge. pp. 54–81.

Vallance, E. (1995) *Business Ethics at Work*. Cambridge: Cambridge University Press.

Victor, B., Boynton, A. and Stephens-Jahng, T. (2000) The effective design of work under total quality management, *Organization Science*, 11(1): 102–17.

Vinzant, J.C. and Vinzant, D.H. (1996) Strategic management and total quality management: challenges and devices, *Public Administration Quarterly*, 20(3): 201–19.

Wall Street Journal (1992) 14 May.

Westphal, J.D., Gulati, R. and Shontell, S.M. (1997) Customisation or conformity? An institutional and network perspective on the content and consequences of TQM adoption, *ASQ*, 42(2): 366–94.

White, R.F. and Jaques, R. (1995) Operationalising the postmodernity construct for efficient organizational change management, *Journal of Organizational Change Management*, 8(2): 45–71.

White, T.I. (1993) *Business Ethics: A Philosophical Reader*. Englewood Cliffs, NJ: Prentice Hall.

Wilber, C.K. (1998) *Economics, Ethics and Public Policy*. Lanham, MD: Rowman & Littlefield.

Wilkinson, A. (1992) The other side of quality: 'soft' issues and the human resource dimension, *Total Quality Management*, 3(3): 323–9.

Wilkinson, A., Redman, T., Snape, E. and Marchington, M. (1998) *Managing with Total Quality Management*. Basingstoke: Macmillan.

Wilkinson, A. and Willmott, H. (1995) (eds) *Making Quality Critical: New Perspectives on Organizational Change*. London: Routledge.

Wilkinson, A., Godfrey, G. and Marchington, M. (1997) Bouquets, brickbats and blinkers: total quality management and employee involvement in practice, *Organization Studies*, 18(5): 799–819.

Wilkinson, A., Marchington, M., Goodman, J. and Ackers, P. (1992) Total quality management and employer involvement, *Human Resource Management Journal*, 2(4): 1–20.

Willmott, H. (1993) Strength is ignorance: slavery is freedom: managing culture in modern organization, *Journal of Management Studies*, 30(4): 515–52.

Willmott, H. (1995) The odd couple?: Re-engineering business processes; managing human relations, *New Technology, Work and Employment*, 10(2): 89–98.

Wright, A. (1997) Public service quality: lessons not learned, *Total Quality Management*, 8(5): 313–21.

Wruck, K.H. and Jensen, M.C. (1994) Science, specific knowledge and total quality management, *Journal of Accounting and Economics*, 18: 247–87.

Xu, Q. (1999) TQM as an arbitrary sign for play: discourse and transformation, *Organization Studies*, 20(4): 659–81.

Young, M. (1992) A framework for the successful adoption of Japanese manufacturing techniques in the United States, *Academy of Management Review*, 17(4): 677–700.

Yukl, G. (1989) Managerial leadership: a review of theory and research, *Journal of Management*, 15(2): 251–89.

Zbaracki, M. (1998) The rhetoric and reality of total quality management, *ASQ*, 43(3): 602–36.

Index

Compiled by Indexing Specialists (UK) Limited, Hove, East Sussex